Contemporary Gulf Studies

Series Editors

Steven Wright, College of Humanities and Social Sciences, Hamad bin Khalifa University, Doha, Qatar
Abdullah Baabood, School of International Liberal Studies, Waseda University, Tokyo, Japan

Salient Features:

- The Gulf lies at the intersection of regional conflicts and the competing interests of global powers and therefore publications in the series reflect this complex environment.
- The series will see publication on the dynamic nature of how the Gulf region has been undergoing enormous changes attracting regional and international interests.
- The series is managed through Gulf Studies Center at Qatar University, which has emerged as the leading institution within the Gulf region offering graduate degrees in Gulf Studies at both masters and doctoral level.

Aims and Scope:

This series offer a platform from which scholarly work on the most pressing issues within the Gulf region will be examined. The scope of the book series will encompass work being done on the member states of the Gulf Cooperation Council (GCC): Saudi Arabia, Oman, United Arab Emirates, Qatar, Bahrain, Kuwait in addition to Iraq, Iran and Yemen. The series will focus on three types of volumes: Single and jointly authored monograph; Thematic edited books; Course text books. The scope of the series will include publications relating to the countries of focus, in terms of the following themes which will allow for interdisciplinary and multidisciplinary inquiry on the Gulf region to flourish:

- Politics and political development
- Regional and international relations
- Regional cooperation and integration
- Defense and security
- Economics and development
- Food and water security
- Energy and environment
- Civil society and the private sector
- Identity, migration, youth, gender and employment
- Health and education
- Media, literature, arts & culture

Tobias Zumbraegel

Political Power and Environmental Sustainability in Gulf Monarchies

palgrave
macmillan

Tobias Zumbraegel
University of Hamburg
Hamburg, Germany

Center for Applied Research
in Partnership with the Orient
(CARPO)
Bonn, Germany

ISSN 2662-320X ISSN 2662-3218 (electronic)
Contemporary Gulf Studies
ISBN 978-981-19-4500-7 ISBN 978-981-19-4431-4 (eBook)
https://doi.org/10.1007/978-981-19-4431-4

Cover image: Fernando Tatay, shutterstock.com
Cover design by eStudio Calamar

This Palgrave Macmillan imprint is published by the registered company Springer Nature Singapore Pte Ltd.
The registered company address is: 152 Beach Road, #21-01/04 Gateway East, Singapore 189721, Singapore

To my parents, Elisabeth and Matthias Zumbrägel

Acknowledgements

First of all, I am most grateful to two anonymous readers who helped me strengthen this book by providing exceptionally thoughtful and comprehensive feedback on drafts. I am also grateful to the experienced editors at Palgrave Macmillan. Special thanks are dedicated to Charlotte McGowan-Griffin, whose copyediting cut a path through my writing for readers to follow.

This book is a revision of the dissertation "Sustaining Power after Oil: Environmental Politics and Legitimacy in Qatar, Saudi Arabia and Kuwait", my Ph.D. thesis for the department of Political Science, Friedrich-Alexander University (FAU) Erlangen-Nuremberg (2020). Especially, I want to thank my supervisor, Professor Dr. Thomas Demmelhuber. He oversaw my research project from the very first moment and provided me with a fantastic environment to strive academically. My debts to him, intellectual and personal, are enormous.

Innumerable people contributed to this book by dedicating their time and sharing their thoughts, above all, the many people I have interviewed and talked to, who remain anonymous. I accrued more debts than I can possibly repay. This book and analysis are a reflection of the combined input of all people I met during this journey although many would probably not agree with it. This work criticizes but hopefully in a fair and balanced way.

Funding to support the research and writing was supplied by German Research Foundation (DFG) and the ZEIT-Stiftung (special thanks to

Anna Hoffmann and Jane Bartels). Sincere thanks are addressed to the King Faisal Centre for Research and Islamic Studies (KFCRIS) and Dr. Saud al-Sarhan as well as the Gulf Studies Program at the Qatar University, and Dr. Abdullah Babood in particular, who gave me the opportunity to become a visiting fellow at their renowned institutes. Statements and opinions of this book are mine and do not necessarily reflect those of the above organizations.

Many further colleagues and friends have helped me in undertaking this research project. Particularly, I want to thank my former colleagues at the University of Erlangen (FAU) and my colleagues at CARPO (Center for Applied Research in Partnership with the Orient), with special thanks to Dr. Sebastian Sons, who provided invaluable guidance on Chapter 6. Finally and most importantly, I want to deeply thank my parents, who have always supported me without any signs of hesitations in what I love to do. This work is dedicated to them.

All errors in judgement, content or otherwise are mine of course.

Note on Transliteration and Translation

Transliteration

The spelling of Arabic words is oriented on the *International Journal of Middle East Studies*, a publication of the Middle East Studies Association (*MESA*) of North America. Names of specific people, places and organizations are capitalized while the usage of the generic term is lower cased. Sometimes, deviations were allowed for in the case of proper names whose bearers spell themselves differently. For instance, Mohamed Bin Zayed vs. Mohammad bin Salman. Furthermore, commonly used words have remained in their English format (Emir, not *ʾAmīr,* or Al Saud and not *Āl Saʿūd).* Arab names have been abbreviated because they can be very lengthy. For instance, the founding father of the United Arab Emirates is simply referred to as Sheikh Zayed.

Translations

Quotations from texts written in languages other than English have been translated by the author into English in order to facilitate reading—except when an authorized translation was at hand or existed. Specific or crucial terms remain, in some instances, in their original language in case this helps in understanding. However, the translation is then given.

Contents

About the Author

Dr. Tobias Zumbraegel is a postdoctoral researcher at the cluster of excellence 'Climate, Climatic Change and Society' (CLICCS) at the University of Hamburg and a researcher at the Center for Applied Research in Partnership with the Orient (CARPO). He studied History, Political Science and Middle Eastern Studies in Cologne, Tuebingen and Cairo and holds a Ph.D. from the Friedrich-Alexander University Erlangen-Nuremberg. He received scholarships from the German Academic Exchange Service (DAAD) and the ZEIT-Stiftung and was a visiting fellow at the Faisal Center for Research and Islamic Studies (KFCRIS) and the Department for Gulf Studies at the Qatar University.

He has over 14 years' experience in the Middle East and has extensively researched the region. He specializes in the intersection of politics and ecology in the Middle East. He is particularly interested in the geopolitics of environmental sustainability, dynamics of climate and conflict as well as questions of political and social transformation.

His Ph.D. thesis (summa cum laude) on environmental policymaking and its legitimizing effects in the oil- and gas-rich Arab Gulf monarchies was awarded with the dissertation prize of the German Middle East Association (DAVO). As a political analyst, he is consulted by German and international political institutions as well as by international journalists to provide expertise on the Middle East and North Africa. He also acts as a reviewer for international journals and funding bodies and is editor-in chief of CARPO's Sustainability Series.

Abbreviations

ACWA	Arabian Company for Water and Power Development
ADNOC	Abu Dhabi National Oil Company
ARAMCO	Arabian American Oil Company
BAPCO	Bahrain Petroleum Company
BOT	Build-Operate-Transfer
CAMRE	Council of Arab Ministers Responsible for the Environment
CCUS	Carbon Capture, Utilization and Storage
CDM	Clean Development Mechanism
CEDA	Council of Economic and Development Affairs (Saudi Arabia)
CMP	Conference of the Parties of the Kyoto Protocol
CO_2eq	Carbon Dioxide Equivalent
COP	Conference of the Parties
DEWA	Dubai Electricity and Water Authority
DNA	Designated National Authorities
ECRA	Electricity and Cogeneration Regulatory Authority (Saudi Arabia)
EPA	Environment Public Authority (Kuwait)
EPC	Engineering, Procurement and Construction
ERWDA	Environmental Research and Wildlife Development Agency (UAE)
FDI	Foreign Direct Investment
FEA	Federal Environment Agency (UAE)
FIFA	Fédération Internationale de Football Association
G20	Group of Twenty
GAMEP	General Authority for Meteorology and Environmental Protection (Saudi Arabia)
GCC	Gulf Cooperation Council
GHG	Greenhouse Gas

GONGO	Government-Organized Non-Governmental-Organization
GORD	Gulf Organization for Research & Development (Qatar)
GSDP	General Secretariat for Development Planning (Qatar)
GW	Gigawatt
IAEA	International Atomic Energy Agency
IEA	International Energy Agency
INDC	Intended Nationally Determined Contributions
IPCC	Intergovernmental Panel for Climate Change
IPO	Initial Public Offering
IPP	Independent Power Producer
IRENA	International Renewable Energy Agency
K.A.CARE	King Abdullah City for Atomic and Renewable Energy (Saudi Arabia)
KACST	King Abdulaziz City for Science and Technology (Saudi Arabia)
KAPSARC	King Abdullah Petroleum Studies and Research Center (Saudi Arabia)
KAUST	King Abdullah University of Science and Technology (Saudi Arabia)
KEPS	Kuwait Environment Protection Society
KISR	Kuwait Institute For Scientific Research
KOC	Kuwait Oil Company
KPC	Kuwait Petroleum Corporation
LEED	Leadership in Energy and Environmental Design
LNG	Liquefied natural gas
MECA	Ministry of Environment and Climate Affairs (Oman)
MENA	Middle East and North Africa
MEPA	Meteorology and Environmental Protection Administration (Saudi Arabia)
MICE	Meetings, Incentives, Conferences and Exhibitions
MME	Ministry of Municipality & Environment (Qatar)
MOCCAE	Ministry of Climate Change and Environment (UAE)
MOEIMR	Ministry of Energy, Industry and Mineral Resources (Saudi Arabia)
MoU	Memoranda of Understanding
MOWE	Ministry of Water and Electricity (Saudi Arabia)
MPMP	Ministry of Petroleum and Mineral Resources (Saudi Arabia)
MW	Megawatt
NAMA	Nationally Appropriate Mitigation Action
NC	National Communications
NDC	Nationally Determined Contribution
NGO	Non-Governmental-Organization
NOC	National Oil and Gas Company
NREP	National Renewable Energy Program (Saudi Arabia)
OAPAC	Organization of Arab Petroleum Exporting Countries

OPEC	Organization of the Petroleum Exporting Countries
PDO	Petroleum Development Oman
PIF	Public Investment Fund (Saudi Arabia)
PME	Presidency of Meteorology and Environment (Saudi Arabia)
PPA	Power Purchase Agreements
PPP	Public Private Partnership
PV	Photovoltaics
QEERI	Qatar Environment and Energy Research Institute
QF	Qatar Foundation
QIA	Qatar Investment Authority
QNFSP	Qatar National Food and Security Programme
QSTP	Qatar Science and Technology Park
REPDO	Renewable Energy Project Development Office (Saudi Arabia)
ROPME	Regional Organisation for the Protection of the Marine Environment
RST	Rentier state theory
SABIC	Saudi Basic Industries Corporation
SCE	Supreme Council for the Environment (Bahrain)
SCENR	Supreme Council for the Environment and Natural Reserves (Qatar)
SDGs	Sustainable Development Goals
SEC	Saudi Electricity Company
SESRI	Social and Economic Survey Research Institute (Qatar)
SMEs	Small and Medium Enterprises
SOE	State-Owned Enterprise
SWCC	Saline Water Conversion Company (Saudi Arabia)
SWF	Sovereign Wealth Fund
UAE	United Arab Emirates
UNDP	United Nations Development Programme
UNEP	United Nations Environmental Programme
UNFCCC	United Nations Framework Convention on Climate
VAT	Value-Added-Tax
WHO	World Health Organization
WTO	World Trade Organization
WWF	Wide Fund for Nature (Formerly: World Wildlife Fund)

List of Figures

List of Tables

CHAPTER 1

Introduction

Locating the 'Environmental Enthusiasm' of the Fossil-Wealthy Gulf Monarchies

Whether there are heatwaves with temperatures higher than ever before in Kuwait and Abu Dhabi or unprecedented snowfall in southern Iraq; whether Iranian cities suffer from toxic air or war-torn Yemen from flash floods: The Middle East and North Africa (MENA) provides a whole package of evidence of a looming climate peril. Many countries already suffer from decreasing water availability, soil degradation, exposure to toxins, waste disposal, threats to food and energy security and biodiversity loss. Long-term effects of climate change (e.g. sea level rise, rise in temperature, increasing evapotranspiration, etc.) exacerbate the deteriorating ecological situation. It is to be expected that environmental degradation and climate change, in combination with socioeconomic developments and political mismanagement, cause further tensions in an already volatile environment.

While the members of the Gulf Cooperation Council (GCC) have been viewed as "being the worst environmental polluters worldwide" (Reiche, 2010, 8) or a "haven of ecocide" (Luomi, 2012, 45), efforts towards sustainability and environmental protection measures are increasingly monitored. Accordingly, one can notice a greater commitment to sustainable principles, an upgrading of environmental institutions and a

T. Zumbraegel, *Political Power and Environmental Sustainability in Gulf Monarchies*, Contemporary Gulf Studies,
https://doi.org/10.1007/978-981-19-4431-4_1

stronger prioritization of renewable energy targets and plans in their policies and frameworks. In this vein, Christopher Davidson already noted some years ago that environmental protection has become "a high profile policy" in some Gulf monarchies and that those states, particularly the United Arab Emirates (UAE) and Qatar, "have transformed what was previously a liability for their regional and international reputations into something of a strength" (Davidson, 2015, 76).

This 'eco noise' about a 'green' turn[1] was certainly accompanied by sustainability milestones including, in 2006, the creation of the eco-city Masdar in Abu Dhabi as first of its kind, along with the decision of the International Renewable Energy Agency (IRENA) in 2009 to establish its headquarters at the city. Only two years later, Qatar received global attention by successfully winning the bid to host the first global climate conference in the region. Nearly concurrently, it promised to host the first carbon-neutral Fédération Internationale de Football Association (FIFA) World Cup in 2022. Meanwhile, all GCC states have also pronounced long-term development plans (so-called visions) that present roadmaps towards a 'post-oil era', and in some of them, environmental sustainability has become a key component (Al-Saidi et al., 2019). Over the last two or three years, the topic of sustainability has experienced another boom in the Gulf, with further large-scale announcements and pledges taking place. Among these was Saudi Arabia's announcement of its futuristic US$500 billion NEOM project, whose first phase will include a 'zero-carbon' city called The Line, due to extend over 170 km and house a million people. Particularly, the year 2021 was seen as a wind change for climate diplomacy, with Saudi Arabia's announcement of 'Middle East and Saudi Green Initiatives', the UAE's 'Regional Climate Dialogue' initiative and its award to host the climate conference in 2023. Several states, such as Saudi Arabia, the UAE and Bahrain, also announced ambitious net-zero targets, a move that was unthinkable some years ago.

This fundamental transformation in the Gulf[2] has also attracted attention by scholars: While in the early 2000s environmental studies in the region constituted a niche (see: Ouis, 2002; Vrojilk, 2003), a little less

[1] For reasons of simplicity and accessibility, terms like 'green', 'clean' and 'environmental' are used interchangeably in this book although they are in itself constructed and contested. They all refer to the here presented idea of environmental sustainability.

[2] Persian/Arabian designates ownership and is politically charged. I am aware of this debate but refer to the area as the Gulf for the rest of the book.

than a decade later this field of research has expanded significantly. For instance, an increasing scholarly interest on climate change and environmental degradation in the GCC region, particularly in Saudi Arabia, has emerged. A number of climatological studies have pinpointed growing threats such as (a) a continuous surge of temperature, (b) an increase in warm days and a decrease in cold days during the year, (c) depletion of groundwater sources, (d) growing pollution of the environmental media (air, water, soil), (e) an increase in occasional natural hazards such as dust storms, heavy rainfall or droughts and (f) a rising number of threatened flora and fauna (Al-Maamary et al., 2017; Almazroui et al., 2012; Batayneh et al., 2014; Williams et al., 2012). Despite the fact that especially local environmental scientists and experts have produced vast knowledge and a better understanding of the region's vulnerability, it has seldom gained greater public interest. Research activity remains largely marginal, with little awareness among the population and political elite, funding and financing gaps and limitations due to lack of available data (Al-Maamary et al., 2017). As an environmental scientist describes the situation:

> We have the committee of the environment in our parliament but it is only cosmetic, it is not that they are not trying but they don't have the technical know-how. Many of us environmental experts have approached this committee and we were faced–not me personally, but colleagues of mine–with statements by the committee that there are more important issues than the environment (...) and I don't blame them because it is not a public movement. People are worried about increasing real-estate prices, security and cheap water and electricity.[3]

Research interest in explaining the oil- and gas-exporting monarchies' 'eco-craze' shifted instead to exploring their socioeconomic motives, dominated by external experts and scholars. As Chapter 3 elaborates, publications such as the Chatham House report *Burning Oil to Keep Cool. The Hidden Energy Crisis in Saudi Arabia* (Lahn & Stevens, 2011) is an early prime example of how the external research community has shaped the discourse.[4] The general reading of the policy shift was the need to harmonize the hydrocarbon-based economic growth and wealth with a

[3] Interview #76.

[4] Interview #44.

pressing need to adapt a low-carbon and climate-resilient development. By the late 2000s, when the global "thirst for oil" was at its peak (Krane, 2019, 65), policymakers across the Gulf realized that the hydrocarbon model of the 'energy kingdoms' was gradually becoming a liability. The hypermodern development and welfare models were under pressure from skyrocketing domestic consumption, growing external criticism of the high ecological footprint (in terms of per capita emissions and resource consumption) and mounting pressure to change this by the international community. At the same time, they intended to warrant the export of oil and gas that assures wealth, influence and (external) protection. The situation deteriorated, however, when the crude oil prices plunged from $113 a barrel in June 2014 to $52 in January 2015, decreasing further until a low point of $36 a barrel in January 2016, resulting in large state budget deficits. In view of the economic fallout caused by the global coronavirus pandemic, the average price of oil dropped again from $64 per barrel in 2019 to $41 in early June 2020 (Fig. 1.1).

In light of these multiple challenges of oil price fluctuations, domestic overconsumption, a high rate of anthropogenic greenhouse gas emissions, a global depreciation of fossil fuels (coal, oil and natural gas), the decarbonization lever and, of course, global warming, many scholars base their main argument on a monocausal claim that the Gulf states "have

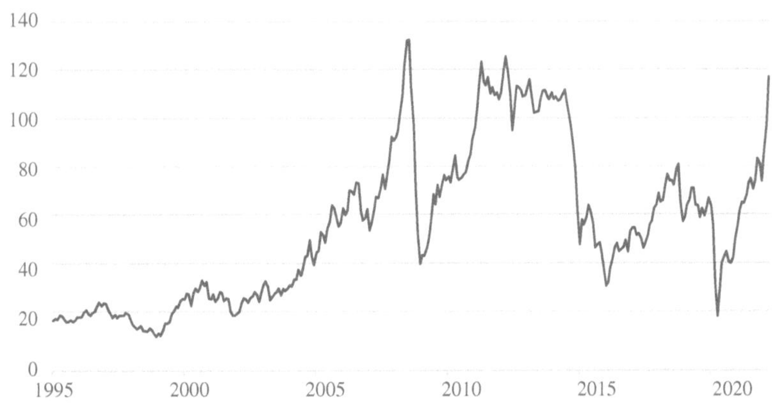

Fig. 1.1 Brent crude oil prices 1995–2022 (U.S. Energy Information Administration, "Petroleum and Other Liquids: Europe Brent Spot Price FOB," April 8, 2022)

reached their limits of 'natural sustainability'" (Luomi, 2012, 1). Within this broader debate, two dominant approaches can be differentiated. On the one hand, a rather pessimistic perspective of 'ecoscarcity' and on the other a more optimistic outlook of 'ecological modernization'.

A comparatively early account of ecological scarcity can be connected to the 'peak oil' debate that dominated the public discourse during the first decade of the twenty-first century. Since a large amount of oil is drilled and exported from a few giant oil fields that were put into operation several decades ago, the question of an imminent depletion of these natural resources was perhaps inevitable. However, the 'peak supply' discussion has been gradually supplanted by talk of 'peak demand' in the last few years. Although predictions are difficult to make and are shaped by many variables, one can suggest that a peak, rather seen as a "plateau with numerous rebounds", will likely occur in light of a global clean energy transition and that this will represent a serious challenge for the oil- and gas-producing states (Krane, 2020, 8). Challenges of energy demand are also being compounded by threats to water and food security (Al-Zubari, 2019; Rambo et al., 2017). Studies within the broader framework of resource scarcity also speak to the above-mentioned climatological analyses that emphasize the growing threat of environmental change. It is not only inefficient and escalating consumption habits, but also rapid deterioration of conventional water resources, increasing pollution, sea level rise and frequent drought cycles that lead to the growing gap between demand and available supply of resources.

Considering these constraints and dilemmas, the large proportion of scholars, however, focus on the economic impact and questions of how to solve the challenges of increasingly scarce commodities (Odhiambo, 2017). Already from early on, scholars also emphasized the (economic) opportunities (Al-Sarihi & Mason, 2020; Raouf, 2008; Russell, 2009). Oftentimes, sustainability has been dealt with as one part of the broader pursuit of economic diversification among the Gulf states (Azar & Abdel Raouf, 2017; Sultan et al., 2011). As Omar al-Ubaydli and colleagues summarize: "Since hydrocarbon combustion sets out large amounts of GHG [greenhouse gas] it can be argued that the diversification towards non-oil sectors is in fact a strategy of climate change mitigation" (Al-Ubaydli et al., 2019, 217). Accompanied by buzzwords such as 'economic efficiency', 'green economy' (Raouf & Luomi, 2016) or 'ecological modernization' (Al-Saidi & Elagib, 2018; Reiche, 2010), another popular research strand asserts that the implementation of innovative and modern techniques and solutions can avert the upcoming ecological collapse and environmental crisis. This perspective of an ‘environmental technological fix’, situated in neoclassical growth theories, has been a key component since the state-building processes, as Chapter 3 will describe more thoroughly (Hamblin, 2019). Sometimes also labelled as ‘weak’ sustainable development (Scoones, 2016), it pretends that economic prosperity and development are still possible without overexploitation of the natural capital. Thus, research in this area is mostly concerned with making assessments of the adaptation and implementation capacities of ‘modern’ and more sustainable technology. For instance, even though the current deployment of renewable energy sources in the GCC is minimal, various scholars have emphasized their opportunities, especially in terms of solar energy (Griffiths & Orkoubi, 2019).

In light of this techno-optimistic ecological modernization perspective, research activity has shifted to the Gulf's energy transition, producing countless studies, while topics of environmental-related politics have lost ground (Akhonbay, 2019; Hertog & Luciani, 2012; Luciani & Moerenhout, 2021; Mills & Sim, 2021). The public and academic discourse has shifted towards the “imagination of climate change as a problem of emissions (...) that are overwhelmingly embedded within the status quo of a global capitalist economy” (Nightingale et al., 2020, 346); associated ecological problems, social values or political dynamics are steadidly downplayed by this dominant narrative.

Despite the fact that the boundaries of both research strands of ‘ecoscarcity’ and ‘ecological modernization’ are often blurry in empirical analyses, what both have in common is the fact that they are “asserting apolitical answers to extremely political questions” (Robbins, 2019, 15). Only occasionally have scholars also included political assessments in their analyses, but these remain rather cursory in addressing only one specific country or aspect such as ‘green branding’ (Sim, 2012), climate diplomacy (Al-Saidi et al., 2019) or most commonly the rentier effects (e.g. Al-Sulayman, 2021; Krane, 2019). Instead of offering another contribution to this fast-growing literature body, this study intends to offer a more comprehensive political-driven approach with a special focus on environmental sustainability. It picks up preliminary thoughts by other authors who critically engage with the political realities in the region (e.g. Luomi, 2012; Spiess, 2008).

Analytical Framework: Bringing Political and Environmental Forces (Back) in

In addition to the dominant paradigms of a dystopian (neo)Malthusian-oriented perspective of climate wars and a rather utopian liberal development and neoclassical growth viewpoint, political ecology can be seen as a third paradigm. It focuses on the human-nature relationship and unravels the political, economic and cultural dynamics behind environmental processes. In brief, political ecology is about "*something people do*" (Robbins, 2019, 4). While the approach covers a broad field of disciplines—for instance, environmental destruction and conflict, environmental history, critical development research, cultural ecology, postcolonial theory—this book is mainly inspired by Harry Verhoeven's viewpoint. In his pioneering volume on *Environmental Politics in the Middle East* (2018), he states:

> With the notable exception of the proliferation of scholarship on rentierism and the oil resource curse and tropes of scarcity-induced 'water wars', discussions of environmental issues still all too often tend to be framed in isolation from wider societal dialectics and broader questions about authority, ideology, identity, legitimacy, and power that form the core of the social sciences (Verhoeven, 2018, 2).

This book adopts this perspective and enriches the discussion about the 'green turn' of the Gulf Arab monarchies by asking how political power can be constituted through advocating environmental sustainability. It draws on the idea of governments "as self-interested actors" that "are interested in staying in power" (Faust, 2010, 518), which is especially the case in the absolutist Gulf monarchies with powerful individual leaders on top of the decision-making and power pyramid. A guiding key assumption is that the climate crisis and increasing environmental degradation as potentially *the* security threat of the upcoming century should not be treated primarily apolitically as before. This is not only because of its normative evaluation ('it is the right thing to do') and apocalyptic element ('we have to save humankind'), climate change and environmental degradation are also powerful catalysts of future conflicts: Global warming is turning into a matter of survival as it threatens long-term inhabitation on the Arabian Peninsula. In combination with a steadily decline of environmental quality, governments face a crisis of legitimacy as continuous damage to the ecosystem results in human insecurity and a loss of provision of basic services. All form parts of the social contract, meaning "sets of formal and informal agreements between societal groups and their sovereign (government or other actor in power) on rights and obligations toward each other" (Loewe et al., 2020, n/a).

In core, climate crisis and environmental degradation belong to the greatest challenges of this century and their mitigation is a key interest that every government needs to fulfil. While the abundance of hydrocarbon natural resources has equipped the Gulf Arab monarchies with considerable political leverage and enabled an unprecedented modernization and expansion of public welfare, environmental sustainability management also offers trajectories for not only capital but also power accumulation. In this vein, sustainability governance should not be seen as a perfunctory greenwash but as a tool for harnessing political power that ultimately helps to strengthen regime resilience. Using this particular field as one of many other policy fields, the book intends to unravel what Gulf monarchs *actually do* in order to uphold their power base or, according to Sean Yom, to understand how certain choices and new policies are made and implemented "in an effort to survive" (Yom, 2016, n/a).

For understanding key decision-makers' perceptions, preferences, choices and decisions, the 'regime' is the key reference point in terms of both the domestic and international levels. It refers not only to a type of government (democratic or autocratic, with gradations between these two ideal types) but also to the "political elite's guiding ideology, the rules of the game, and the structuring of the polity in a given nation" (Cammett et al., 2015, 73). Monarchies can be seen as a distinctive subtype of autocratic regimes that are particularly concentrated in the MENA region. They form a kind of cluster on the Arabian Peninsula ranging from constitutional ones to absolute ones. While the terminology of the different states varies (kingdom, sultanate, emirate),[5] they all combine elements of dynastic rule and absolute power (Herb, 1999). Moreover, Gulf monarchs are unavoidably interwoven with the state organization. This oscillation between political concepts of 'state' and 'regime' becomes most evident in Saudi Arabia, where the kingdom bears the name of the ruling family.

[5] For a more detailed assessment of what the varying terms and titles of King, Emir, Sheikh or Sultan imply, refer to Gray (2019, 113).

Additionally, Mehran Kamrava noticed in the Qatari case that "individuals have not just replaced institutions. They have become institutions" (Kamrava, 2015, 104). Despite the political dominance of a small elite, processes of decision-making do not occur in a vacuum, so that a range of stakeholders and politically relevant figures across different sectors must be analysed, too.

Leaders at the top of the decision-making hierarchy can apply a broad toolbox in consolidating their position and/or in response to challenges the regime faces. This includes strategies such as empowering certain elites (i.e. co-optation) and generating popular support at home (i.e. legitimation) as well as enhancing cooperation and influence (i.e. linkage and leverage) to create dependencies and secure allegiance on the external level (Zumbraegel, 2022). However, these dimensions are not separated: For instance, foreign policy goals and achievement can increase a domestic support base whereas certain elite networks can also be transnational. It is important to note that this is a dynamic process and not static as it is often quite misleadingly expressed by terms such as 'regime survival' or 'persistence'. Instead, one can rather speak of "recombinant authoritarianism", meaning the ability "to reorder and reconfigure instruments and strategies of governance" (Heydemann & Leenders, 2013, 7).

In the following, some of the core concepts underpinning this study will be briefly explained, such as co-optation, legitimation, linkage and leverage. On the one hand, scholars often refer to the deeply rooted 'neopatrimonial logic' of interlocking privileges in the absolutist Gulf monarchies.[6] This comprises not only large-scale patronage through the allocation of specific welfare gifts and benefits but also gaining the support of specific groups via co-optation, for instance (Cammett et al., 2015; Schlumberger, 2008). In core, the 'dynastic enterprises' exercise traditional unlimited authority through a web of cross-cutting coalitions to assure support and limit oppositional forces. In political science, co-optation is a key element of this dynamic state strategy that can be described "as the capacity to tie strategically-relevant actors (or a group of actors) to the regime elite" (Gerschewski, 2013, 22). On the other

[6] As Davidson describes it in simple terms, 'patrimonialism' (in which governance is dominated by the ruler, his family and his friends) and 'neo-patrimonialism' (in which modern-looking institutions and rules serve as a veneer for patrimonialism) (see: Davidson 2021, 6).

hand, political legitimacy, broadly meaning the "acceptance of the incumbents' claim to rule" (Josua, 2017, 303), is a significant feature of any existing regime and plays a decisive role in determining its 'fate and future'. Legitimation is the process that describes all means and efforts to create political legitimacy and is a universal phenomenon inherent to all regimes (Gerschewski, 2013). On the international level, linkage and leverage are core themes. Leverage implies asymmetric interdependencies that enable a powerful actor to exert power and influence in forms of conditionality or incentives. Lastly, linkage effects often describe the density of ties and cross-border flows. They are a more subtle way of soft power and include "the ability to 'shape preferences' and 'get others to want what you want'" (Levitsky & Way, 2006, 385).

Using this as a conceptual springboard, the book study deals with the nascent field of environmental sustainability in the hydrocarbon-rich Arab Gulf monarchies and how it affects state power. It thus relies on the approach of ***environmental sustainability*** as the idea "that environment can maintain its ability to support human life and maintain all existing eco-systems and life into the future despite resource depletion through human activity" (Brinkmann, 2020, 2). It thus relates on a sustainable development approach as designed by the United Nations (UN) in the late 1980s and early 1990s. From this understanding, "economic models seek to accumulate and use natural and financial capital sustainably; environmental models basically dwell on biodiversity and ecological integrity while social models seek to improve political, cultural, religious, health and educational systems, among others, to continually ensure human dignity and wellbeing" (Mensah, 2019, 5). While this three-pillar approach is frequently reiterated in public and scholarly literature, there is disaccord concerning the relative weight of the individual pillars. Different actors have different positions in identifying what 'sustainability' actually means (Connelly, 2007).

Instead of an inclusive approach that reflects on all dimensions in an equal way, in practice the economic and social pillars have received greater attention and priority than the dimension of environment. A common perception among policymakers and experts "was to grow first and clean up later" (Elder & Olsen, 2019, 70). The environmental pillar, however, has received more prominence lately, in the articulation of the Sustainable Development Goals (SDGs) (2016–2030). This revitalized notion of environmental sustainability has also been reflected in some of the long-term development plans of the GCC and other strategic governmental papers (Al-Saidi et al., 2019). In order to delimit the idea of sustainability, this study applies a practical approach and relies on the environmental-related goals of the SDGs. Out of the overall sixteen goals, the following have an explicit reference to environmental sustainability: (6) Clean Water and Sanitation, (7) Affordable and Clean Energy, (11) Sustainable Cities and Communities (12) Responsible Consumption and Production, (13) Climate Action, (14) Life below Water and (15) Life on Land (al-Saidi, 2021; Elder & Olsen, 2019). Relying on the SDGs as a way to contextualize the status and process of sustainability management in the GCC has the benefit that there are already clear-cut indicators (see further: Bayoumi et al., 2022).

This analytical framework used in the book provides a novel explanation of the sustainable transformation in the oil and gas-rich Gulf through a greater political and environmental perspective that has often been ignored by the strong economic and sustainable energy focus of the hitherto literature.

A Few Words on Methodology and Data Collection

This book is mainly based on a qualitative content analysis and interviews derived from mixed-method fieldwork, including semi-structured and structured expert interviews, focus groups interviews and participant observations conducted during four periods of fieldwork in November–December 2016, February–March 2017, October–November 2017 and September 2021. Overall, fifty-three in-depth and personal semi-structured interviews have been conducted across the Gulf (Bahrain, Kuwait, Qatar, Saudi Arabia and the UAE) and Europe (United Kingdom and Germany). A handful of further interviews, especially during the ravaging COVID-19 pandemic, have been conducted virtually. In addition, twenty unstructured interviews were part of private conversations or group discussions. The interviewees included researchers, scientists, policymakers, consultants, civil society sector, businesspeople and technocrats with considerable knowledge in the broad field of environmental sustainability. Interviewees included both inside experts (actors) and outside experts (analysts) in order to receive a holistic picture of the research subject (von Soest, 2022). Leading ministries and other governmental entities that are mentioned in this book were also approached. Interviews were chosen as main methodological approach as there are significant data gabs, especially among the GCC countries, when analysing sustainability (see also: Bayoumi et al., 2022).

Conducting field research in an authoritarian political climate poses several obstacles for a researcher. Moreover, even though one is inclined to think that a 'soft policy' field like environmental sustainability is unproblematic and easy to study in authoritarian contexts, I was subjected to different experiences and was faced with severe constraints and reluctance, especially when it comes to energy security as a highly sensitive topic. The author and the interview partners therefore agreed mutually on anonymity and all interviews were kept strictly confidential. However, some general background information is provided in the list of interviews in the appendix.

Complementing the interview material, primary and secondary documents have been systematically analysed. The analysis draws on a range of texts including government documents, publicly available information on firm and sector-level data, magazines and articles, advertisements, policy papers and studies as well as newspaper articles. With regard to media items, the process of data collection included a systematic review of pro-government newspapers. The chosen media outlets were al-Sharq al-Awsat and Arab News (English) as well as Ar-Riyadh (Arabic) for Saudi Arabia, the Qatar Peninsula (English) for Qatar, Khaleeji Times and The National (English) for the UAE, Oman News Agency (English) for Oman and finally, Kuwait Times (English) for Kuwait. The archives of the newspapers have been searched using selective keywords such as 'climate change' and/or 'sustainability' in the database *LexisNexis*. In addition to the qualitative content analysis, the study was also inspired by a network analysis in order to unpack the involved actors and institutions. In contrast to a structured approach of pre-defined and -categorized types, a more explorative, to some extent even investigative, approach was chosen in order to identify various relevant stakeholders and uncover the multilayered public–private elite power structures.

The research design is based on comparing very similar cases in a proximate geographical space with each other. The analysed states share a broad range of similar characteristics including linguistic, political, cultural, kinship, sectarian and historical background. They also face the dilemma of a hydrocarbon-based development path that follows the 'logic of fossil fuels' and the pressure to fundamentally alter this model. Given their abundance of oil and their relevance in the global (energy) economy, they all share a high degree of international linkages and leverage.

However, this work also acknowledges the heterogeneity of these states that is, for instance, expressed in aspects such as size and demography, the maturity of civil society and the degree of economic diversification. By being sensitive about their differences, this book intends to unravel the common public perception of the GCC as a monolithic bloc.

Structure and Scope of the Book

After this first chapter has outlined the thematic focus and briefly introduced the analytical framework and methodological approach, Chapter 2 will dive deeper into the structure and characteristics of the Gulf countries. It elaborates on the politics and stability of the Gulf Arab states and then asks why they have become so 'unsustainable'. It looks at the rising political, socioeconomic and environmental challenges that are indicating that the countries are experiencing a transformative shift. Despite the fact that these countries face many challenges ranging from political intra-elite rivalry, regional insecurity, rising social frustration, in particular among the youth, as well as grave economic difficulties (see: Davidson, 2015), the book explicitly focuses on the key dilemma of the need to become sustainable while still fulfilling state duties. In core, the states hold a key role as global supplier of oil and gas but, at the same time, are highly sensitive to the severe environmental impacts for which these utilities are responsible. It seems apparent that leaderships need to lower their overreliance on hydrocarbons, invest large sums in renewable energy sources, promote energy efficiency, conserve the environment, combat climate change and radically transform their oil- and gas-reliant rentier economies (Al-Saidi & Elagib, 2018). The key question, however, with which the chapter ends, is how they can undertake such a fundamental policy shift without eroding their power base and influence.

The empirical analysis thus begins with a more detailed contextualization of the subject of investigation. It starts by tracing back the closely interwoven relationship of political power and the environment in the region. Thus, Gulf leaders have used 'environmental power' from early onwards to consolidate their power. The advent of oil and gas only amplified this approach in an unprecedented manner. At the same time, Chapter 3 also explains that one can notice a 'paradigm shift' towards environmental sustainability by the (late) 2000s but that this was nothing the Gulf leaders 'invented' from scratch but rather built upon previous structures and preferences. Here, one landmark is what Karen Young has called "the new Gulf fiscal reality post-2014" (Young, 2019, 80). The outbreak of the COVID-19 pandemic with its economic and social consequences can also be cited as another recent turning point (Al-Sulayman, 2021).

Chapter 4 then explores the state organization of this environmental sustainability management. It looks into the involvement of governmental and semi-governmental institutions and the role of human agency and specific individuals in the sustainable transformation. In a similar way, Chapter 5 concentrates on the economic sector and the importance of environmental sustainability as a business opportunity. It further reveals the close and mutual independence between the previously described public sector and the growing assemblage with the private sector in the Gulf states. In the following part of the book, Chapter 6 turns to the international level. While the first part investigates the intra-regional dynamics within the GCC, the subsequent sections show how sustainability management has been instrumentalized by Gulf leaders to increase linkage and leverage effects. As argued there, this notion can best be captured through specific concepts such as environmental diplomacy, green branding or hedging. Ultimately, the last chapter summarizes the book's findings. It strengthens the previously introduced argument that the political dimension is key to understanding the sustainable transformation in the Gulf states and contextualizes this within broader debates. A final section provides a short outlook of the future dynamics we might expect in the coming years, some earlier than others.

As indicated in the introductory note, this book is a quite comprehensive attempt to understand the manifold facets of the political dimension of the Gulf monarchies' sustainability transformation. However, it is not able to address all aspects in the same manner.

First, this book does not intend to claim that there is a causal relationship between environmental sustainability and political power, but rather present empirically robust and consistent patterns that support this assumption. It also does not evaluate a potential correlation between a certain regime type (in this case authoritarian) and successful climate policies. This debate of 'authoritarian environmentalism' or 'eco-dictatorships', i.e. "the use of authoritarian methods to accomplish environmental goals" (Li & Shapiro, 2020, 14), has been particularly increased with China's greater action on sustainability governance. For many, the country's decisive state interventions have clearly outperformed the oftentimes inaction of liberal democracies in terms of environmental protection (Beeson, 2010). Other, rather long-term studies challenge this perspective and show that democracies are more capable of promoting environmental protection in the long run (Fredriksson & Neumayer, 2013). Instead of contributing to this debate, which is occasionally highly normatively driven and focuses only on the regime type, this book is more interested in the process and functioning of environmental sustainability governance. It attributes that the empirical literature on 'eco-authoritarianism ' has produced valuable insight including the role of specific stakeholders, changing state-society relationships and broader trends of power consolidation and centralization (Eaton & Kostka, 2014; Gilley, 2012). However, those dynamics are not limited to autocracies (Li & Shapiro, 2020). Furthermore, especially Chapter 6 shows the global entanglement of this topic that thwart the general idea of a simple democracy-autocracy dichotomy. In core, the topic reveals a close interconnectedness and various entanglements between the Western world and the Gulf states.[7]

Second, given the explicit focus on regimes in the region, other stakeholders are only treated marginally. While certainly of great importance, civil society actors are not part of this research question but, as has been argued in the conclusion, their voices might become more important and relevant in the near future. Also, the important but tragic role of migrant workers, for instance, in the built environment of sustainability when discussing a steadily marginalization through urban sustainability (Al-Zo'by, 2019, 566) or migrant labour deaths associated with 'sudden death syndrome' caused by inhuman working conditions and a combination of rise of temperature and humidity (Mason & Raouf, 2021), is not part of the analysis. These complex questions of social sustainability are part of a broader discussion of sustainable development and must be addressed separately, requiring more research that exceeds the subject of this book.

Third, and related to the question of agency, the study also does not look at the external perception of the region's shift towards environmental sustainability. For instance, if John Kerry praised the UAE's candidacy for hosting the next climate summit or his senior advisor, David Livingston, stresses "the unique role that the UAE plays in the region" in terms of climate change (Tolley, 2021, June 24), then this is only of secondary

[7] Interview #48.

importance. Fourth, the reader should bear in mind that this book is not a comprehensive list of environmental politics and climate action in the Gulf states. Instead, it takes a social scientist point of view, revealing multiple facets of how environmental sustainability is—or can be—linked to political power games across different sectors and dimensions. Thus, this book cannot cover every (minor) detail across all states, which is already impossible given that the availability of data is a problem in itself. It rather casts empirical spotlights and devotes attention to certain phenomena, in order to sketch out broader developments. Lastly, and related to this, not all GCC states are treated in the same way. While I have tried to cover all countries in each chapter, leading countries such as the UAE, Qatar and Saudi Arabia certainly dominate the analysis.

References

Al-Hinai, A., Espinosa, A., &Vidgen, R. (2017). A systemic approach to integrate SOEs and SMEs in business ecosystem. In A. Mishrif & Y. Al-Balushi (Eds.), *Economic diversification in the Gulf region: The private sector as an engine of growth* (Vol. I, pp. 49–76). Palgrave.

Al-Maamary, H., Kazem, H. A., & Chaichan, M. (2017). Climate change: The game changer in the Gulf Cooperation Council region. *Renew. Sustain. Energy Rev., 76*, 555–576.

Al-Saidi, M. (2021). Cooperation or competition? State environmental relations and the SDGs agenda in the Gulf Cooperation Council (GCC) region. *Environmental Development, 37*. https://doi.org/10.1016/j.envdev.2020.100581

Al-Saidi, M., & Elagib, N. (2018). Ecological modernization and responses for a low-carbon future in the Gulf cooperation council countries. *Wires Climate Change,* e528. https://doi.org/10.1002/wcc.528

Al-Saidi, M., Zaidan, E., & Hammad, S. (2019). Participation modes and diplomacy of Gulf Cooperation Council (GCC) countries towards the global sustainability agenda. *Dev. Pract., 29*(5), 545–558. https://doi.org/10.1080/09614524.2019.1597017

Al-Sarihi, A. (2022). Climate change governance in Saudi Arabia: integrity, politics, challenges and opportunities. In M. Thompson & N. Quilliam (Eds.), *Governance and domestic policy-making in Saudi Arabia. Transforming society, economics, politics and culture* (pp. 225–256). I.B. Tauris.

Al-Sarihi, A., & Mason, M. (2020). Challenges and opportunities for climate policy integration in oil-producing countries: The case of the UAE and Oman. *Climate Policy, 20*(10), 1226–1241. https://doi.org/10.1080/14693062.2020.1781036

Al-Sulayman, F. (2021). The rise of renewables in the Gulf states: Is the 'rentier effect' still holding back the energy transition? In R. Mills & L. Sim (Eds.), *Low Carbon Energy in the Middle East and North Africa* (pp. 93–120). Palgrave.

Al-Ubaydli, O., Abdullah, G., & Yaseen, L. (2019). Forging a more centralized GCC renewable energy policy. In H. Akhonbay (Ed.), *The economics of renewable energy in the Gulf* (pp. 216–234). Routledge.

Al-Zo'by, M. (2019). Culture and the politics of sustainable development in the GCC: Identity between heritage and globalisation. *Dev. Pract., 29*(5), 559–569. https://doi.org/10.1080/09614524.2019.1602110

Al-Zubari, W. (2019, December 13). *Regional water governance and cooperation in the Arab region*. EDA Insight. https://www.agda.ac.ae/docs/default-source/Publications/eda-insight_gear-iii_water_en.pdf?sfvrsn=2

Akhonbay, H. (2019). *The economics of renewable energy in the Gulf*. Routledge.

Almazroui, M., et al. (2012). Recent climate change in the Arabian Peninsula: Annual rainfall and temperature analysis of Saudi Arabia for 1978–2009. *Int. J. Climatol., 32*(6), 953–966. https://doi.org/10.1002/joc.3446

Azar, E., & Abdel Raouf, M. (2017). *Sustainability in the Gulf*. Taylor and Francis.

Batayneh, A., et al. (2014). Environmental assessment of the Gulf of Aqaba coastal surface waters, Saudi Arabia. *J. Coast. Res., 30*(2), 283–290. https://doi.org/10.2112/JCOASTRES-D-13-00112.1

Bayoumi, M., Luomi, M., Fuller, G., & Al-Sarihi, A. (2022, April 17). Arab region SDG index and dashboard report 2022. Mohammed bin Rashid School of Government, Anwar Gargash Diplomatic Academy and UN Sustainable Development Solutions Network. https://arabsdgindex.com/

Beeson, M. (2010). The Coming of Environmental Authoritarianism. *Environmental Politics, 19*(2), 276–294.

Brinkmann, R. (2020). *Environmental sustainability in a time of change* (Vol. 279). Palgrave.

Cammett, M., Diwan, I., Richards, A., & Waterbury, J. (2015). *A political economy of the Middle East* (4th ed.). Westview Press.

Connelly, S. (2007). Mapping Sustainable Development as a Contested Concept. *Local Environment: International Journal of Justice and Sustainability, 12*(3), 259–278. https://doi.org/10.1080/13549830601183289

Davidson, C. (2015). *After the Sheikhs. The coming collapse of the Gulf monarchies* (2nd ed.). Hurst & Co.

Davidson, C. (2021). *From Sheikhs to Sultanism. Statecraft and authority in Saudi Arabia and the UAE*. Hurst & Co.

Eaton, S., & Kostka, G. (2014). Authoritarian environmentalism undermined? Local leaders' time horizons and environmental policy implementation in China. *The China Quarterly, 218*, 359–380.

Elder, M., & Olsen, S. H. (2019). The design of environmental priorities in the SDGs. *Global Pol., 10*(S1), 70–82. https://doi.org/10.1111/1758-5899.12596

Fathallah, D. (2019, April 19). *Challenges of public policymaking in Saudi Arabia: Carnegie endowment for international peace.* https://carnegieendowment.org/sada/79188

Faust, J. (2010). Policy experiments, democratic ownership and development assistance. *Development Policy Review, 28*(5), 515–534.

Fredriksson, P., & Neumayer, E. (2013). Democracy and Climate Change Policies: Is History Important? *Ecol. Econ., 95*, 11–19. https://doi.org/10.1016/j.ecolecon.2013.08.002

Gerschewski, J. (2013). The three pillars of stability: Legitimation, repression, and co-optation in autocratic regimes. *Democratization, 20*(1), 13–38. https://doi.org/10.1080/13510347.2013.738860

Gilley, B. (2012). Authoritarian environmentalism and China's response to climate change. *Environmental Politics, 21*(2), 287–307. https://doi.org/10.1080/09644016.2012.651904

Gray, M. (2019). *The economy of the Gulf states.* Agenda Publishing.

Griffiths, S., & Orkoubi, D. (2019). Energy and climate policies to stimulate renewables deployment in GCC countries. In H. Akhonbay (Ed.), *The economics of renewable energy in the Gulf* (pp. 139–166). Routledge.

Hamblin, J. D. (2019). An American miracle in the desert: Environmental crisis and nuclear-powered desalination in the Middle East. In A. M. Kirchhoff & J. R. McNeill (Eds.), *Nature and the Iron Curtain: Environmental policy and social movements in communist and capitalist countries, 1945–1990* (pp. 205–218). University of Pittsburgh Press.

Herb, M. (1999). *All in the family: Absolutism, revolution, and democracy in the Middle Eastern monarchies.* State University of New York Press.

Hertog, S., & G. Luciani (2012). Energy and sustainability policies in the Gulf states. In D. Held & K. Coates Ulrichsen (Eds.), *The transformation of the Gulf: Politics, economics and the global order* (pp. 236–257). Routledge.

Heydemann, S., & Leenders, R. (2013). *Middle East authoritarianisms: Governance, contestation, and regime resilience in Syria and Iran.* Stanford University Press.

Josua, M. (2017). Legitimation towards whom?: Managing the legitimacy crisis in Algeria during the Arab uprisings. *Zeitschrift Für Vergleichende Politikwissenschaft, 11*(2), 301–324. https://doi.org/10.1007/s12286-017-0331-3

Kamrava, M. (2015). *Qatar. Small state, big politics.* Cornell University Press.

Krane, J. (2019). *Energy kingdoms: Oil and political survival in the Persian Gulf.* Columbia University Press.

Krane, J. (2020). Climate action versus inaction: Balancing the costs for Gulf energy exporters. *British Journal of Middle Eastern Studies, 47*(1), 117–135. https://doi.org/10.1080/13530194.2020.1714269

Lahn, G., & Stevens, P. (2011, January 23). *Burning oil to keep cool: The hidden energy crisis in Saudi Arabia*. Chatham House Report. https://www.chathamhouse.org/sites/default/files/public/Research/Energy%2C%20Environment%20and%20Development/1211pr_lahn_stevens.pdf

Levitsky, S., & Way, L. (2006). Linkage versus leverage. Rethinking the international dimension of regime change. *Comparative Politics, 38*(4), 379–400.

Li, Y., & Shapiro, J. (2020). *China goes green.*

Loewe, M., Zintl, T., & Houdret, A. (2020). The social contract as a tool of analysis: Introduction to the special issue on "Framing the evolution of new social contracts in Middle Eastern and North African countries". *World Development, 145*. 104982. https://doi.org/10.1016/j.worlddev.2020.104982

Luciani, G., & Moerenhout, T. (2021) *When can oil economies be deemed sustainable?* Palgrave.

Luomi, M. (2012). *The Gulf monarchies and climate change: Abu Dhabi and Qatar in an era of natural unsustainability.* Hurst & Co.

Mason, R., & Raouf, A. (2021). Environmental politics in the Middle East. In R. Mason (Ed.). *New perspectives on Middle East politics: Economy, society, and international relations* (pp. 193–214). American University Press.

Mensah, J. I. (2019). Sustainable development: Meaning, history, principles, pillars, and implications for human action: Literature review. *Cogent Social Sciences, 5*(1), 1653531. https://doi.org/10.1080/23311886.2019.1653531

MEWA—Ministry of Environment, Water and Agriculture. (2018, April 11). *Executive summary of the national environment strategy.* https://www.jetro.go.jp/ext_images/world/middle_east/sa/law/pdf/National_Environmental_Strategy_ENG.pdf

MEWA—Ministry of Environment, Water and Agriculture. (2021, April 12). Saudi Arabia joins the world in addressing environmental degradation, securing sustainable future. Press Release. https://mewa.gov.sa/en/MediaCenter/News/Pages/News562021.aspx

Mills, R., & Sim, L. (2021). *Low carbon energy in the Middle East and North Africa.* Palgrave.

Nightingale, A. J., Eriksen, S., Taylor, M., Forsyth, T., Pelling, M., Newsham, A., Boyd, E., Brown, K., Harvey, B., Jones, L., Bezner Kerr, R., Mehta, L., Naess, L. O., Ockwell, D., Scoones, I., Tanner, T., & Whitfield, S. (2020). Beyond technical fixes: Climate solutions and the great derangement. *Climate and Development, 12*(4), 343–352. https://doi.org/10.1080/17565529.2019.1624495

Odhiambo, G. O. (2017). Water scarcity in the Arabian Peninsula and socio-economic implications. *Appl Water Sci, 7*, 2479–2492. https://doi.org/10.1007/s13201-016-0440-1

Ouis, P. (2002). 'Greening the emirates': The modern construction of nature in the United Arab Emirates. *Cult. Geogr., 9*(3), 334–347.

Rambo, K., et al. (2017). Water-energy nexus in Saudi Arabia. *Energy Procedia, 105*, 3837–3843. https://doi.org/10.1016/j.egypro.2017.03.782

Raouf, M. (2008, February 2). *Climate change threats, opportunities, and the GCC countries*. The Middle East Institute Policy Brief 12. https://www.mei.edu/publications/climate-change-threats-opportunities-and-gcc-countries

Raouf, M., & Luomi, M. (2016). *The green economy in the Gulf*. Routledge.

Reiche, D. (2010). Energy policies of Gulf Cooperation Council (GCC) countries: Possibilities and limitations of ecological modernization in rentier states. *Energy Policy, 38*(5), 2395–23403.

Robbins, P. (2019). *Political ecology. A critical introduction* (3rd ed.). Wiley Blackwell.

Russell, J. (2009). Environmental security and regional stability in the Persian Gulf. *Middle East Policy, 16*(4), 90–101.

Schlumberger, O. (2008). Structural reform, economic order, and development: Patrimonial capitalism. *Review of International Political Economy, 15*(4), 622–649.

Scoones, I. (2016). The politics of sustainability and development. *Annual Review of Environmental Resources, 41*, 293–319. https://doi.org/10.1146/annurev-environ-110615-090039

Sillitoe, P. (2017). *Sustainable development. An appraisal from the Gulf region*. Berghahn.

Sim, L.-C. (2012). Re-branding Abu Dhabi: From oil giant to energy titan. *Place Brand. Public Dipl., 8*(1), 83–98.

Spiess, A. (2008). Developing adaptive capacity for responding to environmental change in the Arab Gulf states: Uncertainties to linking ecosystem conservation, sustainable development and society in authoritarian rentier economies. *Global Planet. Change, 64*(3–4), 244–252.

Sultan, N., Weir, D., & Karake-Shalboub, Z. (2011). *The new post-oil Arab Gulf. Managing people and wealth*. Saqi.

Tolley, G. (2021, June 24). *Climate action at centre of the UAE's economic growth*. The National. https://www.thenationalnews.com/uae/environment/climate-action-at-centre-of-the-uae-s-economic-growth-1.1247907

Verhoeven, H. (2018). *Environmental politics in the Middle East*. Oxford University Press.

von Soest, C. (2022, June). Why do we speak to experts? Reviving the strength of the expert interview method. *Perspectives on Politics*, 1–11. https://doi.org/10.1017/S1537592722001116

Vrojilk, C. (2003). Climate governance in the GCC. In T. Najem & M. Hetherington (Eds.), *Good governance in the Middle East oil monarchies* (pp. 119–136). Routledge.

Williams, J., et al. (2012). Climate change and animals in Saudi Arabia. *Saudi Journal of Biological Sciences, 19*(2), 121–130. https://doi.org/10.1016/j.sjbs.2011.12.004

Yom, S. (2016, January 30). *Collaboration and community amongst the Arab monarchies*. POMEPS. https://pomeps.org/collaboration-and-community-amongst-the-arab-monarchies

Young, K. (2019). Prioritizing renewable energy in the time of fiscal austerity. In H. Akhonbay (Ed.), *The economics of renewable energy in the Gulf* (pp. 77–99). Routledge.

Zumbraegel, T. (2022). In search of legitimation: Environmental policy making in Saudi Arabia. In M. Thompson & N. Quillian (Eds.), *Governance and domestic policymaking in Saudi Arabia. Transforming society, economics, politics and culture*. I.B. Tauris.

CHAPTER 2

Unsustainable Development in the Gulf: Under Pressure

Approaching al-Khalīj al-ᶜArabī: Understanding Gulf Politics and Stability

The Arabian Peninsula (*shibhu l-jazīrati l-ᶜarabiyyah*) connects Africa and Eurasia by a small isthmus through the Arabian plate. It is surrounded by the Red Sea to the west and southwest, the Indian Ocean to the southeast and the Persian/Arabian Gulf to the northeast. The member states of the GCC, whose full name is 'The Cooperation Council for the Arab States of the Gulf' (*majlis al-taawun li-duwal al-khalij al-arabiyya*), share a high degree of structural similarity and geographical proximity. The hydrocarbon-exporting and dynastic Gulf Arab monarchies all share homogeneity in terms of their linguistic, political, cultural, kinship, sectarian and historical backgrounds. The states are also unique in terms of state building. Only Saudi Arabia originated from an internal state project. The other countries were under British protectorate, which came to an abrupt but smooth end in 1971. Another unique feature relates to their enormous hydrocarbon wealth. This abundance of oil and gas as well as a strategic geopolitical location has brought power and influence and explains why city-states such as Bahrain, Kuwait, Qatar and the single emirates of the UAE are renowned worldwide. Irrespective of these common traits, the GCC states differ in many aspects such

T. Zumbraegel, *Political Power and Environmental Sustainability in Gulf Monarchies*, Contemporary Gulf Studies,
https://doi.org/10.1007/978-981-19-4431-4_2

as physical size and topography, state-society relations, social composition and cohesion, variances in the amount of oil income or degree of regional and international leverage. Scholarly tradition, however, has mostly treated the GCC monarchies as one monolithic bloc. This regional clustering of monarchies contributed to the perception of the Middle East as exceptional space, defined by 'eccentricities': Many analysts have been consistently concerned with the question how these centuries-old family-based regimes remain stable. Despite the fact that the Gulf monarchies—in contrast to many other countries in the region—were able to avoid civil wars and maintain civil peace, their collapse has been long expected. When many other regional monarchies broke down in the middle of the century, such as Egypt (1952), Iraq (1958), Yemen (1962) and Libya (1969), several prominent scholars had already predicted these regimes' demise, as their institutional settings seemed incompatible with (and anachronistic to) the current dominant paradigm of development and modernization theory (e.g. Lerner, 1958, 6; Huntington, 1968, 177). More recently, in the scope of the Arab upheavals in 2010 and 2011, Christopher Davidson predicted the coming collapse of the Gulf monarchies, stating that the majority of the Gulf Arab states would vanish within the next five years (Black, 2012; Davidson, 2015). Yet, the respective leaderships were able to consolidate their power against all odds. They weathered external shocks such as the revolution in Iran in 1979 or accusations in the wake of 9/11 as place of origin for radical Islamism. Most recently, the GCC states also endured the Arab uprisings of 2010 and 2011 much better than their republic counterparts. They were even perceived as the new centre of power or "heart of the Middle East" (Kamrava, 2020, 3). However, this sense of GCC unity was rather short-lived. Internal strife created multiple power blocs and "developed separate identities, interests and policies, which appear irreversible" (Ottaway & Ottaway, 2019, 132).

Still, scholars are puzzled by this long-term monarchical authoritarian resilience, deliberating over why these regimes rank so high in terms of "YIPPI scores", meaning years in power per incumbent (Aarts, 2007, p. 251). In the following section, three broader explanations will be explored, covering more than three decades of Gulf studies. These include: (a) a historical centralization of power, internal coalitions and a conserved political idea of rule, (b) consolidation through hydrocarbon rents and (c) cultivating dependable regional and international allies (Bank et al., 2013).

First, different scholars have emphasized the preservation of traditional pre-state patterns of dynastic rule (Derichs & Demmelhuber, 2014; Lucas, 2004) and a 'unique' process of state formation ('historical accident') (Anderson, 1991). Other voices have highlighted the "monopolizing of key offices in the state" (Herb, 1999, 235) and the long-term ability to cope with oppositional forces and social contestation. These explanations relate to ideas of a 'monarchical exceptionalism' and inherent 'monarchical legitimacy' first described by Michael Hudson's *Arab Politics: The Search for Legitimacy* (1977). According to Hudson, as well as other more recent scholars (e.g. Menaldo, 2012, 709), a unique cultural legitimacy of the Arab monarchies derives from their longevity, an extensive compatibility of cultural values (such as religious and tribal traditions) and high degree of personalization that establishes close networks and ties between rulers and society, allowing them to govern more effectively than their presidential comrades (for an overview, see Gause, 2013). The longevity of these regimes has also been seen as a touchpoint of their unquestioned political legitimacy. As Abdulla describes it: "The hallmark of continuity is the centuries old ruling families of the AGS [Arab Gulf States], who have survived tough challenges and proved to be adept in the art of survival and ruling (...) their legitimacy is hardly in doubt" (Abdulla, 2012, 110; further: Kamrava, 2018).

Second, perhaps most prominently, have been explanations of a democracy gap in the Gulf which are derived from a political economy viewpoint. Coined as rentier state theory (RST), the reliance on fossil fuels and associated political rents has been viewed as the 'most persuasive' trajectory of authoritarianism by many experts of the Gulf region. Rentier states are defined by the fact that a small number of political elites control large proportions of the state budget that mainly stems from external revenues. They use these rents strategically with the aim of influencing political, social and economic developments in their favour. Rentier theory advocates argue that oil hinders democratization since financial resources from the oil rents are used to buy loyalty among the population, create legitimacy and buy off dissent among the opposition (Gause & Yom, 2012; Ross, 2011). Especially, the distribution of welfare gifts and material allocation in return for social obligation is a key component for stabilizing the autocratic rule in this region (Mishrif, 2018). This social contract has often been seen as the backbone of legitimacy among the monarchies (Kamrava, 2018, 159; Krane, 2019). With the decline in oil price since 2014, scholars have focused on the social context and socioeconomic and political implications that not only threaten "middling rentiers" such as Saudi Arabia, Oman and Bahrain but also "extreme rentiers" such as Kuwait, the UAE and Qatar (Herb, 2014, 14). Whether more engaged with discussing the role of economic diversification and post-oil preparations (Mishrif & al-Balushi, 2017; Sultan et al., 2011) or rather focusing on the political implications of allocative or rentier states with "diminished patronage power" (Hertog, 2020, 95), numerous scholars have readjusted the dominant framework of RST (Moritz, 2020; Selvik & Utvik, 2015). In addition to fostering social cohesion and allegiance among the GCC citizens and buying off dissent, resource wealth is also used to enhance a repressive apparatus as well as strategically co-opt state institutions and politically relevant players (Cammett et al., 2018).

A third pattern of research deals with the international dimension as well as the interplay dynamics of the domestic and international levels. In this way, some authors like Paul Aarts have pointed to the general weakness of the above-mentioned explanations for their exclusive focus on internal causes. Instead, relatively early, Aarts highlighted the existence of an external patron as a source of regime resilience among the Gulf monarchies (Aarts, 2007). As other scholars have also emphasized, particularly the role of the USA is crucial. It acts as a major ally and protector because of Saudi Arabia's irreplaceable role as the global supplier of fossil fuels (Aarts, 2007; Jones, 2012). The kingdom, in turn, receives security assurances and diplomatic support by its foreign patron (Gause & Yom, 2012). The smaller Gulf monarchies are also allied with the USA by, for instance, granting US forces access to their territories. Especially, the smaller GCC countries have received greater attention for their attempts to apply foreign policy strategies of "subtle power" (Kamrava, 2015) or "nation/state branding" (Peterson, 2006) to increase their leverage. Certainly, the Gulf states' deep involvement in the global energy system and their important geopolitical location have also been cited as reasons why not only the regional hegemon Saudi Arabia but also aspiring microstates such as Qatar and the UAE can rely on powerful international allies (Coates Ulrichsen, 2016b).

The combination and entanglement of all these three 'ingredients' have had an impact on explanations of regime resilience of the Gulf monarchies. In the last several years, however, the Gulf Arab monarchies have experienced changing dynamics on both the domestic and international fronts. Despite a firm legitimation base, the GCC states face serious problems in light of growing stressors that include grave economic difficulties and social tensions. All six GCC countries face difficulties in sustaining their welfare allocation regimes while keeping up high export numbers as the most important source of rents. The situation continues to deteriorate through endogenous factors (e.g. uncertainties of succession, demographic trends, socioeconomic imbalance, weak institutionalization and oversized public sectors) and exogenous factors (e.g. regional rivalry, shifting geopolitical conditions, climate change, fluctuation of oil price, low-carbon development). All these developments impact state-society and state-elite relationships as well as shaping regional and even global geopolitics. The following section aims to sketch out this 'confluence of crises' more profoundly.

Political Reconfigurations: A Game of Thrones

Simply put, policymaking in the Gulf region should be understood as a continual strategy to maintain the ruling elites' privileges, authority and power while preventing and obstructing anything that may constitute a challenge to this goal. The current ruling families in the six GCC states have inhabited the Arabian Peninsula for hundreds of years and established their rule during the eighteenth century (Abdulla, 2012). While the Al Saud family gained their independence in 1932,[1] others remained under semi-imperial administration by the British.[2] In the 1960s and 1970s, the British withdrawal resulted in the Eastern Arabian states' independence in Kuwait (1961) and Bahrain, Qatar and the UAE (1971). Local realities, dating to times before the establishment of the modern state, enabled ruling families to become royals and heads of state. The rulers were able to boost their legitimate claim to power by relying on ideational sources of religion and tribalism. In contrast to many republican counterparts, they did not experience a transformation accompanied by a denial and disengagement of the colonial legacy. Quite the opposite, the process of state building was smooth and connected to existing

[1] Two early attempts at state-building were averted by Ottoman rule in 1818 and 1871.

[2] Located at the Ottoman Empire's periphery, the rulers of the various sheikhdoms on the Gulf's coastline enjoyed considerable autonomy and agreed to individual treaties with the British Empire resulting in more or less formal protectorate. While the British had their own interests, they served as a protection shield against internal and external threats such as familial and/or tribal power struggles and piracy. Ultimately, this enhanced the survival and legitimacy of the ruling families and transformed "the traditional Arabian sheikhdoms into proto-state entities" (Coates Ulrichsen 2011, 18).

pre-state patterns and norms that made monarchism "the defining frame of reference" (Demmelhuber, 2015, 99). Eventually, it resulted in the conflation of the regime and the state (Demmelhuber, 2015; Derichs & Demmelhuber, 2014). In other words, the ruling elites saw themselves as inherently linked to the territorial state and considered it and its recourses their personal property. This becomes most apparent in the Kingdom of Saudi Arabia, whose name is inextricably bonded with the ruling family Al Saud. Gulf monarchs developed highly centralized states, in which rulers stand "above the political system" and family members occupy and monopolize key offices (except in the case of Oman) (Kostiner, 2000, 8; Herb, 1999). Consequently, the statehood itself is closely linked to the perception of elites as legitimate leaders, who rule these states (Ehteshami, 2013, 143), whereas policymaking in these states is based mainly on the preferences, choices and decisions of individual patron figures.

Additionally, the formation of a well-advanced security apparatus enhanced the creation of repressive regimes that counter any form of interest articulation and aggregation. In all states, the establishment of political parties and conducting of public demonstrations are both forbidden. In more liberal Kuwait, no political parties exist (legally speaking), but members of the National Assembly are organized along political blocs. At the same time, draconian punishments exist and have been tightened lately, for insulting the ruling families, the state or its security forces (Zumbrägel & Demmelhuber, 2020). This helps promote "the idea of making them [the royals] sacrosanct", supporting what one interviewee dubbed "monarchism as symbolism".[3] Top-down reform processes over the last decades that introduced new constitutions, crafted homegrown systems of consultative bodies such as the place of sitting (*majlis*) or consultation (*shura*) and initiated government-controlled electoral processes of these traditional political structures are "wrapped in a façade of modernity" (Abdulla, 2012, 109). It has all served well to foster the legitimizing narrative of being consistent with national values and is in accordance with the global script of democracy. In sum, despite the development of institutions and formalized procedures of politics, decision-making is highly shaped by a political culture that is tribal,

[3] Interview #6, further interview #1 and interview #5.

centralized, small and rather informal and "fall[s] into the hands of an inner circle consisting of not more than a handful of people".[4]

Such strategies have worked for a long time, but currently these regimes face new challenges on several fronts. First, as the subsequent chapter will elaborate more, the abundance of oil and gas that equipped the monarchies with the financial capacity to exploit incentive-based legitimizing strategies, instead of relying on sheer repression for their own survival, is at stake. Second, all countries except the UAE have experienced political transitions in the last decade. As previous examples in the Gulf Arab states have shown, especially during the 1990s and early 2000s, these transition periods are characterized by profound changes as new leaders tend to legitimize their rule through ambitious new agendas while also building new coalitions to support them (Diwan, 2017). New ambitious leaders on top of the power pyramid raise their profile through a mixture of gaining legitimacy (e.g. by constructing forms of 'hypernationalism' or introducing alleged political reforms), repression (e.g. by silencing dissidents) and the exertion of influence (e.g. taking a more assertive foreign policy approach) (Al-Rasheed, 2020; Davidson, 2021). Third, societal demands are growing due to rising educational levels and new communication technologies. Particularly, "young people appear to want governments that are more inclusive, accountable, and responsive" (Grand and Wolff, 2020, 8; Thompson, 2019). Hereby, actors from civil society start to challenge deeply rooted habits of authoritarian rule. At the same time, new second-tier elites, specialized technocrats (*mudarāʾ fi-l-dawla*) and relevant veto-players from different strata of society such as economy and trade are entering the field and playing a considerable role in decision-making.

Shifts in the Regional and International Order

It is, however, not only the domestic realm where GCC leaderships face new challenges. Also, old patterns of alliance building and international partnerships are in constant flux. On a regional level, the stronger efforts towards regionalism and regional integration that have been observed since the early 2000s experienced a major setback during the Qatar blockade between 2017 and 2021 (Coates Ulrichsen, 2020). Since its

[4] Interview #9.

inception in 1981, the subregional organization has taken substantial steps towards economic, political, societal integration and internal security. Some of these milestones include the creation of customs union, a common market and collective security approaches. Although the subregional organization failed to fulfil its promises of a deeper institutional integration, especially the collective and solidary approach to counter the waves of mass protest in 2010 and 2011 has led to a widespread perception of the 'monarchy club' as the new centre of gravity in the Middle East (Saouli, 2020). Yet, only a few years after this regional turmoil, the often propagated 'GCC brotherhood spirit' began to fall apart. It was replaced by the formation of new power blocs, which included an Abu Dhabi–Riyadh–Manama axis against Doha whereas Kuwait City and Muscat acted as neutral mediators. The first disclosure of a fundamental reconfiguration along different blocs appeared in March 2014 when the trio of Saudi Arabia, the UAE and Bahrain recalled their envoys from Doha. This diplomatic rift ended after six months, only to be renewed in summer 2017 when the 'GCC-3' launched a blockade on Qatar on 5 June 2017. The closing of land, sea and air borders for people and goods meant a new dimension of escalation (see further: Coates Ulrichsen, 2020). Despite various mediation efforts, above all by Kuwait and the USA, the blockade and political impasse (as Qatar managed quite successfully to offer resistance) lasted until January 2021. The development of the GCC 'from hero to zero' reflects a natural structural imbalance of power between the single countries that has only been fuelled by new powerful and ambitious, sometimes reckless, leaders. At its core, the subregional organization is characterized by a dual-level competition between single GCC members. On the one hand, Saudi Arabia is frequently undermining regional power aspirations by other members, demanding compliance from the other GCC fellows as its most powerful member (Kneuer et al., 2018). On the other, there is constant competition between the smaller Gulf monarchies, above all between the two microstates Qatar and the UAE. For a while now, both have competed over strategic 'vanity' niches such as arts, sports, architecture and various industrial sectors but the fault-line between the 'GCC brothers' only intensified when Doha and Abu Dhabi enacted a more muscular policy outside their own territories. Both Qatar and the UAE have pursued a stronger regional leadership role for themselves and were quite successful in branding themselves as tourism- and investment-friendly destinations.[5]

The fact that ambitious Gulf monarchs were able to strive for their own globalization course over the last years was also amplified by major geopolitical shifts. The region's geo-strategically critical location that connects world markets in Europe, America and Asia has been of constant interest to various global powers. The long-term and strong alliance between the US and Gulf monarchies has deteriorated during the last years. Examples of this include several watershed policy choices under the Obama administration (e.g. the dissociation with Egyptian president Hosni Mubarak, the Iranian nuclear deal or the Justice Against Sponsors of Terrorism Act). In Qatar, President Trump's immediate solidarization with the blockading states in 2017 was perceived with massive mistrust by Doha, recalling that Qatar hosts one of the largest US airbases. Despite a short 'honeymoon period' under the Trump administration, the perception in Riyadh and Abu Dhabi over the last two or three years has increasingly been that they no longer enjoy unconditional backing from Washington. This "benign neglect" of US policy (Altermann, 2017) has hastened an ongoing process of hedging and diversifying linkages to other world regions and powers. It has facilitated the Gulf states' reorientation towards Eastern countries and emerging powers such as Russia, China, Japan, South Korea and India (Demmelhuber, 2019; Young, 2019). This 'pivot to Asia' is observable through numerous joint ventures that can be found across such sectors as business, diplomacy, security, energy, food, education and R&D. The concurrence of strategic papers and outlooks such as Saudi Vision 2030 and China's Belt and Road Initiative has further boosted political and economic (mutual) dependencies. In tandem, for the smaller GCC states, the 'Four Asian Tigers', especially Singapore and South Korea, served as an inspirational model on how small nations are able to brand themselves to exert greater influence (Hvidt, 2020).[6]

In sum, on a regional level, the monarchies have experienced significant transformation. The relatively stable regional environment of a 'GCC brotherhood clustering' (in comparison with other countries in the Middle East and North Africa) remains in a state of decay despite the latest reconciliation agreements. Furthermore, although several GCC

[5] Interview #52 and interview #64.

[6] Interview #13.

states possess a high degree of international leverage, the gradual but conscious departure of the US patron creates new uncertainties and more efforts to overcome the challenges and pressures of globalization (*ʿawlamah*).[7] Additionally, occasional terrorist attacks (e.g. 2006 and 2019 on Saudi oil facilities and attacks on oil tankers in the Gulf of Oman in 2019) reveal not only that the region still suffers from terrorist threats but also their interconnectedness with other structural challenges such as domestic energy insecurity, regional instability and a volatile global energy market.

Redefining the Socioeconomic Model: Escaping the 'Sustainable Impasse'

The discovery of oil was a game changer in terms of the unprecedented wealth, opulence and luxury it brought. Surging oil prices and the influx of petrodollars literally changed the outlook of the Gulf Arab monarchies: Urban centres with cutting-edge modern buildings "grow into the sea on one side and into the sky on another" (Kamrava, 2020, 2). Yet, the abundance of resources—thought to be a blessing—became a curse for economic development: The flood of foreign exchange through fossil fuels led to vast domestic expenditures with a focus on non-tradable goods (real estate, foodstuff or services) to the demise of tradable goods (industrial products). At the same time, workforce was imported to overcome the domestic manpower shortage. This phenomenon is known as the 'Dutch disease' (Kamrava, 2018; Luciani, 2021). The term goes back to an experience in the Netherlands in the 1970s after the discovery of a gas field. In essence, it implies a sudden rise of primary commodity within the tradable sector along with the demise of manufactured goods, leading to a deindustrialization. In the case of the GCC states, it impeded the building of an internationally competitive industry from scratch (Tétreault, 2008). For a long time, the monarchs mainly focused on an expansion of the physical and social infrastructure at the expense of a manufacturing industry. The huge reliance on expatriates also caused new problems. The consequences of a skewed labour market became apparent: While young GCC citizens seek jobs in the public sector and reject low-prestige work ('mudir syndrome') (Gray, 2019, 145),

[7] Interview #16.

immigrants from developing and less developed countries, considered as cheap labour, turn into a further source of identity-related conflicts since their numbers quickly exceed the number of nationals (Fargues, 2011). Additionally, rising living expenses and inhumane employment conditions (sponsorship or *kafāla*) occasionally led to societal turmoil (Ehteshami, 2013) and damage the GCC states' international reputation. For instance, labour unrest, mostly caused by the inflationary pressure of rising costs of food and housing, occurred throughout 2007–2008 and 2013 (Coates Ulrichsen, 2011). Furthermore, the long-term economic viability is in question as expatriates remit large portions of their income to their countries of origin, while a steadily decreasing cost of labour negatively impacts labour productivity. Additionally, the large number of low-wage workers stands in contrast to the GCC states' pursuit of developing "capital-intensive industries requiring more sophisticated skills" (Luciani, 2021, 19).

In addition to causing a fundamental economic transformation, rent-derived wealth has also significantly changed the power dynamics of state-society relations. Most attention has been dedicated to the rentier social contract or allocative bargaining: After the first oil boom in 1973, the GCC rulers started to distribute the massive wealth through direct money transfers, subsidies of utilities and granting of specific in-kind benefits such as housing, education and medical care. Nearly all GCC states provide their citizens with free health care and education and free or at least highly subsidized electricity, water and transport fuel below production costs, as well as levying no income taxation (Cammett et al., 2018). Additionally, ruling elites in the Gulf massively expanded the public sector, whose employees were provided with certain privileges (Abdulla, 2012). Over the last 50 years, this has created a large middle class that is highly dependent on the state bureaucracy. This "Gulfbourgeoisie" makes up approximately 80% of the native population and largely consists of bureaucrats and technocrats, who are well-paid through governmental entities (Hertog, 2013, 175). They additionally receive guaranteed job security and social standing and enjoy universal benefits and welfare gains. These factors may generally explain their political loyalty to the ruling families (Abdulla, 2012). As one interviewee noted: "Securing the welfare state is within Gulf monarchies' DNA", which is perceived as a fundamental distinction from the Middle Eastern republics.[8] However, rapid demographic growth has put pressure on the government to provide more public services (education, real estate, utilities, etc.) with lesser revenues from the oil and gas sector. Especially, the lack of jobs and high unemployment rates among young and qualified people is seen as potentially jeopardizing future social stability (Hvidt, 2020; Thompson, 2019).

In addition to this (eudaemonic) source of autocratic legitimation (Krane, 2019; Niblock, 2006), individual rulers have also used the oil wealth and its distribution ('ruling bargain') as a 'legitimizing bedrock' for their personal consolidation: Monetary gifts or grants have often been provided directly from the king or emir, showing his generosity and bolstering his personal legitimation as well as monarchism as a system. These gifts or grants (often stated as *makruma malakiyya* or *minḥa*) emphasize the generosity of a leader and aim at strengthening the individual ruler's legitimation base. A vivid example of the interlinkage between personal image-building and the distribution of wealth can be found in the UAE. When Khalifa bin Zayed succeeded the throne in 2004, the government announced an immediate 25% increase of payments for public sector employees that was "understandably a popular decision" (Davidson, 2015, 54). Thus, rentier parameters of wealth, power and privilege became a key pillar of regime stability, but at a high cost. The regimes spend large proportions of incoming rents to pay the generous public sector salaries and to afford the public subsidies, resulting ultimately in a massive fiscal burden (Crystal, 2014).[9]

However, this strong focus on rent distributions and public spending programmes has obscured many other dynamics of rentierism. In this way, the rentier-based model has had a huge impact on facilitating neopatrimonial structures in the Gulf states. For instance, the system also fostered

[8] Interview #17. However, according to a political scientist based in Saudi Arabia, it is important that benefits and monetary allocations are distributed on a common base (Interview #1). Otherwise, citizens from other Gulf monarchies would demand the same treatment as their neighbours. The diffusion of welfare allocations in the scope of the 'Arab Spring' demonstrated this coordinated action (Zumbrägel 2020a).

[9] Subsidies can be defined as "the gap between regulated sales price of fuel and the cost of its supply", cited from: Wogan et al., (2019, 30). When it comes to energy, a narrow definition of subsidies is erroneous, because the cost of production, too, is comparatively low in the GCC states. Instead, one can also speak of opportunity costs, which measures the forfeited revenues by including the specific circumstances (see: Wogan et al., 2019, 9f.).

a class of crony capitalists, "who grow wealthy on the brokerage of contracts based on political connections rather than on economic principles" (Sorenson, 2008, 140). This business group of so-called crony capitalists or rentier bourgeoisie became a quite autonomous although not coherent force, a heterogeneous class that entails elements both of the old elite capital and of the state bourgeoisie. Usually, these capitalists have close relations with the ruling families and in some instances even manage to gain political positions. At the same time, ruling elites have profited from the successful and large conglomerates that have been established by these businesspeople. Frequently, members of many ruling families were able to exert influence in prospering business sectors. Hence, the formation of a comparatively independent and capitalist-oriented class also constituted a key anchor of ensuring authoritarian power (Hanieh, 2021). There is a realization that Gulf monarchies need to overcome the 'resource curse' and changing the deeply entrenched rentier-based socioeconomic models to escape the 'sustainable impasse'.

Rethinking Rentierism

Over the last decades, the allocative power of these Gulf monarchies—although to a much lesser degree than other semi-rentier states of the Arab region—has gradually decreased. This is as a consequence of disruptions in rent inflows, demographic youth boom and rising living standards, as well as highly energy-intensive industrialization and modernization programmes. The fact that all GCC states, though to a lesser extent the UAE, are almost completely reliant on their oil revenues makes them vulnerable to shifts in the global oil market. Revenues of selling oil and gas account for around 70 and 90 percent of total revenue in many countries, except for the UAE (36 percent). A global demand peak, a global financial recession (as in 2008), a drop in oil price (as in 2014–2016 and 2020–2021), growing pressure to decarbonize, as well as technological advancements that enable the exploitation of new sources of fossil fuels (e.g. shale gas), all of these represent fundamental threats to statehood in the GCC.

In light of these domestic and global erosions, all GCC states have initiated programmes and agendas to diversify their economies in order to pursue growth (Beutel, 2021; Mishrif, 2018). This, however, is not a new phenomenon; in the 1970s, countries started diversification processes by expanding the oil industry (e.g. downstreaming). The more recent phase, in turn, is rather characterized by the development of a knowledge-based economy (Günel, 2019; Luomi, 2012). According to Matthew Gray, the monarchies have entered a state of 'late rentierism' by now. A late rentier economy is characterized by a responsive and open (although not democratic) state with an active foreign policy. Its economy is based on long-term planning and characterized by diversification and entrepreneurial thinking (Gray, 2011). This diversification process is most visible in the individual national development programmes including 'Oman 2020: Visions for Oman's Economy' (1995), Bahrain's 'Economic Vision 2030' (2008), 'Qatar National Vision 2030' (2008), 'Kuwait Vision 2035' (2010), 'Vision 2021' on behalf of the UAE (2010) and 'Saudi Vision 2030' (2016). Particularly, the lower-income states Bahrain and Oman were early advocates of economic diversification but were soon surpassed by Qatar, the UAE and Saudi Arabia (Coates Ulrichsen, 2011).

The rationale behind this economic diversification hyperactivity is based on several aspects such as limiting dependence on a volatile oil market and single commodity, creating new jobs and business opportunities to stimulate the economy, and preparing for a low-carbon global economy. Yet not all GCC states are exposed to these threats in the same way: The 'middling' or 'poor' rentier states, Bahrain and Oman, which are already dependent on the other's oil money, are under great pressure.[10] Also Kuwait, whose economy is heavily reliant on hydrocarbons (with revenues from the export of oil and oil products generating between 80 and 90% of the state income), is highly vulnerable. To a lesser degree, Saudi Arabia and the UAE (except Dubai, which has diversified successfully into a range of economic sectors) face similar difficulties. Qatar, in turn, has a strategic advantage due to its abundance of low-cost gas that is less emitting than other fossil fuels (Mishrif, 2018; Mills & Sim, 2021). Additionally, the GCC states differ in terms of energy supply and demand, requiring different strategies of long-term energy resilience and diversification. Saudi Arabia has the largest installed capacity (around 80.5 GW), followed by the UAE (around 29 GW) and then other states like Kuwait (18.3 GW), Qatar (8.6 GW), Oman (7.8 GW) and Bahrain (3.0 GW) (Wogan et al., 2019).

[10] It is noteworthy that Oman has made substantial efforts in exploiting new gas fields through advanced technology (Dourian 2019).

Energy sustainability is thus a crucial element of economic diversification, and there are good reasons why this is the case: The Gulf region, known to be the global energy powerhouse, is experiencing difficulties meeting the energy demand. In 2008, Kuwait and the UAE became net gas importers (Krane, 2019, 73). Furthermore, GCC states have experienced repeated power cuts during the hot summer months when consumption peaks (Luomi, 2012, 37). This is not because of a depletion of oil in the foreseeable future. Instead, the long-lasting effects of the radical modernization course and the rentier mentality have led to a waste of energy, high energy inefficiency and overconsumption (Krane, 2019). The mantra of development enhanced a reckless usage of energy. Examples include the outdoor energy-intensive air conditioning systems in almost every corner and maintaining extensive garden areas run by high water-usage automatic sprinkler systems (Luomi, 2012). The subsidized cheap transport fuel—partly linked to the harsh climate conditions and an undeveloped public transport infrastructure—has resulted in a car-centred mentality, where people prefer driving petrol-guzzling SUVs. The same is true for the heavily subsidized housing that led to the mushrooming of vast and mostly inefficient architecture such as glazed skyscrapers and indoor ski halls (Rabinowitz, 2020); especially, cooling is a very sensitive and 'hot topic' of a sustainability transformation.[11] The oil wealth also enhanced the unsustainable practice of building artificial islands (e.g. in Dubai, Bahrain and Doha) leading to the destruction of coastal areas and biodiversity. As the following chapter will elaborate in greater detail, growing temperature rise leads to an almost complete dependence on air conditioning during long summer seasons, accounting for around 70% of the annual peak electricity consumption (Günel, 2018a, 2018b). Resource scarcity relates not only to electricity and gasoline but also to other utilities such as water and even food: Potable water is almost exclusively produced through seawater treatment (desalination) since the dry and extremely arid climate offers few groundwater reverses. Despite the fact that the process of desalination has severe environmental impacts (e.g. through saltwater discharge and outflow of untreated wastewater), it is also highly energy-intensive, highlighting the interdependency between water and energy. In other words, at peak times, Gulf countries burn fossil

[11] Interview #50.

fuels, unleashing GHG emissions, in order to secure residential and industrial water usage, which is largely squandered. Simultaneously, water is needed for energy production (e.g. cooling generating plants or refining) and the agricultural sector (e.g. irrigation) (Lahn et al., 2013; Rambo et al., 2017).

In general, the Gulf states have four broader policy strategies to tackle the inherent dilemma of this water-energy-food nexus (see further Abulibdeh et al., 2019). This includes three ways of increasing the supply by (a) investing in more conventional energy sources like oil and gas, (b) diversifying the energy portfolio through non-hydrocarbon energy sources (e.g. solar, wind and nuclear energy) and (c) diversifying the economic structures of their countries to lower the dependence on crude oil. Another option, often associated with higher political risks is (d) to alter the demand side (Krane, 2019). Especially, the latter is seen as sensitive issue as it would fundamentally attack the rentier mentality and the 'social pact'. Across all states, the majority of GCC citizens consider the large subsidies of utilities such as water, fuel or electricity a personal right (Günel, 2018b). Against this backdrop, most regimes have undertaken cautious adjustment to the 'rentier bargaining contract' over the last decade. Although cutting of subsidies and introduction of taxation have been partially modified or reversed, it shows that changing the patterns from exclusive distributive patterns to redistribution without making concessions to a participatory mechanism is not necessarily a Pandora's box (Hamaiza & Moerenhout, 2022).

Expanding the private sector is another crucial issue and key driver of diversification, but success so far has been limited (Mishrif, 2018). For instance, the governments have made stronger efforts to nationalize the private sector (e.g. Saudization, Omanization, Qatarization, etc.). Yet, the welfare state with all its benefits offers few incentives for young and skilled people to pursue jobs in the private sector in favour of more prestigious positions in the bureaucratic sector. One example is Saudi Arabia, where almost half a million new jobs were created in 2015, of which 88% went to non-nationals (Coates Ulrichsen, 2016a, 6). Even more problematic, the GCC economies remain predominantly government-controlled and embedded in neopatrimonial state structures (Crystal, 2014; Gray, 2018). More privatization attempts are also hindered by the fact that a stronger and decentralized private sector beyond the "oligarchic pact" (Valeri, 2017) would tremendously reshape the traditional political custom of state capitalism and centralized authority in the GCC states. Therefore, it comes as no surprise that the economic transformation has almost fully remained in control of the ruling elites. Comparatively early, as the following chapter will put into context, leaderships have supported and promoted only a few internationally competitive firms to avoid the negative effects of the 'resource curse'. Among these 'islands of efficiency' are the oil giant Saudi Aramco and Saudi Basic Industries Corporation (SABIC) (Cammett et al., 2018; Hertog, 2010). Still, large-scale investments by sovereign wealth funds (SWFs)[12] and the emergence of several state-owned enterprises (SOE)[13] in strategic economic niches are seen as a key instrument for such a horizontal diversification (Mishrif, 2018). However, as Mari Luomi rightly points out: "This leads to a limited potential for inward foreign direct investment (FDI)" and a "heavier burden for the governments in job creation, technology transfer and capacity building" (Luomi, 2015, 13). It is in light of these unresolved questions that the GCC states foresee the necessity to act.

The Looming Climate Peril and Environmental Collapse: A Matter of Survival

The above-described mixture of a domestic economic imbalance, neopatrimonial state structures, and demographic and industrial growth, consumption behaviour and increasing industrialization/urbanization is also exacerbated by a fourfold threat of climate change, environmental degradation, resource scarcity and pressure to decarbonize based on changing social preferences. Combating climate change as well as overcoming environmental challenges such as desertification, rising sea levels and saltwater intrusion that impact both urban areas and agriculture need fast and coordinated responses. Apparently most pressing, the aggravation of "desertification in the desert" (Kumetat, 2012, 374) will heat

[12] Traditionally, a SWF is defined as "state-owned investment fund or entity that is commonly established from balance of payments surpluses, official foreign currency operations, the proceeds of privatizations, governmental transfer payments, fiscal surpluses, and/or receipts resulting from resource exports" (cited from: Coates Ulrichsen 2016a, 2016b, 116).

[13] Commonly, a SOE is "a commercial, financial, industrial, agricultural or promotional undertaking–owned by public authority, either wholly or through majority share holding–which is engaged in the sale of goods and services and whose affairs are capable of being recorded in balance sheets and profit and loss accounts" (cited from: Al-Hinai et al., 2017, 54).

up the region by around 3–5 °C over the next century. Even today, the countries regularly experience temperatures that can reach 40–45 °C during summertime. Single countries have already experienced a record high, such as Abu Dhabi with 50.4 °C in summer 2017 and Kuwait with 53.2 °C in summer 2019. According to some studies, there is a high chance that the Arabian Peninsula will become uninhabitable by the end of the century (Pouran & Hakimian, 2019). According to an article in Nature Climate Change, the GCC states will most likely find themselves in scenarios where they exceed a threshold for human adaptability (Pal & Eltahir, 2016).

Rising temperatures and humidity are a further burden to the arid and hyperarid climates of the Arabian Peninsula that is already now a global hotspot of water scarcity. All GCC nations are currently under the water poverty threshold of 500 m^3 per capita of water available annually (Keulertz & Allan, 2019). At the same time, the Gulf monarchies have one of the largest water footprints (including 'virtual water' through importing food and other products) (Sullivan, 2021, November 21). The water crisis and growing scarcity are also caused by anthropogenic pollution of the natural water reserves through, for example, hazardous wastes and undertakings like urban planning (Siddiq et al., 2021). Additionally, the extraction and combustion of fuel affect the water quality in the Red Sea and Arabian Gulf, which may destroy the aquatic environment (Alnatheer, 2006). Weak regulation on waste management (residential and industrial) causes great pollution; artificial coastlines destroy coral reefs. The harm caused through hazardous wastes deposited in the ocean by the private and industrial sector also affects food and health security (Taher & Hajjar, 2014). As Johan Schaar puts it: "The world's largest dead ocean zone is found in the Gulf of Oman" (Schaar, 2020, n/a).

Additionally, long-term climate change includes growing threats from rising temperatures and sea level rise in shared waterways such as the Red Sea and Gulf Sea. The effects will impact food security (e.g. loss of fish stocks), damage and flooding of coastal communities' habitats, industry and infrastructure. Sea level rise poses a major long-term risk. If water level continues to increase, it threatens the densely populated urban centres, in which more than two-third of the all GCC populations reside. It could even destroy large parts of low-lying countries like Bahrain and Qatar. All scenarios would lead to a mass migration of 'climate refugees' (Abdelraouf, 2019). Some projections suggest a rise in sea level of up to 186 cm by 2100 in a worst-case scenario (Beni et al., 2021). Temperature increase in marine environments further aggravates the already tense situation concerning the provision of basic services such as water. Relying almost completely on seawater treatment (desalination), the rise in temperature also stimulates the growth of "harmful algal blooms that can block desalination plants and coastal industrial cooling systems" (Tolley, 2021, n/a). This and other factors such as growing brine discharge, decreasing outflows from Shatt al-Arab as main freshwater source as well as ongoing groundwater extraction leads to a higher concentration of salinity, ergo more desalination. This is particularly true for the northern coastlines of the Gulf, which has less exchange with the Arabian Sea. This all describes why desalination "is not a sustainable solution" (Beni et al., 2021, 14).

Environmental change also disrupts food supplies in the region and above all domestic food production, which is particularly important for Saudi Arabia. The kingdom started to build a large agricultural sector over the last 60 years aiming at food self-sufficiency (Jones, 2010; Woertz, 2013). However, rapid demographic and economic growth has demanded an agricultural expansion along with increase in imports and land acquisition overseas. Despite the fact that only a small amount of the GCC's total area is used for agriculture (approximately 3.9%), the farming industry is the biggest water consumer and uses mainly non-renewable groundwater resources. In addition to the danger of depleting aquifers, there is a risk of increasing salination and growing threat of seawater intrusion (Abulibdeh et al., 2019, 7). Also, the countries' aquafarming industries are under pressure: As Woertz described ten years ago: "The Jeddah coast will be depleted of fish within 15 years if current exploitation rates continue" (Woertz, 2013, 86). Water shortage, salination, degradation of soil fertility and depletion of fish stocks compromise food security and result in greater dependence on importing food. Yet, climate change in other world regions destroys fertile land leading to a rapid rise of global food prices (Woertz, 2013, 198; Al-Saidi, 2020). External shocks such as the global food crisis of 2008, export restrictions, the outbreak of the COVID-19 pandemic in late 2019 and more recently, the war in the Ukraine as one of the largest global exporter of wheat are only exacerbating these trends of insecure and volatile global food supply chains.

Furthermore, occasional environmental hazards occur more frequently (Kumar, 2013). As seen during the summer month in 2022, dust storms happen more often and severely. They are a health issue and can reduce visibility causing a dramatic increase of traffic accidents on land and in the air. Earthquakes and volcanic hazards, as well as cyclones, are frequently occurring events (Al-Bassam et al., 2014; Abdelraouf, 2019). Some areas also experience more erratic rainfalls that lead to flash flooding. Intermittent environmental degradation can also be caused by other human-induced activities such as ignited oil wells, leaking oil tankers or nuclear accidents (e.g. problems with performance under high temperatures or increased risk of terrorist attacks) at the Iranian power plant in Bushehr or the Baraka plant in the UAE, resulting in devastating ecological consequences such as the contamination and irradiation of water and air (Coates Ulrichsen, 2011). Already now, the air quality is negatively affected. High amounts of emissions from the combustion process of hydrocarbons make fossil fuels a 'dirty' energy. Although their overall global share of carbon emissions is low, the GCC states have the highest rates of carbon dioxide (CO_2eq) emissions per capita. In Saudi Arabia, which is a top producer of CO_2eq, most emissions stem from the power and electricity sector, followed by transportation and the industry and construction sectors (Taher & Hajjar, 2014). Poor air quality ultimately impacts human health, especially for people who suffer from lung diseases like asthma. A report by the World Health Organisation (WHO) concluded that GCC citizens "are breathing some of the most toxic air on earth" (cited from: Cooke, 2017, n/a).

In light of these multiple environmental-related challenges, it is surprising that policymakers in the Gulf have turned a blind eye to these issues for such a long time. Quite the contrary, the above-mentioned hydrocarbon path dependency and 'rentier mentality' have had not only economic but also environmental consequences in terms of squandering natural resources. The excessive allocation of resources by the state has led to a lavish and wasteful lifestyle (Taher & Hajjar, 2014). Free or subsidized utilities facilitated overconsumption: The GCC populations have among the highest electricity and water consumption records on earth (Luomi, 2012; Wogan et al., 2019). Almost 100% of the electricity is produced by burning fossil fuels (approximately 40% from crude oil, diesel and fuel oil and 60% from natural gas) (Krane, 2019, 72) causing high amounts of GHG emissions. That the GCC's ecological footprint is significantly higher than the global average has not gone unnoticed. For the last several years, there has been rising criticism and calls for a rigorous reduction.

Growing Environmental Pressure from Inside and Outside

The Gulf monarchies are not known for a 'green lobby' based on the presence of environmental non-governmental organizations (NGOs) or a vibrant scene of environmental activism from civil society actors and stakeholders. Also, the degree of environmental awareness and consciousness has been comparatively low among citizens (Luomi, 2012). The following statement by an influential Saudi businessman is symptomatic: "We are not China, we don't have pollution. Environmental concern is not a major priority".[14] And as environmental experts in Kuwait summarized the situation: "We have a lot of pollution here but the people are not educated. They don't know what is going on. So, no one is pushing the government".[15] Also, "there are no NGOs that push forward this topic".[16] Even more obvious is the lack of environmental awareness: When the Saudi city Jeddah experienced flash floods in Jeddah in 2009 with high numbers of casualties, it was reported that people underestimated the risk of the flood and "decided to take a trip in their cars to 'enjoy' the rain" (Elamir, 2015, 100).[17] At the same time, the natural hazard in 2009 marked a watershed moment, making environmental vulnerability a 'hot topic' of legitimation. For instance, shortly after the incident, a Facebook group 'Popular Campaign to Save the City of Jeddah' was established, which was followed by around 40,000 people within a few days (Aarts & Roelants, 2016, 73). Although the accusations mainly centred on corruption and criticism over the insufficient responses by the municipal authorities, the event also raised concerns over climate change and global warming. According to an interviewee, "It was surely because of corruption but also a sudden realization about environmental threats which had been neglected before".[18] Indeed, while there had been no environmental groups before 2010, except for the government-controlled Saudi Environment Society,[19] some

[14] Interview #3.

[15] Interview #33.

[16] Interview #34.

[17] Interview #30.

[18] Interview #44.

[19] The Ministry of Social Affairs promulgated the creation of the Saudi Environment Society in 2006 under the leadership of H. R. H. Turki bin Nasser bin Abdulaziz. Hence, the alleged NGO is actually registered under the state agency, the Presidency of Meteorology and Environment (see also: Montagu, 2015).

bottom-up initiatives such as Green Jeddah emerged as a result (Luomi, 2012, 75). When Qatar hosted COP18 back in 2012, the Arab Youth Climate movement was formed as largest regional environmental advocacy group. Its chapter in Qatar, founded in 2015, became the first registered independent and youth-led environmental association by 2019 (Shafi, 2019). During the climate summit, around 800 people participated in a climate march through the capital. While there are critical voices to label this demonstration as orchestrated as it was planned and conducted by a 'non-governmental environmental organization', which had been established shortly before through huge financial funding on behalf of the Qatari government, it was still the first ever created civil demonstration in the state (Shafi, 2021, 2022).

There have been further episodes of environmental pollution in other Gulf contexts that have revealed the growing public awareness of environmental sustainability to be a sensitive topic for governments. For instance, there was a public outcry in Qatar when a report published data on poor urban air quality in Doha up to 2014. While the government quickly managed to evade the topic, it showed the sensitive character and vulnerability of the state (Sayyeed, 2016).[20] Shortly afterwards, residents of the village Abu Nakhla, south of Doha, complained about environmental damage and water pollution due to large urban planning projects. Yet, governmental responses remained largely absent. The government only released a study, under the auspices of the Qatar Foundation, which could not confirm the claims about untreated sewage.[21] A similar example is reported from Kuwait. When several oil spills occurred in Kuwait's southern Ras al-Zour area in late summer 2017, the government immediately claimed to have contained all leaks, claims which were disseminated by state-affiliated media outlets. Yet, as environmental groups such as Kuwait's Green Line Society asserted, the government took action way too late and also avoided going into further detail about the damage. The president of the non-profit organization was quoted by foreign news outlets:

> There was no warning people against fishing or entering the polluted area, even though it is close to some of the most popular summer destinations

[20] Interview #22.

[21] Interview #23.

> in Kuwait. (...) This is what happens when under-qualified individuals handle the government's most sensitive environment entity. (...) This media blackout is intentional, and wrong (Associated Press International, 2017, August 13).

Further oil spills in the region soon afterwards provoked more anger, leading to mistrust towards the regime and its functionality. In light of this threat of delegitimization, the government then reacted profoundly and with more transparency. Kuwait's environmental authority released several reports and a map showing the location of the oil slicks as well as detailed information on further procedures to counter this act of environmental destruction (Kuwait Times, 19 March 2018). As these few examples indicate, green grassroots activism in the Gulf is far from constituting a powder keg as in other MENA countries such as Tunisia (Zumbraegel, 2020b). However, there are examples and indications of an increasing environmental advocacy that affects state-society relations. Although data on societal environmental awareness and consciousness is largely missing, the few data sets support these assumptions. In this vein, the Social and Economic Survey Research Institute (SESRI) at Qatar University and the Arab Forum for Environment and Development, both underline a greater awareness and stronger wish for more action to combat climate change (Saab, 2017; SESRI, 2016).[22] Another survey on behalf of the consultancy company PwC supports this perception and finds that there are growing concerns on environmental issues including water conservation and waste pollution (PwC, 2019). Further surveys such as the Arab Barometer in 2019 and the 2021 People's Climate Vote by UNDP also show that environmental awareness has significantly increased over the last ten years (Elmi, 2017; Gaub & Lienard, 2021; Saab, 2017). Observers notice that it is especially the youth that engages more in environmental activism, which might also be linked to the fact that many Arab universities have set up environmental departments and programmes over the last years (Gaub & Lienard, 2021; Sharp et al., 2021). Neeshad Shafi further mentions the radical increase of webinars and virtual workshops around environmental and climate-related topics that turn into forums of exchange and public tools to raise concerns over climate issues (Shafi, 2021).

[22] Interview #21 and interview #23.

Outside pressure is another, perhaps currently even greater force for political leaderships in the Gulf to turn green (Malik et al., 2019; Sever et al., 2019). Global demands to limit emissions as committed to via international accords like the Paris Agreement and the SDGs put further stress on the governments across the MENA. This is particularly true for oil- and gas-exporting nations. Not nearly well-equipped enough for a decarbonizing world economy along the lines of the 2015 Paris Agreement, political decision-makers feel massive pressure to end their 'addiction to oil' and change their hydrocarbon-based socioeconomic models. High amounts of emissions from the combustion process of hydrocarbons and their severe environmental consequences only add strain, reducing the attractiveness of the GCC as a lucrative business and investment destination (Beni et al., 2021). At the same time, commitments to international agreements such as the SDGs may further enhance civil society engagement in monitoring announced goals as well as pressing for implementing environmental activities (Hayman, 2019).

Conclusion

In contrast to opinions that have heralded the dusk of the old-fashioned monarchs, the Gulf monarchies reveal a high capacity to adapt their policymaking to changing patterns and dynamics and transform constraints into opportunities. When the monarchs faced severe threats to their rule, they were able to minimize the losses to their statehood by allocating massive financial reserves, implementing divide-and-rule measures, relying on external networks, and ideational adaptation. Over the last several years, the oil- and gas-exporting Gulf monarchies have become faced with another dual dilemma: The countries need to enhance climate action and reduce their GHG emissions for the sake of preserving their habitability. At the same time, however, this transformation fundamentally threatens their economic and political systems (see also Krane, 2019; Beni et al., 2021).

The abundance of natural resources (i.e. fossil fuels) has created wealth, power and influence. It has secured intra-family and elite cohesion, provided the economic livelihood to transform into full-fledged welfare states and increased regional and international leverage. As we have seen, all are important components for regime resilience. Conversely, it has also led to aggravated corruption, unproductive rent-seeking behaviour, unsustainable consumer habits, environmental damage and social problems (Davidson, 2015). As Kamrava pinpoints, it is the mismanagement that turn natural resources into a curse but not their availability (Kamrava, 2018). Now, all of the six GCC countries (with the partial exception of Qatar) are no longer able to balance the domestic energy consumption and subsidies on electricity, desalinated water and fuels while keeping up the high export numbers, their most important source of rents. In addition, their most precious commodity is less attractive on a global market that transforms to a low-carbon economy. Eroding claims to the country's resources and associated financial influx, as well as control over its distribution, threatens to raise fundamental questions of legitimacy in the Gulf.

In addition to this, the whole region is highly vulnerable to the effects of climate change and environmental degradation for which those fuels are responsible: Be it in terms of carbon emissions resulting from fossil fuel combustion or contamination of the environmental media (soil, water and air). Growing risks of environmental insecurity even exacerbates the diminishing patronage power of the Gulf monarchs and their efforts to lower their dependence on oil and gas. Growing risks of environmental insecurity only exacerbates the situation. For instance, rising temperatures increase the need for air conditioning and water supply. Moreover, climate effects such as sea level rise and increasing temperatures have the potential to hamper the diversification attempts of the GCC states. For instance, these can seriously affect the marine infrastructure and ports of some states or negatively impact the tourist industry through unbearable heat waves or widespread destruction of coral reefs and mangroves.

While the erosion of a social contract may lead to a decrease in loyalty and fidelity to the monarchs and the monarchy as a system, inertia in tackling climate change and environmental degradation can also minimize trust in the governments and their ability to fulfil core tasks. These economic and ecological challenges are combined with political challenges. More bottom-up mobilization and advocacy also translate to the field of environmental sustainability. Growing youth-led demands for sustainable and climate-resilient future development constitutes another challenge and raises questions about the government's core function and legitimacy. Hence, the key question remains how GCC rulers—and especially those quite new in power—can adjust to these increasing risks and challenges while upholding their legitimation base and maintaining authority and power? This book intends to provide some answers to this complex question.

References

Aarts, P. (2007). The longevity of the house Saud: Looking outside the box. In O. Schlumberger (Ed.), *Debating Arab authoritarianism. Dynamics and durability in nondemocratic regimes* (pp. 251–270). Stanford University Press.

Aarts, P., & Roelants, C. (2016). *Saudi Arabia. A kingdom in peril.* Hurst & Co.

Abdelraouf, M. (2019). *Climate change: Partnership opportunities in the framework of EU-GCCrelations.* Bussola Report. Retrieved October 29, 2021 from https://www.bussolainstitute.org/research/climate-change-partnership-opportunities-in-the-framework-of-eu-gcc-relations

Abdulla, A. (2012). The Arab Gulf moment. In D. Held & K. Coates Ulrichsen (Eds.), *The transformation of the Gulf. Politics, economics and the global order* (pp. 106–24). Routledge.

Abulibdeh, A., Zaidan, E., & Al-Saidi, M. (2019). Development drivers of the water-energy-food nexus in the Gulf Cooperation Council region. *Dev. Pract., 29*(5), 582–593. https://doi.org/10.1080/09614524.2019.1602109

Al-Bassam, A., Zaidi, F. K., & Hussein, M. (2014). Natural hazards in Saudi Arabia. In A. Ismail-Zadeh (Ed.), *Extreme natural hazards, Disaster risks and societal implications* (pp. 243–251). Cambridge University Press.

Al-Hinai, A., Espinosa, A., & Vidgen, R. (2017). A systemic approach to integrate SOEs and SMEs in business ecosystem. In A. Mishrif & Y. Al-Balushi (Eds.), *Economic diversification in the Gulf region: The private sector as an engine of growth* (Vol. I, pp. 49–76). Palgrave Macmillan.

Al-Rasheed, M. (2020). *The son king.* Reform and repression in Saudi Arabia.

Al-Saidi, M. (2020). Contributions of water scarcity and sustainability failures to disintegration and conflict in the Arab region–The case of Syria and Yemen. In P. O. Amour (Ed.), *The regional order in the Gulf region and Middle East: Regional rivalries and security alliances* (pp. 375–406). Springer.

Alnatheer, O. (2006). Environmental benefits of energy efficiency and renewable energy in Saudi Arabia's electric sector. *Energy Policy, 34*(1), 2–10.

Altermann, J. (2017). *Benign neglect.* CSIS analysis online. Retrieved October 29, 2021, from https://www.csis.org/analysis/benign-neglect

Anderson, L. (1991). Absolutism and the resilience of monarchy in the Middle East. *Political Science Quarterly, 106*(1), 1–15.

Associated Press International. (2017, August 13). Kuwait battles oil spill in Persian Gulf waters, https://www.cbc.ca/news/world/kuwait-battles-oil-spill-in-persian-gulf-waters-1.4245702

Bank, A., Richter, T., & Sunik, A. (2013). Long-term monarchical survival in the Middle East: A configurational comparison 1945–2012. *Democratization, 22*(1), 179–200. https://doi.org/10.1080/13510347.2013.845555

Beni, A. N., Marriner, N., Sharifi, A., Azizpour, J., Kabiri, K., Djamali, M., & Kirman, A. (2021). Climate change: A driver of future conflicts in the Persian Gulf region? *Heliyon*, 7, n/a. https://doi.org/10.1016/j.heliyon.2021.e06288

Beutel, J. (2021). Economic diversification and sustainable development of GCC countries. In G. Luciani & T. Moerenhout (Eds.), *When can oil economies be deemed sustainable?* (pp. 99–152). Palgrave.

Black, I. (2012, December 28). After the Sheikhs: The coming collapse of the Gulf monarchies by Christopher M. Davidson, *The Guardian*. https://www.theguardian.com/books/2012/dec/28/after-the-sheikhs-christopher-m-davidson-review

Cammett, M., Diwan, I., Richards, A., & Waterbury, J. (2018). *A political economy of the middle east*. Routledge.

Coates Ulrichsen, K. (2020). *Qatar and the Gulf crisis*, Hurst & Co.

Coates Ulrichsen, K. (2016a). *The Gulf states in International Political Economy*. Palgrave.

Coates Ulrichsen, K. (2016b). *Economic diversification plans: Challenges and prospects for Gulf policymakers*. AGSIW Visions of Change Series 2. Retrieved October 29, 2021 from https://agsiw.org/economic-diversification-plans-challenges-and-prospects-for-gulf-policymakers/

Coates Ulrichsen, K. (2011). *Insecure Gulf. The end of certainty and the transition to the post-oil era*. Hurst & Co.

Cooke, K. (2017, September 19). Polluters in chief: Gulf states ahead in poisoned air stakes, *Middle East Eye*. https://www.middleeasteye.net/opinion/polluters-chief-gulf-states-ahead-poisoned-air-stakes

Crystal, J. (2014). Eastern Arabian states: Kuwait, Bahrain, Qatar, United Arab Emirates, and Qatar. In M. Gasiorowski, D. E. Long, & B. Reich (Eds.), *The government and politics of the Middle East and North Africa* (7th ed., pp. 157–95). Westview Press.

Davidson, C. (2021). *From Sheikhs to Sultanism. Statecraft and authority in Saudi Arabia and the UAE*. Hurst & Co.

Davidson, C. (2015). *After the Sheikhs. The coming collapse of the Gulf monarchies* (2nd ed.). Hurst & Co.

Demmelhuber, T. (2019). Playing the diversity card: Saudi Arabia's foreign policy under the Salmans. *The International Spectator, 54*(4), 109–124. https://doi.org/10.1080/03932729.2019.1678862

Demmelhuber, T. (2015). The Gulf monarchies:State-building, legitimacy and social order. In E. Kienle, & N. Sika (Eds.), *The Arab uprisings. Transforming and challenging state power* (pp. 95–113). I.B. Tauris

Derichs, C., & Demmelhuber, T. (2014). Monarchies and republics, State and regime, durability and fragility in view of the Arab Spring. *Journal of Arabian Studies, 4*(2), 180–194. https://doi.org/10.1080/21534764.2014.974322

Diwan, K. (2017). *New generation royals and succession dynamics in the Gulf States. AGSIW Issue 2.* Retrieved October 29, 2021 from https://agsiw.org/new-generation-royals-gulf-states/

Dourian, K. (2019). *Oman: A small oil player with big ambitions.* AGSIW Blog Post. Retrieved October 29, 2021 from https://agsiw.org/oman-a-small-oil-player-with-big-ambitions/

Ehteshami, A. (2013). *Dynamics of change in the Persian Gulf. Political economy, war and revolution.* Taylor & Francis.

Elamir, N. (2015). Awareness-DRM axis: Suggested approach for sustainable development in the Gulf. In D. Bryde, T. Rashīd, & Y. Mouzughi (Eds.), *Sustainable development challenges in the Arab states of the Gulf* (pp. 97–112). Gerlach Press.

Elmi, A. (2017). Risks to critical environmental resources and public wellbeing from climate change in the eyes of public opinion in Kuwait. *Environmental Progress and Sustainable Energy, 37*(1). https://doi.org/10.1002/ep.12662

Fargues, P. (2011). Immigration without inclusion: Non-nationals in nation-building in the Gulf states. *Asian and Pacific Migration Journal, 20*(3–4), n/a. https://doi.org/10.1177/011719681102000302

Gaub, F., & Lienard, C. (2021). *Arab climate futures. Of risk and readiness.* European Union Institute for Security Studies (EUISS) Chaillot Paper 170. Retrieved March 19, 2022 from https://www.iss.europa.eu/content/arab-climate-futures

Gause, F. (2013). *Kings for all seasons: How the Middle East's monarchies survived the ArabSpring.* Brookings Doha Center. Retrieved October 29, 2021 from https://www.brookings.edu/research/kings-for-all-seasons-how-the-middle-easts-monarchies-survived-the-arab-spring/

Gause, F., & Yom, S. (2012). Resilient royals: How Arab monarchies hang on. *J. Democr., 23*(4), 74–88.

Grand, S., & Wolff, K. (2020). *Assessing Saudi Vision 2030: A 2020 review.* Atlantic Council. Retrieved October 25, 2021, from https://www.atlanticcouncil.org/in-depth-research-reports/report/assessing-saudi-vision-2030-a-2020-review/

Gray, M. (2019). *The economy of the Gulf states.* Agenda Publishing.

Gray, M. (2018). Rentierism's siblings: On the linkages between rents, neopatrimonialism, and entrepreneurial state capitalism in the Persian Gulf monarchies. *Journal of Arabian Studies, 8*(Issue supl), 29–45. https://doi.org/10.1080/21534764.2018.1546931

Gray, M. (2011). *A theory of "Late Rentierism" in the Arab states of the Gulf*. CIRS Occasional Paper 7. Retrieved October 29, 2021 from https://papers.ssrn.com/sol3/papers.cfm?abstract_id=2825905

Günel, G. (2018). Air conditioning the Arabian Peninsula. *International Journal of Middle East Studies, 50*(3), 573–579. https://doi.org/10.1017/S0020743818000570

Günel, G. (2018). The backbone: Construction of a regional electricity grid in the Arabian Peninsula. *Eng. Stud., 10*(2–3), 90–114. https://doi.org/10.1080/19378629.2018.1523176

Günel, G. (2019). *Spaceship in the desert. Energy, climate change, and urban design in Abu Dhabi*. Duke University Press.

Hamaizia, A., & Moerenhout, T. (2022). *Five takeaways from a decade of energy subsidy reforms in MENA*. Chatham House. Retrieved March 29, 2022 from https://www.chathamhouse.org/2022/02/five-takeaways-decade-energy-subsidy-reforms-mena

Hanieh, A. (2021). Rethinking class and state in the Gulf Cooperation Council. In J. Beinin, B. Haddad, & S. Seikaly (Eds.), *A critical political economy of the Middle East and North Africa* (pp. 105–122). Stanford University Press.

Hayman, R. (2019). The contribution of civil society to sustainable development in the Gulf and beyond. *Dev. Pract., 29*(5), 646–650. https://doi.org/10.1080/09614524.2019.1589422

Herb, M. (1999). *All in the family. Absolutism, revolution, and democracy in the Middle Eastern monarchies*. State University of New York Press.

Herb, M. (2014). *The wages of oil. Parliaments and economic development in Kuwait and the UAE*. Cornell University Press.

Hertog, S. (2020). Challenges to the Saudi distributional state in the age of austerity. In M. Al-Rasheed (Ed.), *Salman's Legacy. The dilemmas of a new era in Saudi Arabia* (pp. 73–96). Hurst & Co.

Hertog, S. (2013). State and private sector in the GCC after the Arab uprisings. *Journal of Arabian Studies, 3*(2), 174–195.

Hertog, S. (2010). *Princes, brokers, and bureaucrats. Oil and the state in Saudi Arabia*. Cornell University Press.

Hudson, M. (1977). *Arab politics*. Yale University Press.

Huntington, S. (1968). *Political order in changing societies*. Yale University Press.

Hvidt, M. (2020). The emergence and spread of the "Dubai Model" in the GCC countries. In M. Kamrava (Ed.), *Routledge handbook of Persian Gulf politics* (pp. 203–215). Routledge.

Jones, T. (2012). America, oil, and war in the Middle East. *Journal of American History, 99*(1), 208–218.

Jones, T. (2010). *Desert kingdom*. Harvard University Press.

Kamrava, M. (2020). Politics in the Persian Gulf. An overview. In M. Kamrava (Ed.), *Routledge handbook of Persian Gulf politics* (pp. 1–4). Routledge.

Kamrava, M. (2015). *Qatar. Small state, big politics.* Cornell University Press.
Kamrava, M. (2018). Oil and institutional stasis in the Persian Gulf. *Journal of Arabian Studies, 8*(supl), 1–12. https://doi.org/10.1080/21534764.2018.1546929
Keulertz, M., & Allan, T. (2019). The water-energy-food nexus in the MENA region: Securities of the future. In A. Jägerskog, M. Schul, & A. Swain (Eds.), *Routledge handbook on Middle East security* (pp. 157–167). Routledge.
Kneuer, M., Demmelhuber, T., Peresson, R., & Zumbrägel, T. (2018). Playing the regional card: Why and how authoritarian gravity centres exploit regional organisations. *Third World Quarterly, 40*(3), 451–470. https://doi.org/10.1080/01436597.2018.1474713
Krane, J. (2019). *Energy kingdoms. Oil and political survival in the Persian Gulf.* Columbia University Press.
Kumar, A. (2013). Natural hazards of the Arabian Peninsula: Their causes and possible remediation. In R. Sinha & R. Ravindra (Eds.), *Earth system processes and disaster management* (pp. 155–180). Springer.
Kumetat, D. (2012). Climate change on the Arabian Peninsula: Regional security, sustainability strategies, and research needs. In J. Scheffran, M. Brzoska, H. G. Brauch, P. M. Link, & J. Schilling (Eds.), *Climate change, human security and violent conflict. Challenges for societal stability* (pp. 373–386). Springer.
Kostiner, J. (2000). *Middle East monarchies. The challenge of modernity.* Lynne Rienner.
Lahn, G., Stevens, P., & Preston, F. (2013). *Saving oil and gas in the gulf.* Chatham House. Retrieved October 29, 2021 from https://www.brookings.edu/book/saving-oil-and-gas-in-the-gulf/
Lerner, D. (1958). *Passing of traditional society. Modernizing the Middle East.* Macmillan Pub Co.
Lucas, R. (2004). Monarchical authoritarianism: Survival and political liberalization in a Middle Eastern regime type. *International Journal of Middle East Studies, 36*(1), 103–119.
Luciani, G. (2021). Framing the economic sustainability of oil economies. In G. Luciani & T. Moerenhout (Eds.), *When can oil economies be deemed sustainable?* (pp. 9–30). Palgrave.
Luomi, M. (2015). *The international relations of the green economy in the Gulf: Lessons from the UAE's state-led energy transition.* OIES Paper 12. Retrieved October 29, 2021 from https://www.oxfordenergy.org/publications/the-international-relations-of-the-green-economy-in-the-gulf-lessons-from-the-uaes-state-led-energy-transition/
Luomi, M. (2012). *The Gulf monarchies and climate change. Abu Dhabi and Qatar in an era of natural unsustainability.* Hurst & Co.
Malik, K., Rahman, S. M., Khondaker, A. N., Abubakar, I. S., Aina, Y. A., & Hasan A. (2019). Renewable energy utilization to promote sustainability in

GCC countries: Policies, drivers, and barriers. *Environmental Science and Pollution Research, 26*, 20798–20814, https://doi.org/10.1007/s11356-019-05337-1

Menaldo, V. (2012). The Middle East and North Africa's resilient monarchs. *Journal of Politics, 74*(3), 707–722. https://doi.org/10.1017/s0022381612000436

Mills, R., & Sim, L.-C. (Eds.). (2021). *Low carbon energy in the middle east and north Africa*. Palgrave Macmillan.

Mishrif, A., & Al Balushi, Y. (2017). *Economic diversification in the Gulf region, Volume I. The private sector as an engine of growth*. Palgrave.

Mishrif, A. (2018). Challenges of economic diversification in the GCC Countries. In A. Mishrif, & Y. Al Balushi (Eds.), *Economic diversification in the Gulf region, Volume II. Comparing global challenges* (pp. 1–20). Springer.

Montagu, C. (2015). *Civil society in Saudi Arabia: The power and challenges of association*. Chatham House. Retrieved March 28, 2022 from https://www.chathamhouse.org/2015/03/civil-society-saudi-arabia-power-and-challenges-association

Moritz, J. (2020). Rentier political economy in the oil monarchies. In M. Kamrava (Ed.), *Routledge handbook of Persian Gulf politics* (pp. 163–186). Routledge.

Niblock, T. (2006). *Saudi Arabia, power, legitimacy and survival*. Routledge.

Ottaway, M., & Ottaway, D. (2019). *A tale of four worlds. The Arab region after the uprising*. Hurst & Co.

Pal, J., & Eltahir, E. (2016). Future temperature in southwest Asia projected to exceed a threshold for human adaptability. *Nat. Clim. Chang., 6*, 197–200.

Peterson, J. (2006). Qatar and the world: Branding for a micro-state. *Middle East Journal, 60*(4), 732–748.

Pouran, H., & H. Hakimian. (2019). Introduction. In H. Pouran, & H. Hakimian (Eds.), *Environmental challenges in the MENA region. The long road from conflict to cooperation* (pp. 1–9). Gingko Library.

PwC. (2019). Are Arab youth environmentally conscious? Retrieved March 28, 2022 from https://www.strategyand.pwc.com/m1/en/ideation-center/blog/arab-youth-environmentally-conscious.html#:~:text=Arab%20youth%20hold%20the%20potential,the%20development%20of%20the%20region.&text=Our%20research%20suggests%20that%20there,up'%20%2D%20the%20youth%20demographic

Rabinowitz, D. (2020). *The power of deserts. Climate change, the Middle East and the promise of a post-oil era*. Stanford University Press.

Rambo, K., Warsinger, D. M., Shanbhogue, S. J., John H. Lienhard V, J. H., & Ghoniem, A. F. (2017). Water-energy Nexus in Saudi Arabia. *Energy Procedia, 105*,3837–3843.

Ross, M. (2011). *Will oil drown the Arab spring?* Foreign Affairs. Retrieved October 29, 2021 from https://www.foreignaffairs.com/articles/middle-east/2011-08-19/will-oil-drown-arab-spring

Saab, N. W. (2017). *Arab public opinion and the environment AFED 2017 survey in 22 countries*. Arab Forum for Environment and Development (AFED). Retrieved October 29, 2021 from https://www.greengrowthknowledge.org/sites/default/files/downloads/resource/2017%20Report%20of%20the%20Arab%20Forum%20for%20Environment%20and%20Development_Arab%20Environment%20in%2010%20Years.pdf

Saouli, A. (2020). *Unfulfilled aspirations: Middle power politics in the Middle East*. Hurst & Co.

Sayyeed, M. (2016). Qatar's national emission inventory report. QEERI Report. Retrieved October 29, 2021 from https://figshare.com/articles/QATAR_S_NATIONAL_EMISSION_INVENTORY_REPORT/4154238

Schaar, J. (2020). *What the world can do about the Middle East's coming environmental crisis*. The Century Foundation, Retrieved October 29, 2021 from https://tcf.org/content/report/world-can-middle-easts-coming-environmental-crisis/?session=1

Shafi, N. (2022). *As UN climate summit returns to the Middle East, Arab youth fear a lack of representation and opportunities*. Middle East Institute. Retrieved March 17, 2022 from https://www.mei.edu/publications/un-climate-summit-returns-middle-east-arab-youth-fear-lack-representation-and

Shafi, N. (2021). *Young people are leading climate activism in the Middle East*. The Cairo Review of Global Affairs. Retrieved April 5, 2022 from https://www.thecairoreview.com/essays/young-people-are-leading-climate-activism-in-the-middle-east/

Shafi, N. (2019, Januar 18). *The Arab world's best weapon against climate change? Its young peopl*e. World Economic Forum. Retrieved October 29, 2021 from https://www.weforum.org/agenda/2019/01/the-arab-worlds-best-weapon-against-climate-change-its-youth/

Sharp, D., Alshammari, A., & Hameed, K. (2021). The quiet emergency: Experiences and understandings of climate change in Kuwait. LSE Middle East Centre Kuwait Programme Paper Series|13. Retrieved March 21, 2022 from http://eprints.lse.ac.uk/112491/

Selvik, K., & Utvik, B. (2015). *Oil states in the new Middle East*. Routledge.

SESRI. (2016). Climate change and temperature warming inQatar: Issues, public perceptions and policy options. *QU Policy Snapshot* 2. Retrieved October 29, 2021 from http://www.qu.edu.qa/file_source/qu/research/SESRI/documents/Publications/16/Climate%20Change%20and%20Temperature%20Warming%20in%20Qatar.pdf

Sever, S., Tok, M. E., & D'Alessandro, C. (2019). Global environmental governance and the GCC: Setting the Agenda for climate change and energy security. In L. Pal & M. Tok (Eds.), *Global governance and Muslim organizations* (pp. 197–228). Springer.

Siddiqi, A., Abdullah Al-Mamun, A., Baawain, M. S., & Sana, A. (2021). Groundwater contamination in the Gulf Cooperation Council (GCC) countries: A review. *Environ. Sci. Pollut. Res., 28*, 21023–21044. https://doi.org/10.1007/s11356-021-13111-5

Sorenson, D. (2008). *An introduction to the modern Middle East. History, religion, political economy, politics.* Westview Press.

Sullivan, P. (2021, November 21). You need to worry about your 'virtual water' consumption. *The National.* https://www.thenationalnews.com/opinion/comment/2021/11/21/you-need-to-worry-about-your-virtual-water-consumption/

Sultan, N., Weir, D. & Karake-Shalboub, Z. (2011). *The new post-oil Arab Gulf. Managing people and wealth.* SAQI

Taher, N., & Hajjar, B. (2014). *Energy and environment in Saudi Arabia.* Springer.

Tétreault, M. (2008). The political economy of Middle Eastern oil. In J. Schwedler & D. Gerner (Eds.), *Understanding the contemporary Middle East* (pp. 225–280). Lynne Rienner.

The Associated Press. (2017, August 13). Kuwait battles oil spill in Persian Gulf waters. *CBC.* https://www.cbc.ca/news/world/kuwait-battles-oil-spill-in-persian-gulf-waters-1.4245702

Thompson, M. (2019). *Being young, male and Saudi: Identity and politics in a globalized kingdom.* Cambridge University Press.

Tolley, G. (2021, September 21). Gulf waters already changing 'dramatically' due to global warming, research finds. *The National.* https://www.thenationalnews.com/uae/environment/2021/09/29/gulf-waters-already-changing-dramatically-due-to-global-warming-research-finds/

Valeri, M. (2017). Towards the end of the oligarchic pact? Business and politics in AbuDhabi, Bahrain and Oman. In K. Coates Ulrichsen (Ed.). *The changing security dynamics of the Persian Gulf* (pp. 77–98). Oxford University Press.

Woertz, E. (2013). *Oil for food.* Oxford University Press.

Wogan, D., al-Mubarak, I., al-Badi, A., & Pradhan, S. (2019). Overview of energy supply and demand in the GCC. In H. Akhonbay (Ed.), *The economics of renewable energy in the Gulf* (pp. 10–40). Routledge.

Young, K. (2019). The Gulf's Eastward turn: The logic of Gulf-China economic ties. *Journal of Arabian Studies, 9*(2), 236–252. https://doi.org/10.1080/21534764.2019.1768655

Zumbraegel, T. (2020a). Kingdom of gravity: Autocratic promotion and diffusion in Saudi Arabia. In T. Demmelhuber & M. Kneuer (Eds.), *Authoritarian gravity centers. A cross-regional study of authoritarian promotion and diffusion* (pp. 55–88). Routledge.

Zumbraegel, T. (2020b). *The looming climate peril. Sustainable strategies and environmental activism in the Middle East and North Africa*. CARPO Sustainability Study 01. Retrieved October 29, 2021 from https://carpo-bonn.org/en/09-the-looming-climate-peril-sustainable-strategies-and-environmental-activism-in-the-middle-east-and-north-africa/

Zumbraegel, T., & Demmelhuber, T. (2020). Temptations of autocracy: How Saudi Arabia influences and attracts its neighbourhood. *Journal of Arabian Studies, 20*(1), 51–71. https://doi.org/10.1080/21534764.2020.1788785

CHAPTER 3

A Short Environmental History of the Gulf

The Origin of Environmental Power in Arabia

As Toby C. Jones points out, aspects of political regimes such as power and sovereignty have been inevitably connected with energy and the environment in Saudi Arabia. While this is relatively apparent for the discovery of and access to hydrocarbons, as rentier theorists have widely elaborated, Jones argues that this development started even earlier with water and soil management. Controlling natural resources was crucial in consolidating power in the early periods of state formation and ensured the longevity of the Al Saud ruling family throughout the last century. In the words of Jones:

> Environmental power was tantamount to power over people and their movements and also over commerce; ultimately environmental power was derived from and constituted the state's ability to control its own territory (Jones, 2012, 233).

One of these manifestations of environmental power was the earlier push by the Saudi government towards enhancing food security, by expanding the agricultural sector on which most citizens depended during the first decades of the twentieth century. This was even despite the unsuitability of the prevailing hot and dry climate of the Arabian Peninsula for sustaining a large agricultural sector. Farming was mostly confined to a

T. Zumbraegel, *Political Power and Environmental Sustainability in Gulf Monarchies*, Contemporary Gulf Studies,
https://doi.org/10.1007/978-981-19-4431-4_3

few areas that benefitted from winter rainfall and monsoons, or strategic beneficial locations in close proximity to oases and wadis (e.g. al-Hasa and al-Qatif). In the eastern region of the Arabian Peninsula, farmers made use of artificial watercourses called *aflaj* (singular: *falaj*) to transport underground water, or used terraced fields (Woertz, 2013). Oftentimes, it had been small and isolated water resources (oases etc.) and the control over *aflaj* that determined who has access to power and who not (Joseph, 2017).

From the 1920s onwards, the Saudi government expanded irrigation systems (i.e. water pumps, wells, dams and canal systems), imported agricultural machinery and equipment and supported farmers with loans and training. Yet, its overall impact on farming remained marginal in the beginning and only slowly gained momentum (Woertz, 2013). At the same time, the search and control of water reserves became the most important task of military missions. The control, access and distribution of precious resources such as water and fertile land in an arid area mainly characterized by sand and dust storms were a major political weapon for buying allegiance. Distribution of fertile land fostered loyalty and social cohesion among the tribal and Bedouin groups, who had previously helped the Al Saud to gain power. This also facilitated settlement policies of the nomadic tribes and incentivized the establishment of a settled army that was easier to control and maintain. The centralized approach and mastery of water, food supplies and land also limited the power and influence of merchant communities that were perceived as a threat to the Saudi authority. This all helped to transform Saudi Arabia into a modern and sovereign state (Woertz, 2013, 59; Jones, 2010).

Certainly, the signing of the first oil concession with Standard Oil of California (one of their subsidiaries later became the Arabian American Oil Company, ARAMCO) in 1933 marked a watershed (Cammett et al., 2018; Woertz, 2013). The abundance of hydrocarbon resources opened new and unprecedented possibilities of environmental power and an even more centralized way of governance. Among others, oil rents were used to secure domestic food supplies and gain legitimacy on a broad scale. For instance, during World War II almost half of all foodstuff imports were allocated for free to citizens (Woertz, 2013). Oil did not result in the abandonment of the previous strategic instrumentalization of water and agriculture. Quite the contrary, the agricultural sector expanded dramatically with the abundance of energy and the help of American know-how in terms of topographical and geological assessment studies, deep drilling methods, water pumps, sprawling irrigation systems, usage of pesticides and other farming technologies. It was particular the US engineer and geologist, Karl S. Twitchell, who was responsible for gaining environmental power from the desert (Twitchell, 1944; Koch, 2021). This enabled a massive proliferation of wheat cultivation in deserted and infertile areas where nothing could formerly grow except for a few date palms. While considerations of food self-sufficiency were the main rationale for the wheat programme, the latter also helped to perpetuate the by then well-established patronage networks: In contrast to early agricultural modernization programmes that primarily targeted tribes and Bedouins, now royals and Najdi businessmen with little or almost none knowledge of farming benefitted the most from Saudi Arabia agro-investments (Woertz, 2013). During the 1980s, the kingdom became the sixth-largest wheat exporter worldwide although it was economically and ecologically questionable: The kingdom "paid farmers from five to six times the international price of wheat" to support this large-scale agro-business (Cammett et al., 2018, 215).

Furthermore, the professionalized mechanical extraction of water came to the detriment of the groundwater table, that significantly decreased (Al-Saidi et al., 2019). This exacerbated the already bad water situation. And yet, the resource wealth and financial power of oil revenues, particularly since the 1950s, also enabled completely new ways of compensating the lack of freshwater. Certainly, some of those initial ideas and visions appear bizarre today. Among these is the anecdote of King Faisal commissioning a study in 1976 to explore "the feasibility of towing a 100-million-tonne iceberg from Antarctica to the Red Sea, where it was hoped the melting ice would slake the desert kingdom's desperate need for freshwater" (Jones, 2010, 1). Eventually, decision-makers around the king gave up on following this plan, instead turning their focus to a more promising endeavour, namely the desalination of seawater. The first desalination plant had been established in Jeddah in 1970 with the help of the U.S. Department of the Interior's Office of Saline Water (Jones, 2010). By the end of the decade, the Saudi government had invested heavily in building more plants based on the costly and energy-intensive technical approach of desalination. The cost of construction equalled the kingdom's budget spending on education (Jones, 2012). Today, more than thirty desalination projects produce approximately 70% of the total freshwater, of which around 75% is dedicated to agriculture (Rambo et al., 2017).

Besides desalination, Saudi Arabia also constructed several dams, especially during the 1980s, and continued to professionalize expensive and technologically advanced drilling methods to exploit fossil water in order to balance its steadily growing water deficit (Rabinowitz, 2020).

This leadership's centralized control of nature for the sake of regime survival was further facilitated by external help. Especially, the import of agricultural material and knowledge transfer in terms of desalination indicate the important role of the USA. This also applied to the sector of alternative energy sources. During the 1970s, experimentation on several small-scale renewable energy projects started. The most prominent projects included the construction of the so-called solar village near Riyadh. Building works began in 1981 through a joint venture with King Abdulaziz City for Science and Technology (KACST) (est. 1977) and the US-based Renewable Energy Laboratory (Hepbasli & Alsuhaibani, 2011; Koch, 2021).[1] The heavy involvement of the USA was part of a broader environmental-oriented strategy in the Middle East to marginalize Soviet influence and increase US political and military strains (Hamblin, 2019).

Overall, the 1970s marked a climax of prosperous years for the Saudi leadership. Decades of agricultural loans programmes, widespread subsidization of utilities such as water and energy as well as numerous development and modernization projects secured the legitimation basis of the ruling family. The oil boom enhanced the development towards the use of patronage instead of coercion to strengthen power. It was also during this time period that Saudi oil minister Zaki Yamani successfully engaged in transforming the Organization of the Petroleum Exporting Countries (OPEC) into a powerful cartel and leveraged the nationalization of oil giant Saudi Aramco from its American shareholders; a deal that was completed in spring 1980 (Wald, 2018). In the aftermath of 1979 and the 'dual shock' of the seizing of the Holy Mosques in Mecca and social uprisings in the Eastern Province related to the Iranian revolution, the kingdom carefully modified its approach of modernization, belief in the 'technological fix' and heavy reliance on American know-how. Yet, the rulers' "century-long obsession with controlling nature and using science and technology as instruments in political control" did not stop; it was rather reframed (Jones, 2010, 223). For instance, the perception of oil as

[1] Interview #28 and interview #54.

"one of God's blessings" became a key prerequisite "to do God's work" (Jones, 2010, 222).

While the Kingdom of Saudi Arabia provides a vivid example of how environmental power fostered the processes of state-building and consolidated the authority of the ruling family based on a patronage-based system of interlocking privileges, other states on the Arabian Peninsula, however, were just at the beginning of this development. As, for instance, Natalie Koch shows in her assessment of 'desert-to-desert connection' between Arizona and the Emirate of Abu Dhabi, the young and aspiring new ruler of the emirate, Sheikh Zayed bin Sultan al-Nahyan ('Sheikh Zayed'), also relied on US assistance to use the environmental power of natural resources beyond oil and territorialize his authority (Koch, 2021).

The Awakening of the Smaller Gulf States and the Creation of Environmental Infrastructure

In contrast to Saudi Arabia, the state formation of the other Gulf monarchies took much longer. During the 1960s and 1970s, they emerged as independent modern states from protectorate arrangements at different junctures. In the first half of the twentieth century, the discovery of oil irreversibly altered the political, social and economic dynamics. Commercial quantities of oil were found in Bahrain, Kuwait and Qatar in the 1930s, but export was often delayed until the aftermath of World War II. Even in its initial phase, the exploration for oil had a dramatic impact. It not only led to a decline in hitherto economic-based traditions of merchandise, pearling and other sources of livelihood such as farming and pastoralism, but it also altered the balance of power between merchants or tribesmen and ruling sheikhs in favour of the latter (Commins, 2012). The entanglement of both the economic and social dimensions can be best observed by the example of the pearling industry: Alongside other events such as the Great Depression and the rise of Japanese cultured pearls, oil revenues heralded the twilight of the pearl industry. Before the advent of oil, pearling had a significant impact on the inhabitants of the Arabian coast and hinterland. Especially during the pearling boom between 1870 and 1930, this prospering business sector transformed the social setting dramatically. It changed the tribal population and nomadic lifestyle, since many families decided to permanently settle down. It also gave rise to port cities such as Abu Dhabi, Dubai, Sharjah and Ra's al-Khaimaih and facilitated urbanization (Heard-Bey, 1997; Kamrava, 2016). Last, but not least, it created a powerful merchant elite in some countries. Various merchants from Arab countries, Persia or India were in full control of the financial system of this sector: In return for all harvested pearls, merchants lent money and provided boats or other material (Hightower, 2013).

The long-term effects of the existence of such an interest group can be illustrated in Kuwait (Commins, 2012). On June 19, 1961, Kuwait was the first among the Gulf monarchies to become independent from Britain and relatively quickly developed into a modern state. In 1962, the leadership under Emir Abdullah al-Salim al-Sabah promulgated a constitution. The creation of a "constitutional sheikhdom" was the direct consequence of a decade of pressure by the merchants, for the chance to play a defined role in decision-making processes (Heard-Bey, 2008, 33). However, the expansion of the hydrocarbon sector, in which Kuwait became a frontrunner during the 1960s and 1970s, helped to tip the power balance in favour of the ruling al-Sabah family. Besides Saudi Arabia, Kuwait was among the founding members of OPEC in 1960 and headquartered the Organization of Arab Petroleum Exporting Countries (OAPAC) in 1968. Just like Saudi Aramco in the 1970s, Kuwait's national oil champion the Kuwait Oil Company (KOC), which was founded in 1934 by a joint venture of British Petroleum and the American Gulf Oil Company, became fully nationalized in 1975. Controlling the oil giant gave the Kuwaiti ruling family a tacit advantage vis-à-vis its previous dependency on the powerful old merchant elite. Using the revenues to pay their debts and disentangle their financial dependence on the merchants, the latter now became hinged on the goodwill of the al-Sabah (Azoulay, 2020; Crystal, 2014).[2] At the same time, the merchants realized the new business opportunities the private sector would create, following a petrodollar-based modernization (Heard-Bey, 2008).

By the early 1970s, in light of state-building processes and a rapid influx of oil revenues after the oil embargo of 1973, other GCC states also caught up in their development schemes. The British so-called Persian Gulf Residency (since 1763) was terminated in December 1971 leading to the formation of the sovereign states Bahrain (August 1971), Qatar

[2] Interview #71.

(September 1971) and the UAE (December 1971) after talks of a confederated union of emirates failed (Commins, 2012). Only Oman followed a different path. According to Frauke Heard-Bey, this was mainly a consequence of the territorial landscape and natural environment characterized by desert, arid mountains and proximity to the Indian Ocean. Instead of being externally influenced, the creation of modern Oman was foremost "a process of internal coalescence" based on a surpassing importance of tribalism (Heard-Bey, 2008, 42). The country experienced a coup in 1970 after several years of civil war that brought the young Sultan Qaboos to the throne. As Marc Valeri states: "The new ruler possessed no legitimacy at all to rule" with an ongoing revolution in Southern Dhofar (1965–1970) and a delay in oil production, which had only started from 1967 onwards (Valeri, 2017).

The first oil boom caused by a staggering increase in the price of oil (until the mid-1980s) and the increased national ownership of hydrocarbon reserves had a considerable effect on state-building and regime legitimacy in the Gulf states. Like Saudi Arabia, it enabled national development and modernization as well as deepening patronage-based structures. At the same time, the massive investments in infrastructure and urbanization projects as well as industrialization raised concerns among both policymakers and societal actors over a loss of biodiversity and livelihoods as well as increasing environmental effects of pollution from the Gulf oil industry.[3] Concurrent with the greater prominence of environmental issues in the Western hemisphere and concrete events of natural hazards, societal and scientific interest in environmental topics emerged during the 1970s and 1980s. For instance, the UAE's founding father, Sheikh Zayed, known for his interest in the environment, created the Supreme Committee of Environment in 1975. As governing body, it was entrusted with environmental legislations and regulations. Under Sheikh Zayed's rule, large portions of the Ministry of Agriculture's budget went into afforestation. It is estimated that around 800,000 trees were planted between 1965 and 1979 which also fostered "the myth of Sheikh Zayed as a champion of the environment" (Woertz, 2013, 94–95; further Joseph, 2017). However, the massive afforestation programmes, though "close to the heart of Emiratis", were only possible through petro-dollars and large

[3] Interview #41 and interview #42.

amounts of desalinated water, produced from burning oil (Woertz, 2013, 94).

In Kuwait, with its comparatively exceptional model of greater political participation, environmental bottom-up activism emerged relatively early on. Public environmental advocacy increased in light of obvious large-scale environmental issues linked to the country's rapid modernization, the increasing exploitation of fossil fuels and the demographic explosion. As a reaction to the first environmental conference in Stockholm in 1972, "a group of dedicated citizens" created the Kuwait Environment Protection Society (KEPS), which was legally recognized by the government in 1974 (Al-Sultan and al-Bakri, 1989, 63). Although privately organized, KEPS was closely associated with the government as it kept a seat on the country's environmental council. In addition to growing societal environmental demands, increased scientific knowledge about environmental damage had a significant impact on Kuwait's early process of environmental policymaking. This was not only limited to more general scientific interest (e.g. more conferences on environmental-related topics), but also a broader interest that went "hand-in-hand with that of cultural heritage", for example, the conservation of specific places and areas (Caulton & Keddie, 1989, 227). This also started during the 1960s and 1970s—concurrent with the greater prominence of environmental issues in the Western hemisphere and concrete events of natural hazards (Al-Damkhi et al., 2008). In 1967, the Kuwait Institute for Scientific Research (KISR) was created as part of a deal between Kuwait and the Arabian Oil Company of Japan, aimed at scrutinizing the broader (environmental) consequences of the exploitation of oil. In 1973, the government took control of KISR following an emiri decree that ordered the Council of Ministers to be the institution's Board of Trustees. By 1980, the University of Kuwait published an environmental sensitivity index that evaluated the risks of a major oil spillage in the Gulf and its implications for the Kuwaiti coastline (Caulton & Keddie, 1989).

Growing environmental advocacy in Kuwait went along with a further professionalization and institutionalization. In 1976, the government formed the Environment Protection Council, which issued Kuwait's first environmental law in 1980. The law also foresaw the creation of an Environmental Protection Department at the Ministry of Public Health to assist the environmental council. In addition to these domestic developments, Kuwait was deeply involved in regional environmental activities. In 1973, shortly after the UN Stockholm climate conference, Kuwait began discussions with the United Nations Environmental Programme (UNEP) and all Gulf littoral states about marine protection of the waterway. The commonly used waterways of the Persian/Arabian Gulf and Gulf of Oman revealed the dilemma of all neighbouring states: Growing pollution of industrial areas, desalination plants and drilling for oil stood in strong conflict with dependence on the waters for fishing, recreation and transport. It took several years, during which Kuwait organized a series of conferences and gatherings, until the Kuwait Regional Convention for Cooperation on the Protection of the Marine Environment from Pollution (also known as the Kuwait Convention or Kuwait Action Plan) was established. It laid the foundation for the creation of a regional organization to enhance and coordinate regional environmental protection (Nadim et al., 2008; Shuaib, 1988). The creation of the Regional Organisation for the Protection of the Marine Environment (ROPME) in 1979 can be seen as an early and promising step towards a regional integration on environmental issues. The organization included all littoral states (i.e. Bahrain, Iran, Iraq, Kuwait, Oman, Qatar, Saudi Arabia and the UAE) that were represented through a special working group, the Regional Task Force on Climate Change. However, the Iranian revolution that happened in the same year interrupted a joint action within the framework and delayed initiatives for several years (Al-Sarihi & Luomi, 2019).

Kuwait's approach of "equat[ing] committee formation with action" was "not unique" (Caulton & Keddie, 1989, 227). Also other Gulf states enhanced their environmental institutionalization and legislation during the 1980s. In Saudi Arabia, a royal decree created the Meteorology and Environmental Protection Administration (MEPA) and the Environmental Protection Coordinating Committee in 1981. In the following year, MEPA issued their first environmental regulations to combat and limit pollution. Several years later, another institution, the National Commission for Wildlife Conservation and Development was established to prevent illegal hunting and develop and implement wildlife reserves to secure Saudi Arabia's biodiversity. Similar to ROPME, the Saudi kingdom promoted the Regional Convention for the Conservation of the Red Sea and Gulf of Aden Environment (i.e. the Jeddah Convention), which was renamed the Regional Organization for the Conservation of the Environment of the Red Sea and Gulf of Aden by 1996 (Nadim et al., 2008; Vincent, 2008). Also in the early 1980s, Qatar created its first environmental body, namely the Permanent Environmental Protection Committee, while Oman created its Ministry of

Environment in 1984. In addition to that, environmental mobilization efforts increased. One example is the Qatar Natural History Group, which was established in 1978. However, this form of environmental activism was mainly promoted by Western expatriates and their organizations remained of low political profile (Luomi, 2012). Also, social grievances over environmental mismanagement appeared at that time. Critical voices were raised, claiming that the rapid industrialization and urbanization based on oil rents de facto contradicted the previous and long-lasting balance of a human-nature relationship (al-Saidi et al., 2019). Especially, Saudi Arabia's long-term manipulation of nature in its quest to achieve agricultural self-sufficiency experienced a peak in the 1980s. At the same time, it revealed the excessive and indiscriminate use of water resources. The overexploitation of natural groundwater reserves through wells and dams created an environmental crisis in the Shia-dominated and water-rich eastern province in places such as the al-Hasa oasis. During the 1980s, many Saudi Shiites branded the Saudi leadership as "an imperial power" over "the theft of 'Shia' natural resources, including oil and water" (Jones, 2010, 226). It was during this time that the first oil boom came to a sudden end (1986) and the Iran-Iraq war (1980–1988) produced serious environmental problems in the region. All these events indicated that the heyday of ecologically unsustainable management of the natural environment may not last forever.

The Gulf War, Environmental Crisis and the Rise of the 'Dubai Model'

It is not an overstatement to characterize the invasion and occupation of Kuwait by Iraq in 1990/1991 as a traumatic event in terms of environmental degradation. The almost-simultaneous ignition of more than 750 oil wells ordered by Saddam Hussein revealed how environmental destruction is strategically used in a military conflict. It not only severely damaged Kuwait's oil industry but also led to long-lasting negative effects on human health and the ecological system. In addition to the explosion of oil wells that burned for months, Iraqi troops released about 10 billion barrels of oil into the Gulf sea, which also contaminated large areas of Saudi Arabia, Iraq and Iran. It all led to the pollution of the maritime environment, groundwater resources and coastal areas in an unprecedented manner (Warner, 1991). Paradoxically, despite the ecological tragedy, shortly after the firefighting teams managed to extinguish the fires months later, Kuwait resumed oil production. As a consequence of the war, Kuwait intended to compensate the financial loss caused by the invasion by "simply pump[ing] and sell[ing] as much oil as possible" (Kropf, 2016, 29). A heavy increase in GHG emissions was the direct result. High subsidies to appease the citizenries further triggered waste- and overconsumption.

Nevertheless, the environmental crisis of the Gulf war, the creation of a global climate regime as well as a slump in oil price that thwarted previous development and modernization courses provoked a stronger engagement with environmental governance (Al-Damkhi et al., 2009; al-Saidi et al., 2019; Vrolijk, 2003). Oman made serious undertakings in streamlining its environmental sector. It merged the Ministry of Environment (est. 1984) and the Council of the Environment (first established in 1974 with several expansions and relabelling in 1979 and 1985). Both entities were integrated into the Ministry of Regional Municipalities, Environment, and Water Resources in 1991. In the UAE, the Federal Environmental Agency (FEA) was established in 1993 with the purpose of coordinating environmental protection and regulations across the single emirates and raising environmental awareness. Especially Abu Dhabi continued its role as a green leader during this period. In 1996, Sheikh Zayed created the Environmental Research and Wildlife Development Agency (ERWDA). He also launched the UAE's first Environmental Day to raise public awareness and created terrestrial protected areas for the sake of environmental protection and biodiversity (Luomi, 2012; Ouis, 2002).

While especially Oman and the UAE can be seen as early frontrunners of environmental protection, other countries also enhanced environmental governance structures. Saudi Arabia's basic law, created in 1990, makes explicit reference to the environment. Article 32 states that "The state shall work towards the preservation, protection, and improvement of the environment, as well as prevent pollution" (Kingdom of Saudi Arabia, 1992). It was also during the early 1990s that the Saudi kingdom reversed its unsustainable agrarian policy–although it did not completely abandon its programme until 2008. This change helped to reduce the overexploitation of non-renewable aquifers by almost a half (Cammett et al., 2018, 215).

Qatar brought the Permanent Environmental Protection Committee (est. 1981) under the umbrella of the Ministry of Municipal Affairs and Agriculture in 1994. In Bahrain, a decree of 1996 set up the Supreme

Council for the Environment (SCE) as principal regulator for environmental matters. Deeply scarred by the ecological tragedy of the Gulf war, the Kuwaiti government established the Environment Public Authority of Kuwait (EPA) as leading and operating arm of environmental management in 1995. The environmental institution was created by the Ministry of Health as an attempt towards greater centralization and efficiency of environmental-related entities. In this regard, it also absorbed the tasks of the Environmental Protection Council, which was established in 1976. According to one interview: "Everything was mixed up (...) and every ministry was working on its own without a need for more efficiency".[4]

It was also a time when several environmental groups emerged across the Gulf. However, given the limited degree of political participation and widespread control of leaderships, the newly established organizations were directly or indirectly connected with the government. This included the Friends of the Environment Centre, which was founded in Qatar in 1992, but also other "NGO-like environmental organizations" in the UAE (Luomi, 2012, 170). Among them were the Environment Friends Society, established in 1991 by a decree of Abu Dhabi's Ministry of Labour and Social Affairs, and the Emirates Environmental Group under the guidance of the Department of Economic Development, Government of Dubai and Dubai Municipality in the same year (Ouis, 2002).

The growing environmental awareness and institutionalization on a national level in the aftermath of the Gulf war also translated to the regional and international levels. Here, ROPME and its initiatives became very important agents in lowering the marine contamination and pollution by adopting various protocols and programmes between 1990 and 1995 (Nadim et al., 2008; al-Saidi et al., 2019). Another corollary was the launch of the General Regulations of Environment in the GCC States, which came into force in 1997. The regulatory framework marked a watershed in regional environmental governance (al-Saidi, 2021; Sever et al., 2019). Until now, it is the most pivotal framework that promotes a stronger focus on environmental considerations and demands collective action of all GCC states regarding environmental monitoring and assessment in combination with available technology and resources. While some further steps have been taken—including limiting flaring gas, a ban of chlorofluorocarbon and discussions about a regional carbon trading

[4] Interview #33.

platform—the general output has remained modest (Luomi, 2012; Sever et al., 2019; Al-Sarihi & Luomi, 2019). As one interviewee sees it: "There is nice talk about regional integration but countries are lagging behind".[5] Instead, on the international level, GCC states became active in signing and ratifying a number of environmental multilateral agreements during the 1990s. These included, among others, the Basel Convention, Convention on Biological Diversity, Convention on Migratory Species or the United Nations Convention to Combat Desertification. Most importantly, between 1992 and 1996 all the GCC monarchies entered the global climate regime by entering the United Nations Framework Convention for Climate Change (UNFCCC) (al-Saidi et al., 2019; Vrolijk, 2003).

Despite these promising steps, the governments' environmental performance should not be overestimated. The newly formed environmental bodies and agencies remained largely weak and their influence was often downsized by transforming them into an environmental department at another ministry (as seen in Qatar and Bahrain). Additionally, they were incapable of competing with other more powerful ministries. Moreover, environmental governance and climate action were not allowed to harm the carbon industries (Al-Saidi et al., 2019). Paradoxically, despite the growing problems caused by a radical exploitation of the 'black gold' that already appeared during the 1980s, the states continued their unsustainable political and socioeconomic models. Even in times when the oil price plunged to its lowest levels (e.g. during the mid-1980s), GCC states were not willing to sacrifice their patronage-based cradle-to-grave services to their citizens or stop the expansion of the public sector. Instead, some of the states embarked on a governmentally controlled economic liberalization course. They adopted economic reforms that supported the private sector and transferred money into strategic and prospering sectors such as tourism, transportation, heavy industry and finance. Especially Dubai, out of necessity after it experienced its 'peak oil moment', launched reforms with a stronger private-sector approach (Cammett et al., 2018). This development even accelerated when the global oil market recovered by the end of the century, resulting in a second oil boom for the region. The oil boom between 2002 and 2008 heralded an ultramodern period with a lavish lifestyle and reckless consumption habits where environmental

[5] Interview #19.

concerns lost importance. It was the period when the 'Dubai Model' diffused within the GCC countries (Cammett et al., 2018). As Martin Hvidt has stressed, nine parameters characterize Dubai's developmental path: (1) government-led development, (2) fast decision-making and "fast track" development, (3) a flexible labour force, (4) bypass of industrialization— creation of a service-knowledge economy, (5) internationalization of service provision, (6) creation of investment opportunities, (7) supply-generated demand ("first mover"), (8) market positioning via branding and (9) development in cooperation with international partners (see for instance: Hvidt, 2020, 205). In terms of unsustainability, it was rather questionably examples of artificial islands that destroy natural habitats, outdoor air conditioning systems, construction of endless highways and ski halls and glass fronted syscrapers with poor insulation.

While many of the Dubai Model's lavish and often environmentally unsustainable construction schemes aimed at evoking admiration and astonishment (i.e. branding), the development of artificial islands also had other strategic objectives. In so doing, "Dubai invented the concept of 'freehold property'" (...) and "pioneered the idea that artificial islands were in fact not Arab soil and as such could be sold to outsiders" (Hvidt, 2020, 205). One corollary was that this practice provided the fundament for the success of free zones as an important element in the goal of attracting foreign direct investment (FDI). Inherent to this form of modern, western-style architecture and mastery of the geographic situation was a desire to demonstrate force, progress and modernness while neglecting the surrounding environment. Furthermore, certain policy decisions such as allocation of land, subsidization of housing and other utilities, along with an expansion of car-centred urban sprawl resulted in a comfort zone in which citizens are less incentivized to push for more sustainable solutions (Zaidan & Abdulibdeh, 2021, 197). Various other GCC countries competed with each other in this 'hyper-developmentalist' model while the ecological footprint of each country soared.

The Gulf Monarchies Face the Twenty-First Century: A Not-so-New Green 'Paradigm Shift'

Although the second oil boom caused an unprecedentedly excessive consumerist lifestyle, it also led to a new green boom. Particularly, the forward-looking and hypermodern Dubai Model was increasingly perceived as ecologically harmful. It all appeared incongruous in a world that was just realizing the severe effects of climate change—most notably in the 1998 El Niño-related weather disasters that caused 23,000 deaths. It was also a time where many discussed the necessity of ratifying the Kyoto Protocol, which came out as the legally binding framework of the third Conference of Parties (COP3) in Kyoto, Japan, in December 1997. The feeling of a new 'eco era' didn't go unnoticed by the oil- and gas-exporting Gulf monarchies. While they tried a myriad of techniques to block and obscure international climate negotiations as explained in chapter seven (see also: Rabinowitz, 2020, 55; Vrolijk, 2003), concerns increased about peak oil and whether a prospering oil and gas industry would be able to provide sufficient rents in the long term (Fattouh & Sen, 2021).

However, in the early years of the twenty-first century, which were characterized by fast-increasing carbon developments, the Gulf states adhered to their strategy of advancing their environmental governance bodies and infrastructure. Numerous new and leading environmental agencies and institutions were inaugurated such as the Supreme Council for the Environment and Natural Reserves (SCENR) in Qatar (2000), Presidency of Meteorology and Environment (PME) in Saudi Arabia (2001), or the Public Commission for the Protection of Marine Resources, Environment and Wildlife in Bahrain (2002). Previously established environmental bodies were often absorbed into these new structures. For instance, Saudi Arabia's MEPA (est. 1981) became part of the PME. Additionally, new environmental regulations and statutes were issued in the UAE (1999), Saudi Arabia (2001) and Oman (2001). This also went along with a greater climate-oriented advocacy on the international level, as described in chapter seven. Over decades, wide and untouched habitats across the Gulf states had been diminished through reclamation and large-scale construction works owed to the radical modernization course. It was during the turn of the century that the number of protected areas increased significantly indicating a greater awareness of the marine and terrestrial ecosystem. For instance, while there was one protected area in Qatar in 1995, the number reached eight by the mid-2000s (Al-Ghanim, 2017).

This continued reshuffle of environmental institutions and environmental protection measures during the 1990s and 2000s reflected the emergence of environmental politics as a distinctive and individual policy field of governance although it was neither considered 'high' politics nor of such great importance that it deserved an upgrade to the ministerial level. In fact, for most of the first decade of the new century, environmental sustainability remained only of low interest to many policymakers. This changed gradually by the end of this period. While some Gulf leaderships recognized the 'political capital' of environmental sustainability, others faced stronger pressure to change their hitherto economic and social models. While there are various conditions that explain the renewed and more progressive interest towards greater environmental sustainability, three models can be identified for the GCC states: (1) an inward-oriented model of escaping the domestic "natural unsustainability" (Luomi, 2012) ('withinput'), (2) an outward-oriented model of alleged 'greenwashing PR' ('output') to cater Western norms and tastes and (3) an exogenous model of pressure and/or attraction ('input').

The first model of altering the economic model from within applies to the resource-poorer states Oman and Bahrain as well as populous Saudi Arabia. All states recognized increasing difficulties in fulfilling their welfare commitments of distributing free or at least highly subsidized utilities (e.g. electricity, water and transport fuel) far below production cost. Particularly, Saudi Arabia, with the largest population of the GCC, has experienced this with its large-scale energy extravagance based on energy wastage, inefficiency and overconsumption combined with subsidized prices. Additionally, long-term unsustainable development projects such as the kingdom's large agricultural sector, which depends increasingly on potable water produced through energy-intensive desalination plants, accelerated Saudi Arabia's energy crisis (Woertz, 2013). According to several experts, it was in the mid-2000s that then King Abdullah sought solutions to substantially alter the unsustainable Saudi model. An inner circle consisting of modernizers like former King Abdullah and current King Salman intended to strive towards a sustainable transformation but faced resistance by an internal countermovement of conservatives that included key elites such as then oil minister Ali al-Naimi and former UNFCCC chief negotiator al-Sabban.[6] Abdullah needed a persuasion strategy and started a deliberation process with the British Foreign and Commonwealth Office. The result was a report on behalf of Chatham

[6] Ali al-Naimi was the first Saudi to become president of Saudi Aramco in 1983. In 1995, he was appointed Minister of Oil until 2016. Muhammad al-Sabban had been a long-time political advisor to the Minister of Petroleum. In 1991, he became Chief Negotiator and later head of the Saudi Delegation to the UNFCCC. He held this position until 2012.

House entitled *Burning Oil to Keep Cool. The Hidden Energy Crisis in Saudi Arabia* in 2011. The analysis critically summarized Saudi Arabia's business-as-usual manner as being politically and economically unsustainable (Lahn & Stevens, 2011, 26). Eventually, Abdullah used this report's harsh appraisal to convince the sceptics within the elite's segment.[7]

During the same time, oil-rich Abu Dhabi, which had embarked a more cautious development course than its neighbour Dubai, began to evaluate the potential of diversifying its energy portfolio and decoupling carbon-based economic growth. The starting point of this development towards 'ecological modernization' was most vividly reflected in the launch of the Masdar Initiative in 2006 and also signalled a clear distancing from the reckless, ecologically questionable and unsustainable path taken by Dubai. In Abu Dhabi, however, promoting environmental sustainability through large-scale projects such as the world's first carbon-free city was rather seen as the strategic and long-term exploitation of a vanity niche, similar to other fields such as architecture, culture or sports, to brand the country. As will be shown later, the Masdar Initiative and its related milestones such as hosting IRENA were certainly good marketing tools to present the country as environmental champion abroad. Simultaneously, the 'sustainable trend' perfectly fits into the heritage of the revered founder of the UAE, Sheikh Zayed. In fact, his successors continued his environmental-oriented policies by expanding further into clean energy and green industries. This bolstered not only their legitimation but also contributed to the objective of diversifying the country's economy (Coates Ulrichsen, 2017, 114; Davidson, 2009, 138).

Another instance of 'green PR', which however backfired, can be found in the other upper-rich monarchy, Qatar. As sources agree, the foreign office's bid to the UNFCCC for hosting the 18th Conference of the Parties (COP) in 2012, was seen as another marketing opportunity for the country.[8] But for many observers it came as a surprise, in autumn 2011, when it was announced that Qatar had won the race for hosting the next climate conference. At that time the country had no official climate policy and the largest ecological footprint on earth (Luomi, 2012). In fact, Qatar had such high CO_2 emissions per capita that the organization Germanwatch decided to exclude the host in its well-known annual

[7] Interview #44; interview #30.

[8] Interview #22 and interview #20.

Climate Change Performance Index because an "inclusion would have distorted the ranking of all other countries" (Burck & Hermwille, 2013, 5). According to an interviewee:

> It was just at this time that they [the leadership] learned about the measurement of a carbon footprint and that they have the worst record in the world (...). It came as a surprise and during the COP all of this public critique gave the country a hard time.[9]

Within a short period of time, the emirate had to come up with an authentic climate policy to present itself as a reliable host and change its bad image as one of the worst climate polluters. A special task force, the so-called Climate Change and Clean Development Committee, was created and the regime in Doha hired international experts to establish a convincing environmental policy strategy.[10] Although Qatar has been described as having "developed a thick skin" (Luomi, 2012, 168), there is reason to suggest that the external criticism affected the Qatari leadership considerably.[11] Probably because this 'public humiliation' concurred with growing criticism over the World Cup 2022 concerning corruption and human rights violations at that time (Koch, 2014, 1120). According to an expert on the ground: "Qatar is particularly sensitive about international opinion and gets upset when it gets bad press internationally".[12] In brief, by the early 2010s, Qatar's international reputation, authority and legitimacy in diplomatic arenas was at stake and the country was under immense pressure to thrive under these conditions.

Lastly, Kuwait as another wealthy monarchy is a case that reveals the diffusing effects of an 'environmental enthusiasm' in the region. Despite its long tradition of environmental protection and climate action, Kuwait is constantly perceived as a latecomer in advocating sustainability. Despite its long history of advocating environmental politics largely caused by the ecological disaster of the Iraqi invasion in 1990, its record on environmental sustainability is poor. This has often been explained by its high dependence on oil that surpasses all other Gulf monarchies, as well

[9] Interview #24.

[10] Ibid.

[11] Interview #15.

[12] Interview #22.

as the existence of a powerful parliament that is often seen to "paralyze government decision-making, suspend vital projects and forestall economic progress" (Power, 2012, 32).

While several national plans and visions during the late 2000s already emphasized the need for a sustainable transformation, it took until 2015 for the first concrete steps towards installing alternative clean energy sources to be implemented. According to one interview, other GCC micro-states like Qatar and the UAE acted as appealing examples for Kuwait to copy in their attempts at economic diversification and energy sustainability.[13] This assumption concurs with the analysis of Yasemine Atalay and her colleagues, who argue in favour of a policy transfer hypothesis to explain the acquisition of renewable energy technologies in the GCC. They conclude that Kuwait has emulated sustainable policy frameworks from frontrunners like Qatar and the UAE as best practice models (Atalay et al., 2016). Yet, conceivably, the study overstates the (positive) stimulus of policy implementation as the best alternative solution. As several experts on the ground assured, it is not really about convergence and regional cooperation but rather about fierce competition to occupy as many policy niches as possible, particularly among the wealthy smaller Gulf countries.[14] In other words, Kuwait just did not want to be left behind. Furthermore, Saudi Arabia's decision to close two important oil fields (al-Khafji and al-Wafra) in 2014 that are jointly operated with Kuwait was probably another aggregating factor for the Kuwaiti government to diversify its energy portfolio and lower its dependence on oil. In tandem with a drop in oil price in 2014 and stronger commitments from the global community to combat climate change, the need for environmental sustainability was enhanced in the mid-2010s. Particularly, the signing of the Paris Agreement and the adoption of the Sustainable Development Goals (SDGs) in 2015 can be seen as further, rather exogenous, conditions for engaging more seriously in efforts to ramp up the Gulf countries' environmental image. (Al-Saidi et al., 2019). These events occurred simultaneously with a leadership change in Saudi Arabia. Under the ambitious Crown Prince Mohammed bin Salman as the de

[13] Interview #35.

[14] Interview #12. Further: Interview #26 and interview #10.

facto leader, a green agenda has also gained more attention. The new development programme, Saudi Vision 2030, which was launched in April 2016, made prominent references to environmental sustainability. Also in Kuwait, many conversation partners identified the year 2015 as a turning point, as this marked the beginning of sincere interest on behalf of political decision-makers.[15] In addition to the drop in oil price in 2014, they also refer to the Paris Agreement and the launch of the SDGs as important mainsprings for this policy shift. Several news reports support these arguments, as headlines increasingly included terms like 'climate change' (*taghayyur al-munākh*) and/or 'sustainability' (*ʾistidāma*) from 2015 onwards.[16]

Conclusion

This is by no means a comprehensive history of environmental sustainability in the Arabian Peninsula. It rather is an account of broader contexts and a general leitmotiv that drove GCC leaderships towards rethinking their hitherto business models, restructuring energy markets and reconfiguring their policies accordingly. The chapter began by showing how natural resources have strategically been used from early onwards in terms of power consolidation: Provision of water and affordable food was and still is an important part of the social bargaining between citizens and rulers that legitimizes leaderships. The advent of oil did not change this perception of 'environmental power'. It rather built upon this way of governance, though in an unprecedented manner.

The oil booms opened new possibilities of getting cool air almost everywhere, travelling long distance over highways, living in separated houses and working in offices with large glass facades. At the same time, this new lifestyle alienated GCC citizens from the harsh and arid environment they were used to living in (Zaidan & Abulibdeh, 2021). This was immensely triggered by policy decisions and government support that largely neglected principles of environmental preservation and sustainable usage of natural resources. Despite some cautious signs of environmental advocacy during the 1960s and 1970s, this remained marginal. As others

[15] For instance, statements from interviews #31, interview #33 and interview #35.

[16] Examples include Kuwait Times and the wording 'climate change' from 39 (2014) to 56 (2015) and al-Seyassah (Arabic) from 7 (2014) to 16 (2015).

have already noticed, there is a general "irrelevance of societal input in the decision-making process on sustainability policies" (cited from: Atalay et al., 2016, 212). Only in light of severe environmental damage, often caused by oil industries or construction activities, could some societal resentment be seen. This is particularly true for Kuwait, which also holds an exceptional role due to a comparatively vibrant civil society and the ecological damage of the war in 1990/1991. From the 1990s onwards, one can notice an expansion of actors and participation modes in environmental policy, but the emergence of various environmental-oriented organizations did not translate into higher public consciousness. Until now, the authoritarian governments have no intention of changing this status quo and triggering more societal activism (which is rather injected by social media and globally acting environmental networks [Sowers, 2018)). Quite the opposite, leaderships across the region have constantly tried to control this type of bottom-up environmental policymaking. This has mostly been done by building up centralized environmental governance structures and co-opting or incorporating grassroots environmental advocacy and independent research institutions. In sum, a combination of an (incentivized) ecologically unfriendly lifestyle, a controlled setting of environmental organizations and campaigns, as well as a restricted media scene, explains why environmental awareness and consciousness have been relatively low among GCC citizens.

Thus, the GCC states' striving for sustainability is genuinely motivated by a small number of key policymakers at the top of the state. Depending on the personal preferences and choices of individuals, environmental topics have gained more importance, as in the UAE under Sheikh Zayed or Oman under Sultan Qaboos. In other contexts, environmental sustainability has been sidelined by policymakers, both on the domestic and international agendas. This is mostly the case in states with a powerful ministry of energy as well as national oil and gas majors, such as Saudi Arabia, Qatar and Kuwait (Luomi, 2012). In fact, environmental protection has remained a soft security aspect and for the most part of low interest in the agenda setting. The constant creation, abolishment, reshuffling, upgrading and downgrading of environmental-related agencies and institutions reflect the ambiguous role of environmental sustainability in the GCC. As the subsequent chapter will elaborate in greater detail, creating new institutions was a common tool to sustain the bloated public sector as part of the rentier-based social contract. Environmental legislation on the national and international levels, in turn, was welcome as an instrument to secure domestic natural resources as long as it did not negatively impact the oil and gas industry as the driving force of economic prosperity and wealth.

By the (late) 2000s, one can notice a 'paradigm shift'. It took place in parallel with growing indications that an oil demand growth might end some day and a realization that previous development models have equipped the Gulf countries badly for entering this stage. The new thinking was also enhanced by perceiving environmental sustainability as a fresh business opportunity. Sustainable topics gained greater attention in all countries although it took some time until substantial implementation was observable. Some early advocates such as the UAE and Qatar considered the gradually emerging 'green megatrend' as a suitable political instrument to boost their reputations and strengthen their influence while also providing commercial benefits. Other states, in turn, already directly felt the pressure from skyrocketing domestic consumption. Latecomers such as Kuwait also recognized the need for action through comparison with their direct neighbors, be it due to their successful and appealing examples or the looming threat of falling behind. This development accelerated by 2015 when states were faced with several structural constraints: These included increasing pressure towards decarbonization by the international community as well as sinking oil prices caused by global overproduction, weak global growth and decreasing costs of energy production from alternative energy sources such as solar and wind. As a consequence, the Gulf region experienced what can be framed as a revitalization of 'green thought'. At the same time, the broader context of this chapter already indicates that underlying driving forces and trajectories of this policy shift towards environmental sustainability are more complex than simplified explanations of 'post-oil discussion'.

As the following chapters will show, once perceived as constraints, environmental sustainability has turned into a high-profile policy set that constitutes a key pillar of economic transformation for the GCC states. This "tectonic shift" of restructuring the hydrocarbon path dependency has been ongoing for years but more recently, the COVID-19 pandemic has accelerated it (Dourian, 2021). After having clarified some of the most important trajectories, such as a lack of environmental activism and advocacy, the role of the oil and gas industry and the state-led ownership of environmental sustainability, it is now time to dive deeper into the governance structures, processes and stakeholders.

References

Al-Damkhi, A. M., Abdul-Wahhab, S. A., & al-Khulaifi N. M. (2009). Kuwait's 1991 environmental tragedy: Lessons learned. *Disaster Prevention and Management: An International Journal*, *18*(3), 233–248.

Al-Ghanim, K. (2017). Contradictory forces on the Gulf environment. Old and new cultural values and knowledge. In P. Sillitoe (Ed.), *Sustainable development. An appraisal from the Gulf region* (2nd ed., pp. 481–496). Berghahn.

Al-Saidi, M. (2021). Cooperation or competition? State environmental relations and the SDGs agenda in the Gulf Cooperation Council (GCC) region. *Environmental Development*, *37*, https://doi.org/10.1016/j.envdev.2020.100581

Al-Saidi, M., Zaidan, E., & Hammad, S. (2019). Participation modes and diplomacy of Gulf Cooperation Council (GCC) countries towards the global sustainability agenda. *Development in Practice, 29*(5), 545–558. https://doi.org/10.1080/09614524.2019.1597017

Al-Sarihi, A., & Luomi, M. (2019). *Climate change governance and cooperation in the Arab Region.* EDA Insight. Retrieved October 30, 2021 from https://www.agda.ac.ae/docs/default-source/Publications/eda-insight_gear-i_climate-change_en_web-v2.pdf?sfvrsn=8

Al-Sultan, Y., & al-Bakri, D. (1989). The development and experience of Kuwait in environment protection and environmental impact assessment. *Impact Assessment*, *7*(4), 57–68.

Atalay, Y., Biermann, F., & Kalfagianni, A. (2016). Adoption of renewable energy technologies in oil-rich countries: Explaining policy variation in the Gulf Cooperation Council states. *Renewable Energy, 85*, 206–214.

Azoulay, R. (2020). *Kuwait and al-Sabah. Tribal politics and power in an oil state*. I.B. Tauris.

Burck, J., & Hermwille, L. (2013). *Climate change performance index*. Germanwatch. Retrieved October 30, 2021 from https://germanwatch.org/en/5697

Cammett, M., Diwan, I., Richards, A., & Waterbury, J. (2018). *A political economy of the Middle East*. Routledge.

Caulton, E., & Keddie, D. (1989). Environmental conservation problems in Kuwait. *The Environmentalist, 9*(3), 219–228.

Coates Ulrichsen, K. (2017). *The United Arab Emirates. Power, politics and policy-making*. Routledge.

Commins, D. (2012). *The Gulf states. A modern history*. I.B. Tauris.

Crystal, J. (2014). Eastern Arabian states: Kuwait, Bahrain, Qatar, United Arab Emirates, and Qatar. In M. Gasiorowski, D. E. Long, & B. Reich (Eds.), *The government and politics of the Middle East and North Africa* (7th ed., pp. 157–95). Westview Press.

Davidson, C. (2009). *Abu Dhabi: Oil and beyond*. Oxford University Press.
Dourian, K. (2021). *Gulf Countries gear up for a net-zero world*. AGSIW Issue Paper No. 5. Retrieved October 30, 2021 from https://agsiw.org/gulf-countries-gear-up-for-a-net-zero-world/
Fattouh, B., & Sen, A. (2021). Economic diversification in Arab oil-exporting countries in the context of peak oil and the energy. In G. Luciani & T. Moerenhout (Eds.), *When can oil economies be deemed sustainable?* (pp. 73–98). Palgrave.
Hamblin, J. (2019). An American miracle in the desert. Environmental crisis and nuclear-powered desalination in the Middle East. In: A. M. Kirchhof, & J. R. McNeill (Eds.), *Nature and the Iron Curtail. Environmental policy and social movements in communist and capitalist countries 1945–1990* (pp. 205–218), University of Pittsburgh Press.
Heard-Bey, F. (2008). *From tribe to state. The transformation of political structure in five states of the GCC*. CRiSSMA Working Paper No.15. Retrieved March 16, 2022 from https://www.academia.edu/27251096/FROM_TRIBE_TO_STATE_The_transformation_of_Political_Structure_in_Five_States_of_the_GCC_VOLUME_II_BY_FRAUKE_HEARD_BEY
Heard-Bey, F. (1997). The tribal society of the UAE and its traditional economy. In E. Ghareeb (Ed.), *Perspectives on the United Arab Emirates* (pp. 254–272). Trident Press.
Hepbasli, A., & Alsuhaibani, Z. (2011). A key review on present status and future directions of solar energy studies and applications in Saudi Arabia. *Renewable and Sustainable Energy Reviews, 15*(9), 5021–5050.
Hightower, V. (2013). Pearls and the southern Persian/Arabian Gulf: A lesson in sustainability. *Environmental History, 18*, 44–59.
Hvidt, M. (2020). The emergence and spread of the "Dubai Model" in the GCC countries. In M. Kamrava (Ed.), *Routledge handbook of Persian Gulf politics* (pp. 203–215). Routledge.
Jones, T. C. (2012). State of nature: The politics of water in the making of Saudi Arabia. In A. Mikhail (Ed.), *Water on sand: Environmental histories of the Middle East And North Africa* (pp. 231–248). Oxford University Press.
Jones, T. (2010). *Desert kingdom. How oil and water forged modern Saudi Arabia*. Harvard University Press.
Joseph, S. (2017): Farming the desert: Agriculture in the oil frontier, the case of the United Arab Emirates, 1940s to 1990s. *British Journal of Middle Eastern Studies*. https://doi.org/10.1080/13530194.2017.1320977
Kamrava, M. (2016). *Gateways to the world. Port cities in the Persian Gulf*. Hurst & Co.
Kingdom of Saudi Arabia. (1992). Basic law of governance. Retrieved November 3, 2021 from https://www.saudiembassy.net/basic-law-governance

Koch, N. (2014). "Building glass refrigerators in the desert": Discourses of urban sustainability and nation building in Qatar. *Urban Geography, 35*(8), 1118–1139.

Koch, N. (2021). The political lives of deserts. *Annals of the American Association of Geographers, 111*(1), 87–104. https://doi.org/10.1080/24694452.2020.1766410

Kropf, A. (2016). *Oil export economies*. Gerlach Press.

Lahn, G., & Stevens, P. (2011). *Burning oil to keep cool. The hidden energy crisis in Saudi Arabia*. Chatham House. Retrieved October 30, 2021 from https://www.chathamhouse.org/sites/default/files/public/Research/Energy%2C%20Environment%20and%20Development/1211pr_lahn_stevens.pdf

Luomi, M. (2012). *The Gulf monarchies and climate change. Abu Dhabi and Qatar in an era of natural unsustainability*. Hurst & Co.

Nadim, F., Bagtzuglou, A. C., & Iranmahboob, J. (2008). Coastal management in the Persian Gulf region within the framework of the ROPME programme of action. *Ocean & Coastal Management, 51*, 556–565.

Ouis, P. (2002). 'Greening the emirates': The modern construction of nature in the United Arab Emirates. *Cultural Geographies, 9*(3), 334–347.

Power, G. (2012). Parliaments and the process of managed reform in Kuwait, Bahrain and Oman. In D. Held, & K. Coates Ulrichsen (Eds.), *The transformation of the Gulf. Politics, economics and the global order* (pp. 29–46). Routledge.

Rabinowitz, D. (2020). *The power of deserts. Climate change, the Middle East and the promise of a post-oil era*. Stanford University Press.

Rambo, K., Warsinger, D. M., Shanbhogue, S. J., John H., Lienhard, V. J. H., & Ghoniem, A. F. (2017). Water-energy nexus in Saudi Arabia. *Energy Procedia, 105*, 3837–3843. https://doi.org/10.1016/j.egypro.2017.03.782

Sever, S., Tok, M. E., & D'Alessandro, C. (2019). Global environmental governance and the GCC: Setting the agenda for climate change and energy security. In L. Pal & M. Tok (Eds.), *Global governance and Muslim organizations* (pp. 197–228). Springer.

Sowers, J. (2018). Environmental activism in the Middle East and North Africa. In H. Verhoeven (Ed.), *Environmental politics in the Middle East* (pp. 27–52). Oxford University Press.

Shuaib, H. (1988). Oil, development, and the environment in Kuwait. *Environment, 30*(6), 19–44.

Twitchell, K. (1944). Water resources of Saudi Arabia. *Geographical Review, 34*(3), 365–386. https://doi.org/10.2307/209970

Valeri, M. (2017). *Oman: Politics and society in the Qaboos state*. Hurst & Co.

Vincent, P. (2008). *Saudi Arabia. An environmental overview*. Taylor & Francis.

Vrolijk, C. (2003). Climate governance in the GCC. In T. Najem & M. Hetherington (Eds.), *Good governance in the Middle East oil monarchies* (pp. 119–136). Routledge.

Wald, C. (2018). *Saudi, Inc. The Arabian kingdom's pursuit of profit and power*. Pegasus Books.

Warner, F. (1991). The environmental consequences of the Gulf war. *Environment, 33*(5), 6–26.

Woertz, E. (2013). *Oil for food. The global food crisis and the Middle East*. Oxford University Press.

Zaidan, E., & Abulibdeh, A. (2021). Master planning and the evolving urban model in the Gulf cities: Principles, policies, and practices for the transition to sustainable urbanism. *Planning Practice & Research, 36*(2), 193–215. https://doi.org/10.1080/02697459.2020.1829278

CHAPTER 4

Inside the Green State: Institutional Organization, Agency and Governance

Building and Reorganizing Institutional Capacities

The steadily growing importance of environmental sustainability since the Millennium was most profoundly seen across the governmental sector. Here, the GCC-wide trend of environmental sustainability—already noticed during the late twentieth century—was also reflected in a constant institutional reorganization. Interestingly, the single GCC states did not follow a common way of institution-building. Quite the opposite, the countries can be grouped along three different developments: After the establishment of separate environmental ministries in Qatar and Oman, environmental work experienced a setback in terms of institutional downgrading. In contrast, in the UAE and Saudi Arabia it was only recently that the environmental portfolios received an upgrade to the rank of a ministry, whereas the environmental authorities in Bahrain and Kuwait have remained unchanged. A deeper look into these varying pathways also offers more insights into the functioning of the absolutist monarchies of the Gulf.

First, as just mentioned, long-standing continuity can be seen in Bahrain and Kuwait, where the Supreme Council for Environment (SCE) (est. in 1996) and the Environment Public Authority of Kuwait (EPA)

T. Zumbraegel, *Political Power and Environmental Sustainability in Gulf Monarchies*, Contemporary Gulf Studies,
https://doi.org/10.1007/978-981-19-4431-4_4

(est. in 1995), respectively, remain unchanged. These leading environmental institutions do not have the rank of a ministry. Instead, they commission to the Council of Ministers. In the case of Kuwait, the EPA permanently reports to a mediating body, the so-called Supreme Council of Environment, which usually approves the requests. In some cases, these are passed on to the Council of Ministers for further deliberation.[1] The Supreme Council comprises all ministers and special advisors while the EPA's Director-General acts as a rapporteur. Although not a ministry, Bahrain's SCE has substantial executive authority on paper. It is tasked with issuing and monitoring environmental regulations and acts as a rapporteur between other governmental institutions, including ministries, regarding national environmental policy action.[2] However, in reality, environmental entities across the GCC countries, especially when they are not part of the Council of Ministers, are frequently surpassed by other, more powerful governmental bodies (Luomi, 2012).[3]

Second, Oman and Qatar experienced more fundamental institutional shifts. As previously stated, Oman was the first country to already establish a ministry in charge of environmental affairs, in 1984. In 2007, the Directorate General of Climate Affairs was created as main regulatory authority within the Ministry of Environment and Climate Affairs (MECA) that was perceived as a clear sign towards boosting sustainability governance. During a bigger institutional reshuffle in August 2020, which decreased the number of ministers from twenty-six to nineteen, the MECA was also downgraded to an Environment Authority (Al-Sarihi, 2020). While the Royal Decree (106/2020) stated that the newly created Environment Authority should be financially and administratively independent, it also stressed that the new entity is obliged to report to the Council of Ministers, of which it is no longer part. Climate affairs are also no longer part of the responsibilities of the authority, which instead is mainly engaged with wildlife protection and environmental preservation, environmental science as well as the provision and exchange of information. Management of

[1] Interview #33.

[2] See Decree-Law21/1996 on the Environment, available at: http://www.sce.gov.bh/en/Overview?cms=iQRpheuphYtJ6pyXUGiNqj0IIkIp0ipd [in Arabic] and Bahrain's Third National Communication (2020), Kingdom of Bahrain/Supreme Council for Environment, available at: https://unfccc.int/sites/default/files/resource/9143680_Bahrain-NC3-2-SCE%20Third%20National%20Communication%202020.pdf.

[3] Interview #4; interview #9 and interview #49.

natural resources, in turn, has been delegated to the Ministry of Agriculture, Fisheries and Water Resources, which was previously the Ministry of Agriculture and Fisheries. Oman's latest reorganization of environmental work suggests that Sultan Haitham bin Tariq Al Said does not share the same interest in environmental protection as his predecessor. Instead, a stronger focus is dedicated to resource management and especially to ensuring the country's long-term water and food security.[4]

Also in Qatar, the creation of a separate Ministry of Environment in 2008 was considered a major step, but structural barriers did not vanish overnight. Perceived as a "young and weak institution", the ministry's impact remained low (Luomi, 2012, 160). Official documents published in 2009 and 2011 pinpointed frankly that "presently, the knowledge base in Qatar in the area of climate change and environmental management is rudimentary" (General Secretariat for Development Planning, 2009, 122) and that the country "will need sophisticated environmental institutions" (General Secretariat for Development Planning, 2011, 232). It was only in the light of the country's bid to host the climate conference that the ministry's total staff increased significantly to a number of 2,700, of which more than half were Qataris (Luomi, 2012, 164).[5] In early 2014, several emiri decrees declared the establishment of two separate departments for climate change and combating pollution at the Ministry of Environment. Furthermore, Emir Tamim ordered the hitherto Public Works Authority (*Ashghal*) to be brought directly under the Ministry of Municipality and Urban Planning. In January 2016, the environmental institutionalization in Qatar experienced another reorganization: the Emiri Decree No. 4 of 2016 ordered the creation of the Ministry of Municipality & Environment (MME). In a somehow unexpected move that was probably related to a general 'green euphoria' in 2021—linked to the upcoming climate governance in Glasgow and ambitious pledges by neighbouring countries such as Qatar and the UAE—the Qatari Emir once again created a separate environment and climate change ministry (Reuters, 2021, October 21).

Third, in other contexts, environmental and climate affairs were upgraded to the status of a ministry. This was the case in Saudi Arabia, where a new Ministry of Environment, Water and Agriculture was created

[4] Interview #74.

[5] Interview #23.

in 2015. With this step, King Salman seized the opportunity to shift the electricity portfolio of the previous Ministry of Water and Electricity to a newly created "mega ministry", Ministry of Energy, Industry and Mineral Resources (MOEIMR) (Obeid, 2022, 180). At the same time, it was possible to link the highly fragmented governmental bodies of water, agriculture and the environment under one unified institution, the Minister of Environment, Water and Agriculture (MEWA). The ministry has seven directorates that range from environment, water affairs and services, to agriculture, land and survey as well as animal resources or planning and development. It is further associated with other public and private entities including the National Water Company, the Saudi Wildlife Authority or the General Presidency of Meteorology and Environmental Protection, which was the former executing body of environment-related issues.[6] Overall, the latest reorganization on environmental governance in the kingdom has certainly streamlined the process that had been developed and overstretched over decades under the rule of many kings, each with their own vision. For example, in the last year of King Abdullah's rule in 2014, there were over 16 formal entities engaged with environmental issues and each had its own plans and programmes (Taher & Hajjar, 2014).[7] MEWA is also part of the newly created Council of Economic and Development Affairs (CEDA), a new steering body under the supervision of Mohammed bin Salman to streamline policymaking and facilitate the implementation of his transformation plans (Alomari & Heffron, 2021). Since 2018, the MEWA is working on a 'National Environmental Strategy' since 2018, in which all environmentally mandated bodies and many other stakeholders are involved (Alomari & Heffron, 2021). The following graphic published by the ministry on its new governance plan illustrates the complex nature of environmental policymaking in the kingdom and may also explain why there has been no further update on the current status of the national environmental strategy (Table 4.1).

[6] The latter's name was slightly altered to the General Authority for Meteorology and Environmental Protection (GAMEP). According to a royal decree of 2021, it is responsible for the following five areas of environmental sector development: (a) environmental compliance, (b) meteorology, (c) vegetation cover, (d) waste management and (e) conserving wildlife.

[7] Interview #3 and interview #28.

Table 4.1 The steering committee structure of Saudi Arabia's 'National Environmental Strategy' (MEWA, 2018, 7; see also Alomari & Heffron, 2021)

<table>
<tr><td colspan="3">(A) The Steering Committee, chaired by H.E. the Minister of Environment, Water and Agriculture and the membership of 20 members representing all relevant sectors</td><td>(D) "25" Experts in "17" domains</td></tr>
<tr><td>• Ministry of Environment, Water and Agriculture
• Ministry of Economy and Planning
• Ministry of Energy, Industry and Mineral Resources.
• Ministry of Health
• Ministry of Transportation
• Ministry of Municipal and Rural Affairs</td><td>• General Authority for Meteorology and Environmental Protection
• Saudi Wildlife Authority
• Royal Commission for Jubail and Yanbu
• Saudi Commission for Tourism and National Heritage</td><td>• Saudi Energy Efficiency Center
• National Committee for the Clean Development Mechanism
• King Abdullah University o Science and Technology
• King Fahd University of Petroleum and Minerals
• King Saud University</td><td>• Environmental Strategies
• Biodiversity and desert wildlife
• Marine environment
• Soil and desertification
• Air quality
• Climate change
• Water resources and groundwater protection against pollution
• Solid and hazardous wastes
• Meteorology
• Environmental governance and institutional framework
• Privatization and investment in the environment sector
• Environmental and social economy
• Rehabilitation, sustainability and recycling
• Emergency and oil spills response
• Human capital in the environment sector
• Information and Technology in the environment sector</td></tr>
</table>

(continued)

Table 4.1 (continued)

(B) A Scientific Committee consisting of 19 members:		(C) A Study Team consisting of 18 members:
• Ministry of Environment, Water and Agriculture (Departments of Environment, Water, Agriculture, Planning, Privatization and Vision Realization Office) • Saudi Wildlife Authority. • General Authority for Meteorology and Environmental Protection	• King Abdullah University of Science and Technology. • King Fahd University of Petroleum and Minerals • King Saud University • Food and Agriculture Organization (FAO) • Saudi environmental experts	• Team of the Ministry of Environment, Water and Agriculture consisting of "8" persons • A Consulting Office Team consisting of "10" persons • International experts

A similar process of environmental institution-building happened in the UAE, which operates under a two-tier federal and local (emirate) structure. Upon its creation in 1993, the Federal Environment Agency (FEA), under the umbrella of the Ministry of Health, was the leading institution as it replaced the Supreme Committee of Environment (est. in 1975). In 2006, FEA was fully incorporated into the Ministry of Environment and Water which was again changed to the Ministry of Climate Change and Environment (MOCCAE) in 2016 (Luomi, 2021a). The newly named ministry is supposed to oversee and manage integral elements of environmental and climate change governance on the internal and external levels. During the same period, some of the single emirates developed their own environmental authorities. Above all, Abu Dhabi took the lead by creating the Environmental Agency Abu Dhabi from the Environmental Research and Wildlife Development Agency (ERWDA) in 2005 and establishing the Ministry of Environment and Water in 2006.

Despite these different approaches to developing a sustainable and environmental-related institutional landscape there are also some commonalities across the GCC states. The fragmentation as well as constant reorganization of environmental work has created shortcomings such as unclear areas of responsibility and spheres of competence, lack of funding and rivalry with other bodies, leading to an absence of coordination and cooperation. Another shortcoming, which is most apparent in Saudi Arabia, is the "presence of decentralised environmental regulators" with their own environmental regulation schemes, above all the special royal commissions in Riyadh, Jubail and Yanbu (Alomari & Heffron, 2021, 110). Moreover, the continued dominance of the energy and industry sector explains the absence of powerful and effective environmental authorities: Across all Gulf monarchies, hydrocarbon-based energy continues to be the backbone of the countries' political and socioeconomic stability. Given the oil and gas sector's naturally unsustainable ecological footprint it can be seen as a diverging and competing force to the interests of the environmental authorities. Sections of the energy ministries are continually unwilling to share data with the Ministry of Environment or to comply with enforced legislation.[8] According to one individual, who has worked in a high-level position at the Saudi energy ministry for decades: it is "just ignorance". He continues that frequently,

[8] Interview #11; interview #20; interview #21 and interview #22.

the minister was reluctant to sign proposals for environmental improvements even when he was told that not his own ministry, but the private sector, would cover the costs.[9]

At the same time, also the energy sector underwent processes of governmental restructuring. Over the last years, some countries such as Oman, the UAE and Saudi Arabia renamed their previous ministries of oil to include the energy portfolio. In so doing, the newly created ministries of energy broadened their spheres of responsibility and influence by overseeing all forms of energy. It became clear that these new entities would lead the way for the countries' energy diversification as an important part of the sustainable transformation without losing their status as the world's energy gravity centre.[10] In some cases, new implementing bodies were created to hasten the process of finding alternative energy sources to complement fossil fuels. For instance, in 2017, the new leadership in Saudi Arabia created the Renewable Energy Project Development Office (REPDO) as leading body to promote green energy under the umbrella of the newly created "super ministry of energy" (Krane, 2019, 132).

The Role of Knowledge Production and Parastatal Green Energy Fiefdoms

In addition to formal environmental institutions, whose responsibilities were largely executed by ministries of environment, ministries of agriculture and water, environmental authorities and more powerful ministries of energy, a number of new stakeholders entered the field, too. The creation of semi-governmental entities, sometimes also called fiefdoms or "silos of clientelism" (Youngs, 2012, 21), is a common tool of praxis in the Gulf states. Oftentimes, these fiefdoms are constructed on land owned by royals, though it is difficult to assess who exactly owns this land as there is no land registration or cadastre (Bsheer, 2021).[11] As this chapter will show, in some cases 'green' fiefdoms have come to play a crucial role in sustainability governance. Given the lack of know-how and expertise in environmental sustainability, particularly fiefdoms involved in

[9] Interview #61.

[10] Interview #42.

[11] Interview #45 and interview #46.

'green' R&D play a considerable role. By supporting knowledge production in key sustainable areas such as clean energy, energy efficiency or new oil production technologies, these governmental or semi-governmental research institutions constitute a key part of the monarchies' striving for a knowledge-based post-oil economy (Hvidt, 2021). However, they are also instrumental in maintaining the neopatrimonial system of interlocking privileges and interests.

Long-standing research institutes, such as the Kuwait Institute for Scientific Research (KISR), established in 1967, and the King Abdulaziz City for Science and Technology (KACST), established in 1977, have been early movers in researching and developing sustainable solutions on water and energy. However, many of the projects were phased out during the 1980s and 1990s, mostly because of a lack of technical and economic viability (Bachellerie, 2012). Particularly, the creation of the Abu Dhabi Future Energy Company (commonly known as the Masdar Initiative or simply Masdar with its flagship Masdar City) in 2006 is a more recent prime example. Planned as a zero-carbon sustainable enclave, especially in the early years, Masdar received much publicity as a first of its kind eco-city (Cugurullo, 2013). In addition to the world's first carbon neutral urban planning project, Masdar City, the initiative further comprises the company Masdar Power, the Masdar Institute of Science and Technology and the Masdar Clean Tech Fund. The Masdar initiative is supervised by the Abu Dhabi Future Energy Company, which is wholly owned by the state-led holding company and investment fund, Mubadala Development Company (est. in 2002). With the backing and blessing of the highest circle of political power in Abu Dhabi, Masdar possessed the 'financial fire power' to become the leading institute in the sustainability sector. It was (and still is) the key steering instrument in promoting Abu Dhabi's green image both inside and outside of the Emirate (Cugurullo, 2013; Luomi, 2012).[12] In his study, Federico Cugurullo critically unpacks the specific sustainability imaginary of Masdar (City) and concludes that this is far from reality. Instead, Masdar has only managed to meet its commercial expectations as key platform for the "production and circulation of new green technology" (Cugurullo, 2013, 34). This became even more the case from 2013 onwards when renewable energy sources became economically beneficial (Al-Sulayman, 2021). Despite the fact that Masdar fell

[12] Interview #68 and interview #69.

short of expectations in its initial decade, backed by key decision-makers, the project was (and still is) perceived as 'untouchable' and enjoys relative autonomy from other institutions and sectors in Abu Dhabi (Hertog & Luciani, 2012).

Almost at the same time, neighbouring Saudi Arabia followed a similar path. In summer 2007, then King Abdullah created the King Abdullah Petroleum Studies and Research Center (KAPSARC) with the goal of advancing areas of sustainable energy management and efficiency. In September 2009, a mixed gender university near Jeddah, King Abdullah University of Science and Technology (KAUST), opened its doors for the first students only a few weeks after the first students began their studies at the Masdar Institute (Günel, 2019, 65). It has been said that the king invested much of his private fortune to build KAUST (Jones, 2015, 32). The university is independent of the Ministry of Higher Education and has a more liberal orientation. The green campus includes start-up incubators, research institutes and a technology park and is engaged in environmental related areas such as research on nuclear and solar energy (Alnaser & Alnaser, 2011; Moritz, 2020).

Certainly, a significant milestone in the Saudi kingdom was the creation of the King Abdullah City for Atomic and Renewable Energy (K·A·-CARE) with the mission to undertake sustainable transformation. It was tasked with reducing the country's increasingly visible threat of growing demand for utilities such as electricity and water in the face of demographic growth and ongoing subsidized prices. While KAPSARC and KAUST were mandated under the national giant oil company Saudi Aramco, the royal decree, which created K·A·CARE in April 2010, explicitly stressed the government's direct supervision over the 'city'. Some have labelled the launch of K·A·CARE as an act of "dramatic political will" (Alhoweish & Orujov, 2016, 109). According to one interviewee: K·A·-CARE was essentially "a one-man decision", motivated by intentions to find solutions to the growing energy demand and improve the kingdom's environmental image.[13] Being Abdullah's primary fiefdom in exploiting the potential for new energy resources, K·A·CARE was entrusted with altering the Saudi energy outlook, but it failed dramatically. The creation of a new Western-style entity personally overseen by the king resulted in suspicion and a conflict of competence with other ministerial and semi

[13] Interview #28.

state-organized agencies like the then Ministry of Petroleum and Mineral Resources (MPMR), the Ministry of Water and Electricity (MOWE), the King Abdulaziz City for Science and Technology (KACST), Saudi Aramco and the Saudi Electricity Company (SEC).

The launch of the 'white paper' (sometimes also called Vision 2032) in 2013 marked the preliminary peak of this malfunction. It foresaw the installation of 23.9 GW by 2020 and 54.1 GW of renewable energy by 2032 (Al-Sulayman, 2021). In the face of an expected increase in electricity from approximately 55 GW in 2014 to 123 GW in 2032, the mixture of solar (16 GW by PV and 25 GW by CSP), wind (9 GW), geothermal and waste-to-energy (4 GW) would account for around 45% of the total energy mix (Bahgat, 2013, 573; Taher & Hajjar, 2014). Additionally, the projected plan was to generate 17.6 GW nuclear energy from 16 nuclear plants, equivalent to 14% of the total energy production by that time. These ambitious goals certainly reflected the ruling elite's strategic objective to sustain Saudi Arabia's role as a regional energy power beyond oil. Yet, execution was delayed, and deadlines expired without calls for tender, which is why the prevailing opinion is now that the 'white paper' is "a cautionary example of a model to avoid" (Krupa & Poudineh, 2017, 19). Others see also an inherent problem in 'bureaucratic strata' (Aarts & Roelants, 2016, 3), as a typical form of Saudi governance with major shortcomings (Al-Sulayman, 2021). According to an interview partner: "He [King Abdullah, the author] built many fiefdoms with overlapping competences so it was doomed, but it was symptomatic of how the country was governed".[14] Another interview partner agreed that K·A·CARE "lacks labs, human resources, structure" and was not able to compete with Saudi Aramco and SEC.[15] Eventually, since "K·A·CARE wanted everything and lost everything in the end (...) nuclear is now the only niche they can take"[16] (Luomi, 2021a).

[14] Ibid.

[15] Interview #28.

[16] Interview #29.

Info Box: King Abdullah City for Atomic and Renewable Energy (K·A·CARE)

Among all newly created or already existing (semi) fiefdoms, K·A·CARE certainly was the beacon of Abdullah's sustainable development plans: It was planned as the biggest and most expensive project in the MENA at that time, but instead of a city on Riyadh's outskirts costing an estimated $10 billion, it became an office block in the centre of the capital. K·A·CARE was created to centralize and optimize all stakeholders (Bachellerie, 2012, 152), but existing entities, above all SEC and Saudi Aramco, formulated great protest and resistance. Due to the fact that Abdullah commissioned K·A·CARE with the task of licensing non-hydrocarbon energy sources, it should have become the mainstay of the sustainable transition (Krupa & Poudineh, 2017). Additionally, Abdullah ensured control of the scientific city through article 2 of the royal decree where it's stated that it is "administratively linked to the Prime Minister", as well as article 14, which stresses the obligation of submitting "its closing account and an annual report on the activities" to the Prime Minister (Kingdom of Saudi Arabia, 2010). Another royal decree appointed Dr. Hashim bin Abdullah Yamani as the president of K·A·CARE, a Harvard-educated physicist. Yamani has a distinctive record of previous positions and a broad network. For instance, he occupied the position of Minister of Commerce and Industry (2003–2008), where he was also a member of a special committee under the auspices of King Abdullah that was responsible for the accession talks to the World Trade Organization (WTO) in 2005. Furthermore, he was vice-president of KACST in his early career stages and he held the positions of Minister of Electricity and Industry, where he was also chairman of the state-owned Saudi Basic Industries Corporation (SABIC) from 1995 to 2003.

Despite the fact that King Abdullah's sustainable hubs and entities did not meet initial expectations, cultivating his own fiefdoms helped the king to widen and strengthen his power base. It could be suggested that Abdullah did so to legitimize his policies, to build constituencies and to bypass powerful family branches such as his powerful family members, the Sudairis (see also: Stenslie, 2012, 68).[17] As Steffen Hertog summarizes it: both KAUST and K·A·CARE "were entrusted to old technocratic

[17] Interview #44. The Sudairi branch or the so-called Sudairi seven constitutes a powerful bloc within the Saudi family comprising seven sons of the founding father Ibn Saud's favourite wife, Hussa bint Ahmed al-Sudairi (Davidson, 2021).

confidants of the royals and both operated in parallel to an existing system of less efficient institutions to which they have little organic linkage" (Hertog, 2012, 235). The change in leadership in 2015 intended to centralize and streamline policymaking and overlapping entities more thoroughly.[18] Separately acting state-led and hybrid bodies were more streamlined under the control of the new leadership. K·A·CARE as the former king's showpiece "clearly fell out of favor" and was mandated under the umbrella of the Ministry of Energy, Industry and Mineral Resources (Al-Sulayman, 2021, 107). Nowadays, it is tasked with monitoring the energy transformation that is supervised by the new agency REPDO. Furthermore, a new national organization under the Ministry of Economy and Planning, entitled *Mashroat*, was installed under the advice of McKinsey. It was tasked with implementing Project Management Offices in all major state organs thus overcoming the barriers of non-cooperation that result from the long-term 'bureaucratic stretching' of forming and implementing policies in Saudi Arabia. However, as Faris al-Sulayman emphasizes, the new leader did not abandon this system altogether (Al-Sulayman, 2021).

Finally, also Qatar provides an example of a proliferation of parastatal institutions. Particularly, the Qatar Foundation for Education, Science and Community Development, or for short Qatar Foundation (QF), emerged as the centrepiece or "hero" of sustainable transformation in the little emirate (Alnaser & Alnaser, 2011, 3094). The fiefdom was founded in the same year that Emir Hamad took power in 1996. Labelled as a non-profit organization, it is said that the QF is "by far the most comprehensive and ambitious of government-controlled NGOs" (Kamrava, 2009, 407). Considering this, one can rather concisely speak of a government-organized non-governmental-organization (GONGO). Regarding the structure, after its inauguration QF was divided into three different sections, whereby the Qatar Environment and Energy Research Institute (QEERI) is the most important one (Luomi, 2012, 189; Wright, 2018). It was established in 2011 with the aim of advancing the potential uses of renewable energy sources. Additionally, the Qatar Science and Technology Park (QSTP), under the auspices of QF and located in Education City, focuses among other topics on themes of energy and environment. The QSTP explicitly highlights Qatar's development

[18] Interview #25.

towards a post-carbon and knowledge economy as a major goal, while aiming to contribute to this by fostering domestic expertise and know-how (Luomi, 2012, 187; Richer, 2014). Especially, the QSTP as "the Education City's R&D oriented business incubator" (Luomi, 2012, 189), acts as a central hub to link research and commercialization that also favours new network-building inside and outside the country.[19]

Of particular note is also a $70 million research cooperation that was agreed between QSTP, Qatar Petroleum, Shell and the Imperial College to establish the Qatar Carbonates and Carbon Storage Research Centre (Luomi, 2012; Hertog & Luciani, 2012). Additionally, during the UN climate summit in 2012, the Centre for Climate Research was created in cooperation with the German-based Potsdam Institute for Climate Impact Research (Abdelraouf, 2019), which was framed as a pioneering project and 'ground-breaking initiative'. Other institutions include the Gulf Organization for Research & Development (GORD) (2009) and the Sustainable Energy Research Laboratory (2003).[20] Together with the Qatar Carbonates and Carbon Storage Research Centre, they are all under the banner of QF in one way or another; either they are directly controlled by QF or indirectly through cooperation with QSTP (Luomi, 2012, 184; Meltzer et al., 2014).[21] For convenience, the different QF-related research institutes and their main focal points are recapitulated in the following Table 4.2.

Meanwhile, Qatar University established its Centre for Energy and Sustainability Law in 2011, which was designed as a forum in which governmental entities, energy companies, industry and academia "can debate and discuss how to balance energy policy against environmental sustainability" (Wright, 2018, 256). The think tank was also designed as first of its kind in the region to provide long-term research on energy law and is one of the very few initiatives that stemmed from the education sector.

As can be seen, the field of environmental sustainability provides a suitable 'playground' for (over)stretching the already bloated bureaucratic apparatus in the GCC. While new fiefdoms were established across

[19] Interview #75.

[20] GORD was originally named Barwa and Qatari Diar Research Institute under the umbrella of the Barwa Real Estate Group and the Qatari Diar Real Estate Investment Company (Luomi, 2012).

[21] Interview #14.

Table 4.2 Overview environmental- and climate-related institutions in Qatar (see also: Luomi, 2014, 47)

Research institute	*Research focus*
Qatar Environment and Energy Research Institute (QEERI) (est. 2011)	Renewable energy resources; Part of QF
Qatar Science and Technology Park (QSTP) (est. 2009)	Premier hub for innovation, incubation and entrepreneurship that also includes sustainability; Part of QF
Centre for Climate Research (climate change research institute) (est. 2012)	Mitigation strategies and investigation of climate change impacts; Member of QF
Gulf Organization for Research & Development (GORD) (est. 2009)	Managing energy and resources efficiently; Sustainable construction in Qatar and the Gulf; Member of QF
Sustainable Energy Research Laboratory, Texas A&M University at Qatar (university campus est. 2003)	Solar technology and environmental policy; Member of QF
Qatar Carbonates and Carbon Storage Research Centre (est. 2008)	Development of carbon capture, utilization and storage (CCUS); General reduction of GHG emissions; Member of QF

the countries, other powerful bodies largely remained. This proliferation certainly did not result in achieving goals of efficiency or functionality as the individual entities barely worked together (Al-Saleh & Vidican, 2013). A major question remains, why do governments pursue such an inefficient and resource-draining praxis of policymaking? Much of the answer to that lies in a closer look at the individual level of agency.

Human Agency and the Inclusion of Key Actors

Looking at the manifold governmental and semi-governmental bodies and institutions involved in sustainability governance as did above, help the reader to get a better understanding of endemic practices of 'networked policymaking' in the Gulf region. On the one hand, it shows the green involvement of the royal families or individual members of other well-known and politically relevant families. On the other hand, it also highlights the growing importance of loyal and trustworthy specialized technocrats (*mudarāʾ fi-ldawla*) and advisers, who are entering the state apparatus.

First, the involvement of royals has been crucial in those monarchies with a high degree of elite cohesion and absence of an organized merchant or tribal elite such as Qatar (Kamrava, 2015, 43). Interestingly, Emir Tamim held several environmental-oriented posts prior to his reign, including head of the Upper Council of the Environment and Natural Sanctuaries and chairman of the Supreme Council for the Environment and Natural Reserves (SCENR). Furthermore, before Sheikh Tamim became emir in 2013, he supervised newly created bodies like the General Secretariat for Development Planning (GSDP) (2006) and the Qatar National Food and Security Programme (QNFSP) (2008).[22] In the early stage of the green paradigm shift, both institutions constituted important entities in formulating visions to tackle Qatar's unsustainable development path (Luomi, 2012). In both positions, he assigned positions of responsibility to other important family members (e.g. the prime minister's nephew, Sheikh Hamad bin Jabor Al Thani) (Kamrava, 2017; Luomi, 2012). In so doing, the young Sheikh Tamim strategically consolidated his power base from early onwards. Another key role in this field was assigned to Tamim's mother and former 'first lady', Sheikha Moza bint Nasser. She has been described as "by far the second most visible face of the Qatari state", who allegedly has a genuine interest in environmental protection (Kamrava, 2015, 119). As chairperson of QF, she is seen as a pioneer in the role of women in society and is primarily concerned with aspects of education, culture and social welfare issues (Wright, 2018). In the meantime, she has also become increasingly involved with questions of sustainability. During a reshuffle in 2011, she was able to consolidate her undisputed leadership role within the organization by putting her children into important positions.[23]

In Bahrain and Kuwait, both leading environmental bodies are headed by members of the royal family. In Bahrain, the highest levels of the Supreme Council for Environment are occupied by royal members. The president of the environmental body, Abdullah bin Hamad bin Isa Al Khalifa, is the second in line and personal representative of the heir apparent of the Kingdom of Bahrain. In Kuwait, Sheikh Abdullah Ahmad

[22] While the QNFSP seems to be shut down and its responsibilities have shifted to other ministries, Tamim merged the GSDP with the Qatar Statistics Authority to the Ministry of Development Planning and Statistics in the year of his succession (Rahman, 2017; Woertz, 2016).

[23] Interview #13.

al-Humoud al-Sabah has been chairman and director-general of the Environment Public Authority of Kuwait (EPA) since 2014. He was directly appointed ("just assigned"[24]) by the prime minister and since the EPA is not part of the Council of Minister, the chairman position is not subject of governmental changes. According to a Kuwaiti environmental, specialist, he is a man with a genuine interest in environmental protection but unable to enforce "bigger plans" due to the weak role of his institution that, for instance, "cannot control the energy plants".[25] In some instances, royals also control the powerful portfolios of energy and oil. This has been especially the case in Kuwait, where various members of al-Sabah ruling family held the position of energy minister between 2002 and 2007 as well as between 2009 and 2011. For a long time, the Al Sauds in Saudi Arabia have avoided putting members of the royal family at the top of the energy authority. Supposedly, they did so in order to maintain the pretence that the kingdom's natural wealth and the ruling dynasties are disconnected from one other.[26] However, this commonsense approach ended in September 2019 when King Salman appointed his fourth son, Prince Abdulaziz bin Salman, as first royal minister of energy (Davidson, 2021). It is worth noting that Abdulaziz bin Salman has over 35 years of experience in the energy sector and accompanied three non-royal and Aramco-reared technocrats before gaining control over the country's energy empire. With this step, Abdulaziz became one of the most important individuals in the kingdom (Blas, 2021).

As important as binding royal members is the attempt to co-opt important non-royal political and business elites. One succinct example of strengthening politically relevant families and major tribes through positions in environmental policymaking is the al-Attiyah family in Qatar. A key member of the elite, who occupied the position of minister of energy from 1992 to 2011, is Abdullah bin Hamad al-Attiyah. He is not only a childhood friend of the former emir but stems from one of the most important Qatari family branches, that even made claims to the Qatari throne in the pre-state period. Al-Attiyah has a "reputation

[24] Interview #76.

[25] Ibid.

[26] Interview #26.

for his outspokenness" and belonged to the closest circle of decision-makers under the former emir (Luomi, 2012, 159).[27] Symptomatically of the microstate's neopatrimonial logic, besides the role of energy minister al-Attiyah occupied different positions as deputy prime minister (2007–2011), temporary head of the Emiri Diwan (2011), Director of Qatar Petroleum and member of numerous other boards of directors (Kamrava, 2015, 117; Luomi, 2012, 157). Occasionally, he was also Chairman of the United Nations Commission on Sustainable Development in 2006. In 2012, he was appointed president of the UNFCCC climate summit in Doha. It is said that al-Attiyah's relationship to former Emir Hamad, who made him one of his most trustworthy advisors, was characterized by "fierce loyalty" (Kamrava 2015, 120; 2017). Additionally, his son and former Chairman of the QNFSP, Fahad bin Mohammed al-Attiyah, was head of the sub-committee. Another son, the well-known Qatari rally driver Nasser al-Attiyah, was appointed to help raise awareness as a Goodwill Ambassador for Environment Protection on the occasion of Qatar's Environment Day in 2013. Parallel to his official positions, Hamad al-Attiyah established his own fiefdom by 2015: The Abdullah Bin Hamad Al-Attiyah Foundation for Energy and Sustainable Development is an independent energy think tank that carries out studies and analysis of national and international energy policies (Wright, 2018). Further examples stem from Oman and the UAE. In Oman, members of the Salalah-based al-Rawas branch of the Bait Kathir tribe, characterized by their long-standing loyalty to Muscat and the ruling Al Said dynasty, have benefitted economically and politically. In addition to building a large business empire (i.e. the Al Rawas holding), several tribe members received political positions with responsibilities for environmental sustainability. One of them is Sheikh Abd Allah bin Salim, who was Minister of Regional Municipalities, Evironment and Water Resources from 2004 to 2007 as well as of municipalities and water resources from 2007 to 2011 (Valeri, 2017, 101). In the UAE, the current minister of energy Suhail Muhammad Faraj al-Mazroui, who was appointed in 2013 after his predecessor faced a long prison sentence over financial crimes, is close with the Al Nahyan ruling family (Almezaini, 2013; Hedges, 2021). In fact, he stems from the same tribe as the Crown Prince Mohamed Bin Zayed, namely the important Marazi section of the Bani Yas. Al-Mazroui

[27] Interview #24.

has benefitted from the strategic reorganization of the power sector since 2016 and acted for a long time as 'number two' of the Mohamed bin Zayed-led investment fund, Mubadala (Hedges, 2021). Given also his role as alumni of Abu Dhabi's national oil company, the Abu Dhabi National Oil Company (ADNOC), and his long-standing expertise in this sector, he can be described as someone who stands in between the two classifications of a politically relevant actor and a rather meritocratic technocrat (Hedges, 2021).

In the relatively new field of environment, a third group of actors appears crucial. Especially in accompanying the critical transformation of the energy sector towards a low-carbon economy, the role of specialized technocrats and advisers is indispensable. Frequently, these individuals have had a distinguished career in the oil and gas sector before occupying the top positions of important enterprises or entering ministerial posts in the state apparatus. A well-known example is Dr. Sultan Ahmed al-Jaber, an Emirati technocrat and—in his role of head of energy of Mubadala—founding CEO of Masdar, Abu Dhabi's pioneering renewable initiative (since 2014 he has acted as chairman). In 2016, the time of low oil prices, he was also appointed CEO of ADNOC (see further Chapter 5). Since 2010, he is also special envoy for climate change and heads the Directorate of Energy and Climate Change at the foreign ministry (Luomi, 2012, 98, 105). In 2020, this position was reaffirmed and expanded to include all relevant international forums, bodies and agencies (e.g. UNFCCC, IRENA and relevant NGOs). In the same year, he was also appointed minister of industry and advanced technology to promote Abu Dhabi's sustainable transformation. In addition to these roles, he sits on numerous corporate boards and remained CEO of ADNOC, where he once started his career as engineer (Davidson, 2021). Described as "Masdar's most visible and influential figure", he has an extensive outreach and was not only deeply involved in Masdar's successful bid for headquartering IRENA in 2009, but also appointed as a special adviser to UN General Secretary Ban Ki Moon's Advisory Group on Energy and Climate Change in the same year (Luomi, 2012, 121, 217). In 2012, al-Jaber was awarded the UNEP's prestigious Champion of the Earth award, which also boosted his international profile (Luomi, 2012, 128). In 2020, he was further elevated to the rank of a minister and in his position as the UAE's first minister of industry and advanced technology, and he took over some of al-Mazroui's previous tasks as minister of energy and infrastructure (Davidson, 2021). Like al-Mazroui, al-Jaber was relatively young when appointed to these powerful positions but unlike him, he stems from a rather uninfluential tribal background (i.e. the al-Ali tribe) which could lead to the assumption that his political rise is rather the result of loyalty and meritocracy (Hedges, 2021).

A similarly rapid promotion was experienced by Khalid al-Falih in Saudi Arabia. In the scope of Vision 2030 and broader institutional restructuring that also relieved long-term oil minister Ali al-Naimi of his post, Saudi Aramco's CEO Khalid al-Falih was named as head of the newly formed Ministry of Energy, Industry and Mineral Resources (MOEIMR) in 2016 (Thompson, 2018, 293). Like al-Naimi, al-Falih has a record as long-serving key technocrat of Saudi Aramco (Stenslie, 2012, 153). During 2009 and 2015, he was CEO at Aramco and between 2015 and 2016 minister of health, before obtaining his position at MOEIMR, which he kept until October 2019. In his role as minister, he has not only overseen the board of directors of Saudi Aramco but also KAUST and KAPSARC, where he has exerted considerable influence in the decision-making processes of the company. At the same time, he served, inter alia, as Chairman of the Board of Directors for the Royal Commission for Jubail and Yanbu, the Water and Electricity Regulatory Authority, KACST and K·A·CARE.[28] In 2016, Forbes declared him one of the most powerful men in the world and one interviewee described him as the person Mohammed bin Salman relies on the most (Forbes, n/a).[29] Meanwhile, loyal technocrats of former King Abdullah, such as Hashim Yamani (who headed K·A·CARE), were gradually marginalized under the new leadership. As another interviewee stressed: Al-Falih became the 'royal mouthpiece' and replaced Hashim Yamani, who previously reported directly to the king.[30] However, during 2019, al-Falih was replaced by the paternal brother of the crown prince, Abdelaziz, as already described. Additionally, al-Falih also lost his position as Aramco's CEO to a relative newcomer in Mohammed bin Salman's 'inner circle' of technocrats: Perceived as "a relatively unknown local banker" (cited from Davidson, 2021, 120), al-Rumayyan steadily gained power in his position as managing director of the Public Investment Fund; a previously insignificant sovereign wealth fund (SWF) that was elevated under Vision 2030

[28] Interview #4.

[29] Interview #44.

[30] Interview #46.

and Mohammed bin Salman's quasi ownership. It was further reported that Yasir al-Rumayyan and Mohammed bin Salman jointly performed leisure activities such as hiking, pointing to a trusting and somehow friendly relationship (Davidson, 2021).

A deeper look into the state apparatus using the example of sustainability governance reveals interesting findings about the functioning and operationalization of policymaking in one of the opaquest countries worldwide. Both governmental and semi-governmental entities constitute a strategic element of "inclusionary co-optation" (Albrecht & Schlumberger, 2004, 383). This includes different segments of actors. On the one hand, members of ruling families occupy important positions within the board of directors and take care of the selection of leadership. Sometimes, they also act as presidents and figureheads while content-related tasks are rather executed by individuals from the non-royal segment (frequently high-paid and high-skilled expatriates or nationals with considerable international leverage) (Hertog, 2012). In some instances, the strategic occupation of governmental entities or fiefdoms helps to consolidate a specific family branch. This can be best observed in Saudi Arabia in the light of the recent succession. As a member of the powerful Sudairi clan, the leadership under King Salman privileged this family branch and marginalized the constituencies of his predecessor King Abdullah. While this can be seen in various policy fields such as the security sector, the field of environmental sustainability underscores how the Salmans converted the traditional mechanism of a decentralized system of patronage ('segmented clientelism') into a family-based vertical top-down-hierarchization (Davidson, 2021; Demmelhuber, 2019, 109).[31]

On the other hand, in the dynastic monarchies—which are characterized by a high concentration of power by the ruling emir, sultan or king surrounded by his closest relatives—regime stability also depends on non-royal but politically relevant players. Those key elites are often connected through personal friendship or tribal belonging and stand out for their loyalty and high degree of trustworthiness (also: Stenslie, 2012, 67).[32] In sum, this group of actors can be described as "the set of people whose endowments include the qualities or characteristics institutionally required

[31] Interview #26.

[32] Interview #46.

to choose the government's leadership and necessary for gaining access to private benefits doled out by the government's leadership" (Bueno de Mesquita et al., 2003, 42). Interestingly, these non-royal key elites often oversee some of the most important governmental fiefdoms quite independently (Crystal, 2014, 177). The first and second group of actors are unified by the fact that the second group either has enough power or else possesses certain benefits, so that they cannot be ignored or disregarded by the regime. In short, appointments in the (semi)governmental sector are not often based on meritocracy. This explains why political staff have often been seen as rather inexperienced and unqualified for the position (Luomi, 2012). This neopatrimonial and favouritism (*wasta*) logic results in structural inefficiency and a lack of professionalism (Gray, 2019, 127).[33] This not only relates to the top of leading environmental decision-making bodies but is transmitted all the way down to sublevels of the administrative levels (Spiess, 2008). According to one interviewee in Qatar: "There are non-professional Qataris, who want to keep their jobs. This is why they don't rely on external professional assistance and experts. If the government would know how unprofessional the locals are, they would fire them and that's why they conceal everything".[34]

The lack of competence caused by the neopatrimonial logic of governance tends to be gradually compensated for by a last group that includes specialized technocrats (*mudarā fi-ldawla*). Especially during the last years, this group has been increasingly involved in sustainability governance that goes along with a greater professionalization in that sector. The reliance on these extremely well-turned-out technocrats has several benefits: First, it enhances an (alleged) perception of improved policymaking process, since the formal nomination of non-royals not only avoids the allegation of corruption and nepotism, but also may enhance the rationalization and efficacy of governance processes. Second, royals can rely on a broad segment of loyal but non-royal individuals to foster their own grip on power. For instance, for most parts, Abdullah primarily relied on (independent) specialized technocrats as he did not possess a similar family-based power base to other relatives (Niblock, 2006; Stenslie, 2012).[35] Third, in contrast to powerful elites or family members

[33] Interviews #34; interview #36 and interview #37.

[34] Interview #24.

[35] Interview #44.

it is easier to put second-tier technocrats in place "because it is also easier to kick them out when necessary".[36]

National Sustainability Governance: The Gap Between Pledges and Implementation

Especially during the last two to three years, Gulf monarchies have made noticeable efforts towards a green transition. Leaderships across the region realize that promoting climate action outweighs the benefits of their previous path of hydrocarbon-based dependency. Climate action, once only a sidenote of GCC policymaking, has become a top priority; even if environmental policies focus rather on adaptation than mitigation: The countries aim to lower their high ecological footprint (in particular carbon emissions) without threatening the hydrocarbon industry as long as it is economically meaningful and viable (i.e. as long as there is demand). The COVID-19 pandemic has accelerated the speed of implementation as global lockdown and curfew measures have significantly reduced the demand for oil, for instance in the transport sector. The breakdown of global supply chains (in terms of many commodities but particularly food) evinced once again the high dependence of the GCC countries on exports and their unsustainable consumption habits (for instance of 'virtual water') (Luomi, 2021c; Noach & Guzansky, 2021).[37] Despite the fact that much of this sustainable transformation is based on climate mitigation and energy resilience, it is overall good news for limiting global warming as outlined in the Paris Agreement of 2015. Certainly, such a shift does not occur overnight, rather gradually over a longer transitional period. However, when reading the news in the Gulf, it appears that a radical reorientation and even a "green revolution" is taking place in the oil- and gas-exporting region (Quaile, 2013). Government-owned newspapers across the region declare exclusively good news in eye-catching headlines. Especially, the UAE, Qatar and Saudi Arabia race to compete for being the greenest leader in the region. Such perceptions are also closely linked to repeated promotions of new and groundbreaking green superlatives.

[36] Ibid.

[37] The concept of 'virtual water' encompasses a measure of a product's water footprint within the entire supply chain (Allan, 2011).

The following list of English and Arabic news headlines are only some examples and should provide a better understanding of the strategic instrumentalization of the media to foster a green image: For instance, in Qatari-based The Peninsula, one can find headlines such as "Qatar a role model in water conservation" (The Peninsula, March 22, 2013), "Qatar makes headway in emission cuts" (The Peninsula, October 5, 2015), "Over 121 GW renewable energy installed in 2015" (The Peninsula, June 5, 2016), "Qatar set to revolutionise global solar industry" (The Peninsula, August 15, 2016), "Qatar tops the region in energy transion" (Qatar Tribune, April 22, 2021), "Qatar will remain world's top clean energy producer" (The Peninsula, November 23, 2017) or "Qatar major contributor to tackling climate change" (The Peninsula, December, 18 2018). Similarly, media outlets in Saudi Arabia have applied superlatives from very early on, for example referring to the kingdom as "the most attractive country for renewable and nuclear energy investments after China and India" (Ar-Riyadh, May 10, 2012) or stating that it will shortly become the "world's biggest contributor of solar energy" (Ar-Riyadh, November 7, 2013) or one of the "world's leading solar exporters in the future" (Ar-Riyadh, April 19, 2010). Particularly, the Saudi newspaper al-Sharq al-Awsat paid a lot of attention to the announcement of Solar Plan 2030 with SoftBank, which foresaw the installation of 200 GW of solar power but was shelved shortly afterwards. Several articles celebrated it as the "world's biggest solar power project" and "greatest energy source worldwide" (Al-Sharq al-Awsat, March 29, 2018; April 1, 2018; Ar-Riyadh, April 3, 2018). Another article stressed that this project shows the country's willingness for alternative energy, which some "anti-Saudi lobbies" have tried to ignore (Ar-Riyadh, March 30, 2018). Also, the Emirati media outlets helped in crafting the image of a green leadership role. This included headlines such as "UAE is a leading state regionally in the field of green development" (Emirates News Agency, February 3, 2016), "UAE among top 10 countries for LEED Green Building" (Emirates News Agency, August 8, 2015), "Mohammed bin Rashid Al Maktoum Solar Park Highlights Dubai's International Position in Sustainable Development" (UAE Government News, May 4, 2016) or "Dubai harvests abundance of solar energy" (Emirates News Agency, February 14, 2015). Further topics in government-affiliated The National emphasized new achievements such as the inauguration of "the largest single-site solar park" (The National, June 24, 2021) the "largest solar-powered car park"

(The National, June 1, 2021) or the launch of the "largest coral reef rehabilitation project in the region" (The National, June 9, 2021). However, as a short comparison between the announced targets and implementation in terms or renewable energy production shows (Table 4.3), there still exists a huge gap.

In short, one can say that reports have overemphasized "good-news stories about the environment" (Alraouf & Clarke, 2017, 126) while being reluctant to publish negative or contentious environmentally related issues (see also: Al-Sarihi, 2022). As other scholars have also stressed, there is a gap between 'green noise' or self-determined goals and practical implementation in the Gulf (Luomi, 2012). For instance, Agatino Rizzo emphasized that it is "difficult—arguably impossible—to overlook the mismatch between the stated intentions and the actual policy" (Rizzo, 2017, 11). As the examples show, promoting a certain narrative can help to increase the ruling elites' legitimacy base (Zumbraegel, 2019, 2020). In this vein, environmental decisions and actions are strategically tailored in order to foster personal image-building and boost the leader's charisma, to underline the country's superiority and to brand a distinctive model of development and modernization. The following insights

Table 4.3 Overview national targets of renewable energy and actual share in 2019 (based on: Sim, 2022; Al-Sarihi & Mansouri, 2022)

Country	*National level target*	*Actual share of generation in 2019*	*2020*
Bahrain	5% of generation by 2025 10% of generation by 2035	0.03%	0.1%
Kuwait	15% of generation by 2030	0.22%	0.5%
Oman	10% of generation by 2025 30% of generation by 2030	0.01%	1.3%
Qatar	6% of generation by 2020 20% of generation by 2030	0.26%	0.3%
Saudi Arabia	50% of generation by 2030	0.04%	0.5%
The United Arab Emirates	Federal: 23.5% of generation mix by 2021, 50% of generation mix by 2050 • Dubai: 7% renewable energy generation by 2020, 25% by 2030, and 75% by 2050 • Abu Dhabi: 7% of installed capacity by 2020	3.21%	7.2%

from case studies will help to re-evaluate the status quo and contextualize sustainability governance in the region. The following subsections look at the environmental governance processes and climate actions of each of the GCC countries. Research is mainly based on national climate action plans (where existent) national development plans (visions) or other initiatives such as the recently promoted net-zero targets by some states. Additionally, it looks at the GCC states' submitted National Communications (NC), Intended Nationally Determined Contributions (INDC) as non-Annex I countries under the UNFCCC, as well as their Nationally Determined Contributions (NDCs) under the framework of the Paris Agreement of 2015, which all Gulf monarchies have signed and ratified.[38] The country subsections look at different aspects of environmental sustainability such as environmental protection and climate action, clean energy targets and energy efficiency measures.

The United Arab Emirates (UAE)

Of all the states, the UAE has established the most advanced level and structure of environmental policymaking that not only acts in a horizontal way but also leaves space for vertical interaction and coordination. A special committee, the UAE Council on Climate Change and Environment, which was established in 2016 as part of the UAE Green Agenda 2030, constitutes the central steering body between different agencies across ministries and local authorities as well as with the private sector and academia. At the federal governance level, since its inauguration in 2016 the already mentioned MOCCAE is the leading body (Luomi, 2021a). The energy sector is dominated by two technocrats close to the Crown Prince, Mohamed bin Zayed (Cahill, 2021; Hedges 2021). This includes the above-mentioned Suhail Muhammed Faraj al-Mazroui as minister of energy and Sultan bin Ahmad Sultan al-Jaber, who is minister of industry and advanced technology, CEO of Abu Dhabi's oil company and also special envoy for climate (Al-Sarihi & Mason, 2020). It all culminates

[38] With the Paris Agreement of 2015, a new international climate agreement came into force. Through submitting Intended Nationally Determined Contributions (INDC) every five years, countries describe their efforts and commitments towards the Paris Agreement. The word "Intended" was used prior to 2015, as countries were communicating proposed climate actions ahead of the Paris Agreement being finalized. At the time countries officially signed up to the Agreement, an INDC was converted into a Nationally Determined Contribution (NDC) (see Griffiths & Orkoubi, 2019, 146).

in the lead of Crown Prince and recently announced President Mohamed bin Zayed, who controls the UAE's economic reform to which alternative energy and sustainability-related initiatives belong (Luomi, 2012).

Particularly, the UAE National Climate Change Plan 2017–2050, which was launched in 2017, constitutes the pivotal framework for the country's environmental sustainability agenda. Being the first of its kind in the GCC region, the climate action plan is overseen by the Council of Climate Change and Environment and built upon three core principles—managing GHG emissions, stronger climate adaptation and an economic diversification agenda through innovative solutions. Consequently, the plan reflects the aim of building climate resilience while sustaining economic growth. It is also underpinned by further development plans. One of them is the National Energy Strategy 2050, which intends to raise the share of non-carbon energy sources (renewables and nuclear) to 50% by 2050 and reduce both the carbon footprint of power generation by 70% and the final energy demand by 40% in the same year. According to the information of the official portal, the plan builds on an energy mix using clean energy (44%), gas (38%), clean coal (12%) and nuclear (6%). These targets are underpinned by the UAE Green Agenda 2030 (2015) that enables the public and private sectors to implement a shared vision of a competitive and sustainable economy (Al-Sarihi & Mansouri, 2022). As an intermediary goal, the UAE's second NDC (2020) stresses a reduction of 23.5% in GHG emissions by the year 2030 (Al-Sulayman 2021; Krane 2021). In October 2021, the Emirates bolstered their commitment towards decarbonization—it was the first country in the region to announce a net-zero carbon target by 2050. The goal stands in line with the objectives outlined by previous plans such as the Climate Plan (2017) and the national agenda described in Vision 2021 (2011). As leading body, the MOCCAE should coordinate efforts to execute the net-zero initiative. This contrasts many other GCC countries, where aspects of promoting renewable energy, limiting emissions and increasing energy efficiency are overseen by the separate ministries of energy and not environmental institutions. Another, rather long-term strategy is the UAE's desire to become a global leader in the hydrogen industry. In this regard, the leadership officially launched its Hydrogen Leadership Roadmap during the climate conference in Glasgow in 2021.

In addition to these mitigation efforts, the country has also fostered adaptation measures. In November 2020, the UAE cabinet approved a new Environment Policy as a national guide that will be overseen by the minister of industry and advanced technology, Sultan al-Jaber, as the UAE's special envoy for climate change. The strategy shall serve as a reference point for all federal and local environmental policies and includes more than a hundred initiatives across key priorities such as (a) limiting the impacts of climate change, (b) accelerating the efforts to conserve natural resources, (c) boosting air quality and (d) ensuring safety of food products. Since September 2021, the ministry is chaired by the former minister of state for food and water, Mariam bint Mohammed Saeed Hareb Almheiri. For several observers this also indicates a stronger future focus on (d) ensuring the country's long-term food and water security.[39]

Meanwhile, the individual emirates have developed their own plans and initiatives, with Abu Dhabi succeeding the other six emirates. Among these programmes are Abu Dhabi's Masdar Initiative, its urbanization initiative Plan Abu Dhabi 2030 and the recently unveiled Environment Vision 2030. In addition to the federal plans, the latter identifies five key areas of sustainability governance for further improvement. These are (a) minimizing the impact of climate change, (b) clean air and noise pollution—contributing to safe and healthy living conditions, (c) efficient management and conservation of water resources, (d) biodiversity, habitats and cultural heritage and (e) enhanced value creation through optimized material flows and waste management.

In terms of concrete outputs, the UAE has taken steps in achieving some of the above-outlined objectives. By having two large-scale solar parks, namely Dubai's 5 GW Mohammed bin Rashid Al Maktoum Solar Park and Abu Dhabi's 2 GW Al Dhafra Solar Project, the UAE has the highest solar energy capacity in the Middle East and North Africa.[40] Additionally, it was the first Arab country to build a major nuclear power plant, in Barakah, which started operation in August 2021. Abu Dhabi has also taken steps to enhance sustainable urban planning by developing the Estidama framework in 2008 and launching its own green building rating system. Dubai and the smaller emirate, Ras Al Khaimah, have also implemented green building regulations. Both emirates Dubai and Abu Dhabi have also undertaken an incremental approach to cut subsidization of hydrocarbons. Between 2008 and 2014, the government

[39] Interview #63 and interview #66.

[40] For further smaller renewable energy projects, see overview Karen Young's publication (ibid., 2019, 84)

lifted energy subsidies for commercial and industrial consumption that facilitated the development of solar PV as alternative energy source (Al-Sulayman, 2021). Starting in 2015 the UAE reduced subsidies on petrol and diesel prices and removed them altogether by 2018 (Moerenhout, 2021). At the same time, a 5% VAT rate was applied to hydrocarbon use (Al-Sarihi & Mason, 2020).

In terms of education and research, the UAE has also advanced. Environmental awareness played a leading role in the UAE's National Strategy for Awareness and Education 2015–2021. Meanwhile, MOCCAE conducts an annual national environmental awareness and behaviour survey. Numerous federal and national initiatives are further applied such as Sustainable School Initiative, Sustainable Campus Initiative, Be'ati Watani programme, Eco-Schools Program or the My Sustainable Lifestyle programme that all target different segments of society. In order to address the lack of environmental data collection and validation that is endemic in the region, Abu Dhabi launched a multi-year project in 2002 to study ecosystems across the local, national and regional levels. The Abu Dhabi Global Environmental Data Initiative works closely with the federal and national leading environmental institutions to assess the impact of climate change and environmental degradation.

However, databases such as the Climate Action Tracker sees the Emirates' overall performance still as 'highly insufficient'. This is mainly due to an expected increase in emissions due to the continuation of hydrocarbon-based sources of electricity and the consideration of coal as part of the country's future energy mix (Climate Action Tracker, 2022). Coal is the only hydrocarbon resource that is not naturally available in the region, which contributes to an almost doubling of emissions per unit of energy delivered, in comparison with other hydrocarbons such as natural gas (Krane, 2020). Coal has some advantages, for instance in terms of cost or reliability of supply, but it is considered a backward technology. Even though Dubai's 2.4 GW Hassyan Power Complex has been described as a 'clean' coal-fired power plant due to improved energy efficiency and less emissions (in comparison to other coal plants), one has to question what 'clean' or 'green' means in this context (Al-Sarihi, 2018). As Jim Krane puts it: "Even low-particulate 'clean coal' will worsen air quality" (Krane, 2021, 78), and thus its use stands in sharp contrast to many of the above-outlined key environmental priorities in the UAE's climate campaigns. Meanwhile, the government in Dubai has apparently recognized this schizophrenic approach of 'clean coal' and announced in February 2022 that it will convert its Hassyan project to natural gas, which is less emission intensive.

In sum, the UAE remains the poster child with having the third highest rank from all Arab countries and leader within the GCC. It shows an improving trend on SDGs such as (6) Clean Water and Sanitation, (7) Affordable and Clean Energy, (11) Sustainable Cities and Communities, (13) Climate Action and (15) Life on Land. Even more, it is on track or maintaining SDG achievement in two environmental sustainability goals, namely (12) Responsible Consumption and Production and (14) Life below Water (Bayoumi et al., 2022).

Saudi Arabia

As already outlined, the Kingdom of Saudi Arabia is an interesting case because we have seen major shifts and disruptions between the reign of former King Abdullah and current King Salman. This also applies to visions and strategic plans for achieving environmental sustainability. With no clear mandate over environmental protection and climate change and many authorities with partially overlapping competences, sustainability governance has long taken a backseat. Initially, Saudi Arabia's main environmental institution, the Presidency of Meteorology and Environment, released a principial environmental statute, which lacks any legally binding targets and has not been updated since its implementation in 2001. Instead, in the scope of the tenth development plan (2015–2019), the government issued nine environmental by-laws with a comprehensive list of standards and guidelines in 2012. It has not until summer 2020 when the kingdom issued a new environmental law that will supersede all parallel existing environmental laws. However, large parts of this law have not been finalized by the time of writing. The same applies to the above-mentioned 'National Environmental Strategy', which has not produced any tangible results since its release in 2018 (Alomari & Heffron, 2021). In summer 2021, the vice minister declared that altogether 64 initiatives will run under the strategy and "work is underway" (MEWA, 2021). Generally, it has been remarked that the enforcement of environmental regulations often failed in reality.[41] In the words by Taher and Hajjar: "A critical look at the various environmental laws and regulations over

[41] Interview #28.

the past decades suggests that, on paper, these regulations are as good as can be found anywhere in the world, but what is lacking is effective enforcement of the rules" (Taher & Hajjar, 2014, 17). It needs to be seen whether the inauguration of an 'environmental police', the Special Forces for Environmental Security in 2020 with the mandate of environmental surveillance, enforcing regulations and pursuing prosecution over environmental crimes will change this lack of implementation (Alomari & Heffron, 2021).

With the launch of the Saudi Vision 2030 in 2016, environmental sustainability (*al-istidāma al-bīʾyya*) was explicitly named as a principle of the country's future development. The vision, which was planned with the assistance of foreign management consultancy companies (e.g. McKinsey and Boston Consulting Group), considers environmental sustainability in terms of reducing pollution, increasing waste management and recycling facilities and protecting the environment and biodiversity. In another core theme, the vision also makes reference to the expansion of clean energy. As accompanied addendum document to operationalize the vision, the so-called National Transformation Program 2020 provided more details on delivery. The area of sustainable use of resources has the most concrete objectives. Most of the strategic targets have been formulated in accordance with international indices. For instance, the document aims to reduce all forms of environmental pollution, which includes above all air pollution, but also noise, water, soil, thermal and light pollution. It aims to improve the kingdom's rank in the Yale Environmental Performance Index from 95 (2016) to at least 53 in 2020. Using the Global Food Security Index as a baseline, the kingdom intends to upgrade from a baseline of 71.1 (2016) to 72 in 2020. Additional water access shall be increased from 87% (in 2015) to 92% in 2020. At the same time, the rate of treated wastewater shall be enhanced from 13% (2015) to 35% and the proportion of renewable water consumption in the agricultural sector from 16% (2016) to 35% in 2020. Further core objectives include measures for improved protection from environmental hazards and conservation of the natural landscape and biodiversity. This shall be achieved by increasing the accuracy of forecasting from 60% in 2017 to 80% in 2020. Additionally, the scale of rehabilitated natural vegetation shall more than quadruple in the same period. It further seeks an improvement in the Biodiversity and Habitats Index from rank 82 (2016) to 87 in 2020.[42]

In terms of clean energy goals, the kingdom further modified its energy transition strategy. The Vision 2030 revised previous plans by outlining an 'initial target' of producing 9.5 GW via RES by 2023 and 54 GW by 2040, framed under the so-called National Renewable Energy Program (NREP). The newly created body REPDO, under the umbrella of the Ministry of Energy, was commissioned to overlook and supervise NREP. In 2018, plans were ramped up to 27.3 GW (including 20 GW of PV and 7 GW of wind) by 2023 and 58.7 GW by 2030 (40 GW of PV, 16 GW of wind and 2.7 GW of concentrating solar power) (Luomi, 2021a). In March 2021, a new goal of targeting 50% of renewable energy by 2030 was declared (Kiyasseh, 2022). Execution is commissioned to REPDO, which shall tender 30% of the projects in a competitive process whereas the other 70% are awarded to a national sovereign wealth fund, the Public Investment Fund (PIF) (Kiyasseh, 2022). The role of the PIF, which was added later, was justified by a pledge to speed up the process through developing giga-scale projects "via direct negotiations with developers" (Luomi, 2021a, 312; further: Al-Sulayman, 2021).

The kingdom's energy transition has become a personal priority of the Crown Prince Mohammed bin Salman. He is not only the chairman of the PIF but also of a newly formed Supreme Committee for Energy Mix Affairs for Electricity Production and Enabling Renewable Energy, which he created in April 2020 (Luomi, 2021a). In the scope of the NEOM initiative, in January 2021, he announced the founding of The Line, a huge zero-carbon city that is powered entirely by renewables and has no cars. Only several weeks later, he introduced the Saudi and Middle East Green Initiative. On a national level, the initiative emphasizes the country's commitment to generating 50% renewable energy by 2030 and offsetting emissions by planting 10 billion trees in the kingdom, as well as creating 30% protected Saudi land, including coastal ecosystems. In addition to that, the plan foresees the planting of an additional 40 billion trees across the Middle East and aims at a 60% reduction in carbon emissions

[42] See official website Saudi Vision 2030/National Transformation Plan: https://www.vision2030.gov.sa/v2030/vrps/ntp/.

regionwide.[43] Shortly after neighbouring UAE announced their net-zero target, Saudi Arabia followed suit. In October 2021, Riyadh pledged to achieve "Net Zero" emissions by 2060 (Al-Sarihi, 2021). The plans for a so-called Circular Carbon Economy Program that the Saudi government presented as part of its G20 Presidency in 2020 was a major prerequisite for elaborating a net-zero target (Kiyasseh, 2022). The concept is based on mitigating emissions through the 'four Rs'—Reduce: Energy efficiency, renewable energy and other low-carbon energy such as nuclear; Reuse: Converting emissions into industrial feedstock (e.g. through enhanced oil recovery); Recycle: Natural sinks such as forests and oceans, bio-energy and hydrogen; and Remove: Carbon capture, utiliziation and storage (CCUS), planting flora and direct air capture (Al Shehri et al., 2022). Already since 2015, Saudi Arabia is experimenting with these technologies. One succinct example is the pilot project, the Uthmaniyah Carbon Dioxide Enhanced Oil Recovery, in the Eastern province (Al-Sarihi, 2021). In the scope of the net-zero announcements, Saudi Arabia joined the so-called Net-Zero Producers Forum and made pledges to invest around $100 billion in clean energy and updated its NDC with a 35% emissions reduction target (Al-Sarihi, 2021; Kiyasseh, 2022). Even more remarkable, in March 2022, the PIF announced the creation of the region's first voluntary carbon market. In so doing, it signed agreements with several partners from the private sector including Saudi Aramco, the airline company Saudia, the mining company Maaden, the energy company Arabian Company for Water and Power Development (ACWA Power) and a subsidiary of NEOM.

Furthermore the kingdom also made some more casual steps, in pricing utilities to alter the demand side. In contrast to his predecessor, the new leadership under the auspices of the crown prince, did not hesitate to introduce regulations on subsidies and initiate an energy reform. The plan, which foresaw a radical change of the long-perceived "'untouchable' cradle-to-grave subsidies on energy" (Krane, 2019, 124), was based on the efforts undertaken and data collected by the Electricity and Cogeneration Regulatory Authority (ECRA) over more than fifteen years. Between 2012 and 2013, ECRA had already revealed plans to reduce energy consumption (Alhoweish & Orujov, 2016) but it was only under the new leadership that this gained momentum: In January 2016 and

[43] See official website of Saudi Green Initiative: https://www.saudigreeninitiative.org/.

2018, Saudi citizens experienced 'ad hoc' fuel price reforms (Moerenhout, 2021). On January 1, 2016, the prices of, for instance, natural gas and diesel increased significantly. Additionally, in the scope of a complex tariff rate, every household which consumed more than 4,000 kWh per month faced considerably higher electricity bills. These steps had been necessary, but the regime feared political repercussions in the form of public disfavour.[44] In addition, the government introduced a VAT of 5% in January 2018, which marked a break with the 'social contract' of no taxation to the demise of political participation and representation. In the light of the ravaging COVID-19 pandemic and a radical drop in oil price, the Saudi government further increased the VAT to 15%.

So far, the country's output contradicts these above-mentioned green pledges and its claim to green leadership. By the time of writing, Saudi Arabia has less than 1 GW in capacity to produce green electricity (Al-Sarihi & Mansouri, 2022). It includes the 300 MW solar-powered Sakaka IPP PV project, the 50 MW Al-Jowf Solar Power Plant by the SEC and the 400 MW wind farm at Dumat al-Jandal, which is not only the country's first wind farm but also the largest in the Middle East and North Africa.[45] Having said that, several new solar plants are in the construction phase and these should aim at increasing the capacity to around 2.5 GW within a short period since many projects have been awarded and are expected to be comissioned in later 2022 and early 2023 (Noach & Guzansky, 2021; Obeid, 2022).[46] However, this is still far from any previously announced clean energy goals. In fact, even if the current solar projects come online during the year 2022, it would make only "12.5% of the revised 2023 target" (Kiyasseh, 2022), leading to great pressure and extraordinary efforts to fulfil the target by the end of 2023.

Consequently, it is not surprising that the country scores poorly in various indices. According to the Climate Action Tracker, Saudi

[44] Interview #44.

[45] There are also a number of small-scale solar-powered plants. For example, this includes PV solar rooftop systems at KAUST and the King Abdullah Financial District in Riyadh as well as open-land solar installations at Aramco's headquarter in Dharan and KAPSARC in Riyadh (see further: Alnaser & Alnaser, 2011; al-Ubaydli et al., 2019; Young, 2019).

[46] The solar PV projects include: The Sudair project (1,500 MW); Qurayyat IPP PV (200 MW) and Shuaibah IPP PV (600 MW); Jeddah IPP PV (300 MW); Rabigh IPP PV (300 MW); Aljumaih, and Rafha IPP PV (20 MW) and Al Madinah IPP PV (50 MW).

Arabia's environmental performance is "highly insufficient" (Climate Action Tracker, 2022). Also, in the Climate Change Performance Index the kingdom holds the position of "the second lowest ranked performer" (Climate Change Performance Index, 2021). Moreover, despite the ambitious objectives outlined in the kingdom's strategic papers, none of the SGD goals have been achieved so far. Quite the opposite, in terms of clean water and sanitation (SDG 6), sustainable consumption and production of resources (SDG 12) as well as climate action (SDG 13) the country faces major challenges. 'Significant' challenges remain on a wide range of sustainability-related areas such as sustainable cities (SDG 11), life below water (SDG 14) and life on land (SDG 15) (Bayoumi et al., 2022; Sachs et al., 2021). Moreover, in terms of overall environmental performance as measured by the EPI, Saudi Arabia underperforms on aspects including air quality, biodiversity, access to water and climate action (overall rank 90 out of 180 in 2020) (Environmental Performance Index, 2020). As several authors have noticed, there are various obstacles that explains the explains the kingdom's low performance on environmental sustainability. Some of them include significant lack of data and research, a hyper-centralized organization of decision-making, vertical and horizontal overlapping jurisdictions among institutions and authorities as well as lack of human skills with still "too few academically qualified, high-quality bureaucrats who can coordinate longer-term policies, and too many high-level advisors who lead government projects but leave the ministry whenever the minister changes" (Fathallah, 2019; further: al-Sarihi, 2022).

Against this backdrop, it is questionable in what way and to what extent newly announced large-scale initiatives on behalf of the Crown Prince Mohammed bin Salman mark a turning point in the country's transformation, or whether these are rather short-term and diverting examples of 'green dreams'. Moreover, there seems to be inconsistency among the Saudi leadership. While Mohammed bin Salman frequently announces new over-ambitious projects and pledges splashy commitments, his brother, the minister of energy Abdulaziz, appears to have a more realistic perspective on the kingdom's energy transition. He has not only emphasized that the last drop of oil will certainly be produced in Saudi Arabia, but he also interpreted a renewable energy roadmap by the International Energy Agency as "a sequel of [the movie] La La Land" (Noach & Guzansky, 2021, 4).

Qatar

So far, the country submitted its first National Communication (NC) to the UNFCCC in 2011 and its first Paris Agreement contribution (NDC) in 2015. The NC points to a number of voluntary initiatives such as decarbonization projects, climate finance and potential future projects of clean energy and concludes with recommendations for a national action framework, but misses clear measures and goals to address climate change and environmental sustainability objectives. The NDC is also largely descriptive in style and refers to the Qatar National Vision 2030 (launched in 2008) as its baseline. Yet, the vision as well as its underlying planning documents, Qatar's first National Development Strategy 2011–2016 (2011) and second National Development Strategy 2018–2022 (2018) treat environmental sustainability cursorily. They point to climate change adaptation and mitigation, sustainable use of resources, conservation and protection of the natural environment, stronger environmental awareness and more environmental policy frameworks but not at the expense of technology, efficacy, economic prosperity and welfare. For instance, the strategic plans highlight that "environmental degradation can be reduced [and should be compensated] through investment in advanced technologies" (cited from: Luomi, 2012, 11).

More concrete is the underlying so-called Environmental Sustainability Strategy (2011–2016 and 2017–2022 respectively) of both development plans. Although Qatar had been active in terms of environmental conservation and biodiversity prior to its environmental strategies (Richer, 2009), progress has been slow so far, as the new environmental plan admits: Only two out of twelve targets have been achieved so far, including the reduction of gas flaring. As for the other targets, it was said that they were partly too ambitious, including the previous goal of planting a billion trees across the country (Kamrava, 2015). Especially during 2000 and 2004, the Ministry of Environment released numerous laws and regulations relating to wildlife conservation, the trafficking of endangered wildlife, usage of fertilizer and pesticides to improve the soil and water, as well as the sustainable use of fish. However, the practical enforcement of these regulations has been continually brought into question (Al Othman & Clarke, 2017; Luomi, 2012). One interviewee even brought forward an explanation: "People have not made up their minds and this is why you do not see lots of regulations coming out".[47] What appears to be a rather more fruitful approach is the country's efforts to push the environmental sustainability agenda within the educational system. In this sense, Qatar University has—as first in the region—established a degree programme of environmental science for both bachelor and master's students. The programme provides students with knowledge of how to conserve marine and desert ecosystems, how to manage and preserve natural resources energy and waste and how to conduct sustainable urban and regional planning. Furthermore, both the Hamad Bin Khalifa University and Texas A&M University have launched several undergraduate, masters and PhD programmes in sustainable development (Al Othman & Clarke, 2017).

Especially in the light of hosting the climate summit, the country promoted environmental sustainability as an (alleged) key principle. This included the creation of the energy efficient and solar-powered convention centre, the launch of numerous environmental initiatives such as the Qatar Environmental Action Programme (2011), the Tarsheed (Rationalization) Campaign (2012) or Green Car Initiative (2012) as well as small-scale PR initiatives during the summit such as a shuttle service of electric buses, waste and recycling schemes (e.g. recyclable water bottles) or giveaways like iPad cases, pens and memory sticks derived from bamboo. However, most of these greenwashing campaigns were of "low-impact and lack(ed) consistency" (Luomi, 2012, 169) indicating the cursory nature of these projects that were rather implemented to cater to the taste of a well-connected and steadily increasing environmentally aware global population. Moreover, many previously announced RES projects have been scrapped since then as a result of the sinking global oil and gas prices that began in 2014.[48] These include the many solar-powered plants that had been announced by various entities such as the Ministry of Energy and Industry, the Qatari power and water distribution company (*Kahramaa*), the Qatar National Food Security Programme (QNFSP) or other subsidiaries of QF. In total, all these plans were aimed at producing more than 1.5 GW of solar energy in the country (Alnaser & Alnaser, 2011; Ferroukhi et al. 2016, 41; Meltzer et al., 2014). Even though the Vision 2030 outlined a target of generating 20% of renewable

[47] Interview #20.

[48] Interview #20.

energy (Al-Ubaydli et al., 2019), Qatar's de facto deployment of RES was (and still is) low and it has not achieved its first goal of 6% renewable energy generation by 2020 (see also: Table 4.3).[49]

Only lately, and in the light of covering the energy supply needs of the Fédération Internationale de Football Association (FIFA) World Cup 2022, Qatar has started to build an 800 MW solar PV plant at Al-Kharsaag, which should start operation in 2021 (Al-Sulayman, 2021; Al-Sarihi & Mansouri, 2022). This is a great leap forward as the country's alternative energy output was previously limited to a biomass plant, the Mesaieed Domestic Solid Waste Center, completed in 2006, that produces around 30 MW (Al-Sarihi & Mansouri, 2022). Given Qatar's abundance of natural gas that can be produced at very low cost and is relatively clean in contrast to other fossil fuels such as coal and oil, leadership invests large sums into low-carbon technology and cleaning up their large liquefied natural gas (LNG) business. Qatar is the global leader of LNG and gas-to-liquids and lower-emission natural gas is seen to have a crucial role in a future energy mix in the light of global low-carbon development (al-Saffar, 2021; Krane, 2020).[50] For over a decade, it has invested heavily in clean energy R&D development to sustain this vibrant business sector and backbone of the country's wealth (Wright, 2018). This has been done by improving infrastructure (e.g. updating pipeline networks) or installing new compressors that avoid the excess of gas flaring. Prestigious landmark projects include the al-Shaheen Oilfield Gas Recovery and Utilization Project and the Jetty Boil-Off Gas Recovery Project in the city of Ras Laffan that aim at reducing gas flaring by 80 and 65%, respectively (Hertog & Luciani, 2012; Meltzer et al., 2014; PourMirza, 2017). Companies like Qatar Petroleum and Qatargas have commissioned their own systems to monitor the supply chain to decrease fugitive emissions (Luomi, 2014). For instance, the Qatargas Flare Management System declared that it has reduced flaring by 88% since 2011. Much has also been undertaken in the field of diversifying the downstream industries of petrochemicals, which are considered "climate-proof" (Krane, 2019, 168). Given other countries' efforts towards decarbonization, Qatar has lately updated its NDC. In a move that can be interpreted as minimal

[49] Interview #19.

[50] Natural gas produces approximately 60% less CO_2eq than coal so it serves as the "perfect excuse" to reduce any external pressure to mitigate domestic GHG emission (Luomi, 2012, 186).

commitment in the light of the climate summit in Glasgow 2021, the Qatari leadership announced a 25% emissions reduction target by 2030 (Climate Action Tracker, 2022).

As wealthiest country in the world in terms of GDP per capita, Qatar's environmental performance is poor, according to various indices in the last years. For instance, Yale's Environmental Performance Index states that "Qatar shows the lowest overall performance on Climate Change of any country, and shares the bottom score on GHG emissions per capita with Saudi Arabia, UAE, Kuwait, and Bahrain" leading it to rank 122 from 180 countries (Environmental Performance Index, 2020). Similarly, in the Sustainable Development Report of 2021, Qatar occupies rank 94 out of 165 countries (Sachs et al., 2021). However, with the launch of a national environmental and climate strategy and the re-creation of a separate environment and climate change ministry, it can be expected that the country will perform better on a number of SGDs, where it is now stagnating (Bayoumi et al., 2022).

Oman

Until recently, the implementation of climate and sustainable energy plans was neither backed up by a national action plan nor incorporated into national strategies such as the country's 9th Five-Year Development Plan (2016–2020). It was only in the scope of the Paris Agreement 2015 that the government committed to the goal of reducing GHG emissions by 2% by 2030 and to increasing the share of renewable energy production to 30% by 2030. As a result of these commitments, the government launched the Oman Energy Master Plan 2040 supervised by the Public Authority for Electricity & Water. The roadmap towards green transition aimed to include twelve key sustainable energy projects, which will account for at least 2.6 GW of new electric generating capacity on completion (Al-Sarihi & Mason, 2020). One of these was the 1 GW solar thermal field at Miraah but beyond that progress stalled (Al-Sarihi & Mason, 2020). In Spring 2017, the Ministry of Environment and Climate Affairs issued a catalogue with new environmental regulations but despite imposing occasional fines, its enforcement was rather weak. During the last two years, however, the country revitalized plans of environmental sustainability. It was in 2019 when the government ratified the Paris Agreement and launched a comprehensive national climate change strategy for Adaptation and Mitigation to Climate Change, 2020–2040 (Al-Sarihi, 2020). Apart from the UAE, until 2019 Oman was the only country that had developed a national climate action plan. While this indicated a proactive approach, no details of the document have been published so far (Al-Sarihi & Mason, 2020). Further concrete action followed these grand announcements: In 2019, Oman completed a 50 MW wind farm, the Dhofar Wind Project, that was the first of its kind in the GCC. In the same year, the government started an auction process for the 500 MW Ibri II solar power project, which was completed in 2021 and inaugurated in late January 2022. In January 2021, the oil company Shell launched a 25 MW solar PV plant in the port and free zone of Sohar.

Also, since 1 January 2021, single-use plastic bags have been banned in Oman. Additionally, hydrocarbon subsidy reforms are presented as a key element of the energy plan to lower demand and become more energy efficient: As first country in the GCC to do so, Oman cut subsidies on petrol and diesel in January 2015, although with exceptions (price caps) for low-income groups (Al-Sarihi & Mason, 2020; Moerenhout, 2021). In spring 2021, with much delay, the sultanate introduced a VAT of 5%, though with a series of exemptions (Mogielnicki, 2021).

Oman's proactive sustainability governance and its environmentally conscious profile was mainly linked to Sultan Qaboos but frequently faced financial challenges that prevented the country from doing more. Under the new leadership, minimizing the economic challenges appears to have become the new top priority. At the same time, environmental concerns are taking a backseat, unless they are linked to areas of economic development such as the tourist sector, for instance (Al-Sarihi, 2020).[51] In its second NC (released in November 2019), Oman sketched out the potential for renewable energy resources, which could not only satisfy domestic electricity demands but also be used for export. In terms of energy efficiency, the report sets out that up to 25% of electricity consumption could be saved by 2035. This is also reflected in Oman's second NDC, which was submitted in summer 2021. There, the government pledges to reduce emissions by 7% by 2030, which is a more ambitious target that outlined in its first NDC (Climate Action Tracker, 2022). This goal is closely linked to the national economic Vision 2040 that describes economic diversification and a shift to a low-carbon economy as key principles for sustainable

[51] Interview #74.

growth (Luomi & al-Sarihi, 2021). Oman's overall performance in the SDG ranking is comparatively high with rank 6 out of 21 across all Arab countries. The country is moderately improving in several SDG goals but is also stagnating in important environmental goals such as SGDs (12) Responsible Consumption and Production, (13) Climate Action, (14) Life below Water (Bayoumi et al., 2022).

Kuwait

In comparison with the other GCC states, Kuwait can be considered a latecomer in taking meaningful action towards economic diversification in order to lower its dependence on oil. This is also highlighted by the fact that Kuwait did not make any attempt to establish development plans for over fifteen years after the Gulf War in 1991 (Alsayegh et al., 2018). A first cautious sign of a new direction was the launch of a strategic paper by the Central Bank of Kuwait in 2008. The so-called Kuwait Vision 2035 was approved by parliament in 2010. The four-year development plan (2010–2014) was enforced under the former prime minister, Nasser Mohammed al-Sabah in his role of overseeing the Supreme Council for Planning and Development, with the help of an international consultancy business, Tony Blair Associates. Due to unrealistic objectives in the light of shrinking government budgets caused by the financial crisis, the sharp decline in the oil price, ongoing internal turbulences (i.e. boycott by the opposition) and a lack of public support, the plan slowly disappeared together with the removal of prime minister Nasser in 2011 (Coates Ulrichsen, 2016). The plan's main focal point was the development of Kuwait as a regional commercial and financial hub but it left out key social and environmental topics (Mishrif, 2017). Both social and environmental themes were then picked up in a new development vision, the 'New Kuwait' plan, which was unveiled in early 2017. The vision is organized around seven pillars, including global position, human capital, healthcare, living environment, infrastructure, economy and public administration. These pillars can, in turn, be summarized into five general directions of (1) citizen participation and respect of law, (2) effective governance, (3) prosperous economy, (4) nurturing nation and (5) globally relevant player. Interestingly, in contrast to other visions of the GCC states, the emphasis is on citizen participation. In terms of environmental protection, the vision relies on several steps that had been previously taken by the government. The main backbone is the

Kuwait Environmental Governance Initiative of 2016. That initiative, in turn, was preceded by other policies such as the new environmental law (Environment Protection Law No. 42) of 2014, as well as longitudinal research and monitoring projects like the Environmental Monitoring Information System of Kuwait (eMISK) (2009) and the Kuwait Integrated Environmental Management (2012). In core, the vision 'New Kuwait', aims to enforce aspects of the environmental law and to enhance Kuwait's environmental policy in accordance with international environmental standards and agreements.[52] Kuwait's initiative led to the launch of the National Adaptation Plan in 2019, which addressed numerous challenges of climate stressors and risks. In total, a number of 56 initiatives divided in short-, medium- and long-term have been designed towards adaptation measures in key areas such as fisheries and the marine sector, water sector, coastal zone sector and health sector.[53] However, Kuwait is the only Arab country that shows a declining performance on SDG 13 (Climate Action) (Bayoumi et al., 2022).

In terms of clean energy, the development plan has made three modest sets of commitments towards a greener energy transition: Around 15% of its electricity generation shall be produced by renewable energy resources by 2030 and energy efficiency improved by 5% by 2020 and 15% by 2030 (Al-Sulayman, 2021). Similarly, it aims to reduce energy consumption by 30% by 2030. While nuclear energy used to be considered as a viable non-hydrocarbon way to generate electricity, plans to study its feasibility were completely shelved after the nuclear accident of Fukushima in 2011 (Alsayegh et al., 2018). Instead, the Ministry of Electricity and Water, as the responsible entity, shifted its focus to more feasible renewable energy sources like solar energy and wind. The above-mentioned target of approximately 15% of the country's energy production through RES shall be based on solar-generated CSP (5.7 GW) and PV (4.6 GW) as well as wind (0.7 GW) (Griffiths, 2017, 3; Wogan et al., 2019, 33). However, until now, Kuwait's energy system remains largely unsustainable. Two-thirds of the country's power generation still stems from oil and the great majority of GHG emissions in the country come from fuel combustion activities (Atkinson & Gelan, 2021). Furthermore, the main clean energy projects have been halted or shelved due to bureaucratic

[52] Interview #32.

[53] See: Kuwait National Adaptation Plan, https://epa.org.kw/en-US/NAP.

procedures, growing fiscal imbalance and a political stalemate. As Faris al-Sulayman explains: "all credible short-term plans are focused on the 1500 MWp solar PV plant set to be built at Al Dibdibah" as a further extension of the country's prestigious solar-power project Al Shagaya. However, in summer 2020, the government cancelled this project in the light of the economic shock caused by the COVID-19 pandemic (Al-Sulayman, 2021, 101). Like other GCC states, Kuwait updated its NDC regarding GHG emissions in view of the climate summit in 2021. It pledged to cut its emissions by 7.4% under business-as-usual levels by 2035 (Climate Action Tracker, 2022).

Bahrain

Although highly exposed to long-term climatic effects such as sea-level rise, the small island state has not devoted much attention to the biophysical ecological shifts and damage due to climate change and environmental degradation. Bahrain's first two INDCs submitted to the UNFCCC in 2009 and 2012 largely discuss these challenges and threats but remain vague in strategy formulation. Concretely, the second INDC stated that a "clear action plan is not yet in place" but pointed to several initiatives such as its Economic Vision 2030, along with energy efficiency plans by the hydrocarbon sector.[54] Similar to all other Gulf countries, Bahrain became more proactive within the last five years. The National Energy Efficiency Action Plan and National Renewable Energy Action Plan constituted the first documents with a set of concrete targets towards green policies in Bahrain. The plan identified twenty-two new initiatives across all sectors to achieve a reduction in energy use of 6% by 2025 relative to a business-as-usual scenario. Additionally, identifying solar, wind and biogas as feasible renewable energy options for Bahrain, two targets of 5% of renewable electricity production by 2025 and 10% by 2035 were outlined (Al-Sulayman, 2021). These modest commitments were also reiterated in Bahrain's submitted NDC of 2021. Proposed mitigating measures include green building certification and energy efficiency codes, implementing energy labelling and minimum energy performance standards for lighting, air conditioning, appliances as well as district cooling. In addition to implementing CCUS, the government also intends to alter

[54] Second National Communication Report, http://unfccc.int/resource/docs/natc/bhrnc2.pdf, p. 51.

the demand side by gradually enforcing price reforms on gasoline and diesel as well as electricity; a process that has been underway since March 2015 (Moerenhout, 2021). However, proposed taxes on public utilities and a planned decrease in fuel subsidies have been scrapped due to growing fiscal imbalance and political tensions. Lately, it was announced that the government plans to increase the 5% VAT to 10% from January 2022 onwards (Al-Ubaydli, 2021).

Also in other sectors Bahrain underperforms. In terms of environmental legislative frameworks, the government has not updated its initial plans, such as the formal environmental strategy of 2006 and the first National Biodiversity Strategy and Action Plan (2007). While there have been minor efforts by the authorities (e.g. to implement a ban on shrimp fishing due to dramatic decline of fish stocks), protection measures and legal instruments remain weak. In February 2019, it was reported that a consortium around the Saudi-based developer ACWA Power has won Bahrain's tender for a 100 MW solar park at the Askar landfill site. While such a large-scale solar project would have substantially altered the smallest grid in the region in favour of renewable energy, development has been postponed several times and no updated information on the project's status can be found. Until now, Bahrain's renewable energy output only includes several small-scale solar and wind projects that account for around 5–6 MW (al-Sulayman, 2021; Young, 2019). Probably, the most well-known example to the outside world is the three parallel turbines of the Bahrain World Trade Center that account for 770 kW (Alnaser & Alnaser, 2011). Considering Bahrain's weak sustainability endeavours so far, one should be sceptical of whether Bahrain is able to fulfil its ambitious net-zero target by 2060, which it announced in October 2021—a day after Saudi Arabia declared a similar goal (Climate Action Tracker, 2022): In the SDG ranking of all Arab states, it holds rank 13 out of 21 and major challenges remain in all environmental sustainability-related SDGs (Bayoumi et al., 2022).

Conclusion

This chapter reveals insights about the processes and logic of governance in the absolutist monarchies in the Gulf. First, environmental institutions underwent a continual approach of reorganization. In some cases, environmental departments which were previously attached to other environmental bodies experienced an upgrade to a separate ministry. In other cases, already existing environmental ministries were downgraded by attaching their administration to the ministries of urban planning, foreign policy, agriculture, water or local administration. Moreover, environmental competence is often dedicated to rather inexperienced or uninfluential leading figures (Luomi, 2012). The practice of providing jobs to nationals in the public sector ('mudir syndrome') transmitted incompetency further to sublevels of the administrative levels (Spiess, 2008). This all points to an assumption that environmental policy making is perceived as 'nice to have', or good for marketing 'green PR' but is not a constitutive element of governance. This suggestion is further highlighted by the fact that the environmental bodies have constantly been controlled and curbed by the ministries of energy. In fact, sustainability governance is mostly confined to efforts towards economic diversification and mitigation strategies to lower the countries' GHG emissions, efforts which in turn are beholden to other governmental sectors such as energy and industry. This narrow focus of environmental policy also explains why several previous and current environmental ministers in Oman, Qatar or Abu Dhabi, for instance, began their careers in other areas of expertise, above all the energy and industry sectors. Moreover, there is often a micromanagement process behind environmental policymaking, which fragments the process and outcomes. Here, Hadi Fathallah describes how conflicting strategies such as MEWA's national water conservation programme (*Qatrah*) and the creation of water-intensive urban green spaces such as the King Salman Park and Green Riyadh were inaugurated concurrently (Fathallah, 2019). Even more obscuring, both projects, King Salman Park and Green Riyadh, are planned and developed by a newly created independent body, a special 'delivery unit' under the umbrella of Vision 2030 instead of the responsible local authorities and municipalities (Fathallah, 2019).

Second, this tendency of proliferation of parastatal entities or fiefdoms of environmental sustainability is even more apparent in the field of 'green R&D'. In many cases, environmental policymaking (research, development and in some cases also implementation) is not undertaken by the responsible political agencies but by state-controlled or parastatal fiefdoms. Notable examples include the QF in Qatar and Saudi entities such as K·A·CARE or KAPSARC and (not to forget) Abu Dhabi's Masdar initiative, with all its sub-entities. The existence of (semi)governmental bodies creates an "intermediate stratum within the political structure" leading to the emergence of (sometimes very powerful) second-tier and non-royal technocrats that significantly shape the process of policymaking (Thompson, 2018, 297). Princes or kings often rule over these personal fiefdoms in a system of "segmented clientelism" (Hertog, 2010, 21–29) that safeguards their interests and preserves their power base. Oftentimes, specific individuals, who are both trusted confidants and specialized technocrats *(mudarā' fi-ldawla)*, have been appointed to lead these fiefdoms. These technocrats possess expertise and professional experience from different fields than sustainable development and are characterized by having a close (maybe friendly) relationship to the persons in power, which underlines that these appointments are not based on meritocracy alone but also on loyalty, degree of trustworthiness and sometimes tribal belonging (Stenslie, 2012, 67).[55] The massive expansion of governmental and semi-governmental bodies as a strategy to bind specific elites closer to the regime is a tricky trade-off: On the one hand, this broadening has the positive effect of including more people and thus providing a bigger support base, even if the bond to the ruler might be looser and more fragile. On the other hand, strengthening certain elites can empower specific individuals dramatically or create envy among marginalized individuals. Still, the involvement of experts rationalizes decision-making and ultimately can equip the government with greater legitimacy.

Overall, the high number of various actors and agencies results in a loss of efficiency that is also a major explanation for countries' poor records on environmental policymaking, which became apparent in the second part of this chapter. Typically, state-owned or semi state-owned bodies do not cooperate with each other or exchange information. This has even created 'turf wars' in some instances, as the Saudi case shows. In addition to the lack of reporting, professionalism and coordination, ill-defined competencies, overlapping responsibilities and insufficient supervision have exacerbated the problem.[56] The lack of genuine interest and poor institutional and 'absorptive' capacity (Al-Saleh & Vidican, 2013, 158) can be seen as major barriers. Furthermore, one cannot neglect the fact that there is an explicit focus on energy resilience and a general disconnect between self-determined goals and their practical implementation until now: Projected targets by the states have been delayed or not achieved at all and concrete strategies, roadmaps and policy frameworks

[55] Interview #44.

[56] Interview #18 and interview #24.

are largely missing as well. What explains this mismatch? Underlying reasons may include fast-track decision-making, rushed implementation and over-optimistic expectations (Coates Ulrichsen, 2016). Despite these shortcomings it should be acknowledged that there is a new dynamic that's discernible and some countries, particularly the UAE and Saudi Arabia, are managing to perform increasingly better in terms of environmental sustainability (Luomi, 2021b). Still, the Gulf countries have a long and bumpy road ahead if they want to fulfil their own ambitious pledges, that were announced lately.

References

Aarts, P., & Roelants, C. (2016). *Saudi Arabia. A kingdom in peril.* Hurst & Co.

Abdelraouf, M. (2019). Climate change: Partnership opportunities in the framework of EU-GCC relations. *Bussola report*. Retrieved October 29, 2021 from https://www.bussolainstitute.org/research/climate-change-partnership-opportunities-in-the-framework-of-eu-gcc-relations

Albrecht, H., & Schlumberger, O. (2004). "Waiting for Godot": Regime change without democratization in the Middle East. *International Political Science Review, 25*(4), 371–392.

Alhoweish, B., & Orujov, C. (2016). Promoting an effective energy efficiency programme in Saudi Arabia: Challenges and opportunities. In M. Raouf & M. Luomi (Eds.), *The green economy in the Gulf* (pp. 100–122). Routledge.

Allan, T. (2011). *Virtual water: Tackling the threat to our planet's most precious resource*. I.B. Tauris

Almezaini, K. (2013). Private sector actors in the UAE and their role in the process of economic and political reform. In S. Hertog, G. Luciani, & M. Valeri (Eds.), *Business politics in the Middle East* (pp. 43–66). Hurst & Co.

Alnaser, W., & Alnaser, N. (2011). The status of renewable energy in the GCC countries. *Renewable and Sustainable Energy Reviews, 15*(6), 3074–3098.

Alomari, M. A., & Heffron, R. J. (2021). Utilising law in the transition of the Kingdom of Saudi Arabia to a low-carbon economy. *Environmental Innovation and Societal Transitions, 39*, 107–118. https://doi.org/10.1016/j.eist.2021.03.003

Alraouf, A., & Clarke, S. (2017). From pearling to skyscrapers: The predicament of sustainable architecture and urbanism in contemporary Gulf cities. In Sillitoe, P. (Ed.), *Sustainable development. An appraisal of the Gulf region* (pp. 313–342). Berghahn Books.

Alsayegh, O., Saker, N., & Alqattan, A. (2018). Integrating sustainable energy strategy with the second development plan of Kuwait. *Renewable and Sustainable Energy Reviews, 82*(3), 3430–3440.

Atkinson, G., & Gelan, A. (2021). *Sustainability, natural capital and climate change in Kuwait*. LSE Middle East Centre Kuwait Programme Paper Series 12. Retrieved December 10, 2021, from http://eprints.lse.ac.uk/110972/1/Sustainability_Natural_Capital_and_Climate_Change_in_Kuwait.pdf

Al-Saffar, A. (2021). Outlook for producer economies. In L. Giacomo & T. Moerenhout (Eds.), *When can oil economies be deemed sustainable?* (pp. 55–72). Palgrave

Al-Saleh, Y., & G. Vidican (2013). Innovation dynamics of sustainability journeys for hydrocarbon-rich countries. *International. Journal of Innovation and Sustainable Development, 7*(2), 144–171.

Al-Sarihi, A. (2018). *Why oil- and gas-rich Gulf Arab states are turning to coal.* AGSIW Blog Post. Retrieved December 7, 2021, from https://agsiw.org/oil-gas-rich-gulf-arab-states-turning-coal/

Al-Sarihi, A. (2020). *Oman's tradition of environmental protection runs into economic headwinds*. AGSIW Blog Post. Retrieved December 10, 2021, from https://agsiw.org/omans-tradition-of-environmental-protection-runs-into-economic-headwinds/

Al-Sarihi, A. (2021). *Saudi Arabia and the Paris climate agreement*. KFCRIS Commentaries. Retrieved December 8, 2021, from https://kfcris.com/en/view/post/363

Al-Sarihi, A. (2022). Climate change governance in Saudi Arabia: integrity, politics, challenges and opportunities. In M. Thompson, & N. Quilliam (Eds.), *Governance and domestic policy-making in Saudi Arabia. Transforming society, economics, politics and culture* (pp. 225–256). I.B. Tauris

Al-Sarihi, A., & Mansouri, N. (2022). Renewable energy development in the Gulf cooperation council countries: Status, barriers, and policy options. *Energies, 15*, 1923. https://doi.org/10.3390/en15051923

Al-Sarihi, A., & Mason, M. (2020). Challenges and opportunities for climate policy integration in oil-producing countries: The case of the UAE and Oman. *Climate Policy, 20*(10), 1226–1241. https://doi.org/10.1080/14693062.2020.1781036

Al-Sulayman, F. (2021). The rise of renewables in the Gulf states: Is the 'rentier effect' still holding back the energy transition? In: R. Mills & L. Sim (Eds.). *Low carbon energy in the Middle East and North Africa* (pp. 93–120). Palgrave.

Al-Ubaydli, O. (2021). *VAT hike in Bahrain points to fiscal challenges, unattractive choices government faced*. AGSIW Blog Post. Retrieved January 15, 2022, from https://agsiw.org/vat-hike-in-bahrain-points-to-fiscal-challenges-unattractive-choices-government-faced/

Al-Ubaydli, O., Abdullah, G., & Yaseen, L. (2019). Forging a more centralized GCC renewable energy policy. In H. Akhonbay (Ed.), *The economics of renewable energy in the Gulf* (216–234). Routledge.

Al Othman, W., & Clarke, S. (2017). Charting the emergence of environmental legislation in Qatar: A step in the right direction or too little too late? In P. Sillitoe (Ed.), *Sustainable development. An appraisal of the Gulf region* (pp. 116–132). Berghahn Books.

Al Shehri, T., Braun, J. F., Howarth, N., Lanza, A., & Luomi, M. (2022). Saudi Arabia's climate change policy and the circular carbon economy approach. *Climate Policy*, 1–17. https://doi.org/10.1080/14693062.2022.2070118

Bachellerie, I. (2012). *Renewable energy in the GCC countries: Resources, potential, and prospects*. Gulf Research Center. Retrieved December 22, 2020, from https://gssd.mit.edu/search-gssd/site/renewable-energy-gcc-countries-resources-60069-tue-03-26-2013-0758

Bahgat, G. (2013). The changing Saudi energy outlook: Strategic implications. *The Middle East Journal, 67*(4), 565–579.

Bayoumi, M., Luomi, M., Fuller, G., & al-Sarihi, A. (2022). Arab Region SDG Index and Dashboard Report 2022. Mohammed bin Rashid School of Government, Anwar Gargash Diplomatic Academy and UN Sustainable Development Solutions Network. Retrieved April 17, 2022 from https://arabsdgindex.com/

Blas, J. (2021, July 22). *The Saudi prince of oil prices vows to drill 'every last molecule'*. Bloomberg.com. https://www.bloomberg.com/news/features/2021-07-22/saudi-prince-abdulaziz-bin-salman-seeks-to-tame-oil-prices-opec-russia

Bsheer, R. (2021). *Archive wars. The politics of history in Saudi Arabia*. Stanford University Press.

Bueno de Mesquita, B., Smith, A., Siverson, R. & Morrow, J. (2003). *The logic of political survival*. MIT Press.

Cahill, B. (2021). *Everything at once: Transformation of Abu Dhabi's oil policy*. AGSIW Issue Paper 1. Retrieved December 17, 2021 from https://agsiw.org/everything-at-once-transformation-of-abu-dhabis-oil-policy/

Climate Action Tracker. (2022). *Country reports/CAT climate target update tracker*. Retrieved December 7, 2021, from https://climateactiontracker.org/

Climate Change Performance Index. (2021). *Country reports*. Retrieved December 9, 2021, from https://ccpi.org/

Coates Ulrichsen, K. (2016). *The Gulf states in International Political Economy*. Palgrave.

Crystal, J. (2014). Eastern Arabian states: Kuwait, Bahrain, Qatar, United Arab Emirates, and Qatar. In M. Gasiorowski, D. E. Long, & B. Reich (Eds.), *The government and politics of the Middle East and North Africa* (pp. 157–195). Westview Press.

Cugurullo, F. (2013). How to build a sandcastle: An analysis of the genesis and development of Masdar City. *Journal of Urban Technology, 20*(1), 23–37. https://doi.org/10.1080/10630732.2012.735105

Davidson, C. (2021). *From Sheikhs to Sultanism. Statecraft and authority in Saudi Arabia and the UAE*. Hurst & Co.

Demmelhuber, T. (2019). Playing the diversity card: Saudi Arabia's foreign policy under the Salmans. *The International Spectator, 54*(4), 109–124. https://doi.org/10.1080/03932729.2019.1678862

Environmental Performance Index. (2020). *Global metrics for the environment: Ranking country performance on sustainability issues*. Retrieved December 10, 2021, from https://epi.yale.edu/

Fathallah, D. (2019). Challenges of public policymaking in Saudi Arabia. *Carnegie endowment for international peace*. Retrieved April 19, 2022 from https://carnegieendowment.org/sada/79188

Ferroukhi, R., Khalid, A., Hawila, D., Nagpal, D., El-Katiri, L., Thenakis, V., & Al-Fara, A. (2016). *Renewable energy market analysis: The GCC region*. IRENA Analysis. Retrieved December 10, 2021, from https://www.irena.org/publications/2016/Jan/Renewable-Energy-Market-Analysis-The-GCC-Region

Forbes. (n/a). #49, Khalid Al-Falih. *Forbes* https://www.forbes.com/profile/khalid-al-falih/?sh=2f2b735e7cc7

General Secretariat for Development Planning. (2009). *Advancing sustainable development. Qatar National Vision 2030: Second National Human Development Report*. Retrieved January 13, 2022, from http://hdr.undp.org/sites/default/files/qhdr_en_2009.pdf

General Secretariat for Development Planning. (2011). *Qatar National Development Strategy 2011-2016: Towards Qatar National Vision 2030*. Retrieved January 14, 2022, from https://www.psa.gov.qa/en/nds1/Documents/NDS_ENGLISH_SUMMARY.pdf

Gray, M. (2019). *The economy of the Gulf states*. Agenda Publishing.

Griffiths, S. (2017). Renewable energy policy trends and recommendations for GCC countries. *Energy Transitions, 1*(1), 1–15. https://doi.org/10.1007/s41825-017-0003-6

Griffiths, S., & Orkoubi, D. (2019). Energy and climate policies to stimulate renewables deployment in GCC countries. In H. Akhonbay (Ed.), *The economics of renewable energy in the Gulf* (pp. 139–66). Routledge.

Günel, G. (2019). *Spaceship in the desert. Energy, climate change, and urban design in Abu Dhabi*. Duke University Press.

Hedges, M. (2021). *Reinventing the sheikhdom. Clan, power and patronage in Mohammed bin Zayed's UAE*. Hurst & Co.

Hertog, S. (2010). *Princes, brokers, and bureaucrats. Oil and the state in Saudi Arabia*. Cornell University Press.

Hertog, S. (2012). Good, bad, or both?: The impact of oil on the Saudi political economy. In M. Kamrava (Ed.), *The Political Economy of the Persian Gulf* (pp. 221–250). Hurst & Co.

Hertog, S., & Luciani, G. (2012). Energy and sustainability policies in the Gulf states. In D. Held, & K. Coates Ulrichsen (Eds.), *The transformation of the Gulf. Politics, economics and the global order* (pp. 236–257). Routledge

Hvidt, M. (2021). *Reaching for the stars: How and why do the Gulf states aim to transform their economies to 'knowledge-based economies'?* LSE Blog Series. Retrieved December 11, 2021, from https://blogs.lse.ac.uk/mec/2021/08/19/reaching-for-the-stars-how-and-why-do-the-gulf-states-aim-to-transform-their-economies-to-knowledge-based-economies/

Jones, T. (2015). The dogma of development: Technopolitics and power in Saudi Arabia. In B. Haykel, T. Hegghammer, & S. Lacroix (Eds.), *Saudi Arabia in transition. Insights on social, political, economic and religious Change* (pp. 31–47). Cambridge University Press.

Kamrava, M. (2009). Royal factionalism and political liberalization in Qatar. *The Middle East Journal, 63*(3), 401–420.

Kamrava, M. (2015). *Qatar. Small state, big politics.* Cornell University Press.

Kamrava, M. (2017). State-business relations and clientelism in Qatar. *Journal of Arabian Studies, 7*(1), 1–27. https://doi.org/10.1080/21534764.2017.1288420

Kingdom of Saudi Arabia. (2010). *Royal Decree establishing King Abdullah City for atomic and renewable energy: Royal Order A/35.* Retrieved April 13, 2022 from https://www.kacare.gov.sa/en/about/Documents/KACARE_Royal_Decree_english.pdf

Kiyasseh, L. (2022). *Strong momentum in Saudi Arabia's drive toward renewables and infrastructure.* Middle East Institute Policy Analysis. Retrieved January 13, 2022, from https://www.mei.edu/publications/strong-momentum-saudi-arabias-drive-toward-renewables-and-infrastructure

Krane, J. (2019). *Energy kingdoms. Oil and political survival in the Persian Gulf.* Columbia University Press.

Krane, J. (2020). Climate action versus inaction: balancing the costs for Gulf energy exporters. *British Journal of Middle Eastern Studies, 47*(1), 117–135. https://doi.org/10.1080/13530194.2020.1714269

Krane, J. (2021). Pairing coal with solar: The UAE's fragmented electricity policy. In R. Mills & L. Sim (Eds.), *Low carbon energy in the Middle East and North Africa* (pp. 57–92). Palgrave.

Krupa, J., & Poudineh, R. (2017). *Financing renewable electricity in the resource-rich countries of the Middle East and North Africa: A review* (OIES Paper 22). Retrieved December 13, 2021, from https://www.oxfordenergy.org/publications/financing-renewable-electricity-middle-east-north-africa-review/

Luomi, M. (2012). *The Gulf monarchies and climate change. Abu Dhabi and Qatar in an era of natural unsustainability*. Hurst & Co.

Luomi, M. (2014). *Mainstreaming climate policy in the Gulf Cooperation Council states*. OIES Paper 7. Retrieved December 11, 2021, from: https://www.oxfordenergy.org/publications/mainstreaming-climate-policy-in-the-gulf-cooperation-council-states/

Luomi, M. (2021a). Climate change policy in the Arab region. In R. Mills & L. Sim (Eds.), *Low carbon energy in the Middle East and North Africa* (pp. 299–332). Palgrave.

Luomi, M. (2021b). *From the year of climate ambition to action in the Gulf*. AGSIW Blog Post. Retrieved January 15, 2022 from https://agsiw.org/from-the-year-of-climate-ambition-to-action-in-the-gulf/

Luomi, M. (2021c). *Pressure builds on Gulf countries to take climate action*. AGSIW Blog Post. Retrieved December 7, 2021c, from https://agsiw.org/pressure-builds-on-gulf-countries-to-take-climate-action/

Luomi, M., & al-Sarihi, A. (2021). *Oman's Second Nationally Determined Contribution (NDC)*. KAPSARC Data Insight. Retrieved December 10, 2021, from https://www.kapsarc.org/research/publications/omans-second-nationally-determined-contribution-ndc/

MEWA—Ministry of Environment, Water and Agriculture. (2018). *Executive summary of the National Environment Strategy*. Retrieved April 11, 2022 from https://www.jetro.go.jp/ext_images/world/middle_east/sa/law/pdf/National_Environmental_Strategy_ENG.pdf

MEWA—Ministry of Environment, Water and Agriculture. (2021). *Saudi Arabia joins the world in addressing environmental degradation, securing sustainable future*. Press release. Retrieved April 12, 2022 from https://mewa.gov.sa/en/MediaCenter/News/Pages/News562021.aspx

Mishrif, A. (2017). Introduction to economic diversification in the GCC region. In A. Mishrif & Y. al-Balushi (Eds.), *Economic diversification in the Gulf Region. Volume I: The private sector as an engine of growth* (pp. 1–26). Palgrave

Meltzer, J., Hultman, N., & Langley, C. (2014). *Low-carbon energy transitions in Qatar and the Gulf Cooperation Council region*. Brookings Papers on Economic Activity. Retrieved December 11, 2021, from: https://ssrn.com/abstract=2408743

Moerenhout, T. (2021). Fuel and electricity reform for economic sustainability in the Gulf. In G. Luciani & T. Moerenhout (Eds.), *When can oil economies be deemed sustainable?* (pp. 191–214). Palgrave.

Mogielnicki, R. (2021). *Oman's VAT implementation is necessary and not enough*. AGSIW Blog Post. Retrieved January 15, 2022, from https://agsiw.org/omans-vat-implementation-is-necessary-and-not-enough/

Moritz, J. (2020). Rentier political economy in the oil monarchies. In M. Kamrava (Ed.), *Routledge handbook of Persian Gulf politics* (pp. 163–186). Routledge.

Niblock, T. (2006). *Saudi Arabia. Power, legitimacy and survival.* Routledge.

Noach, K., & Guzansky, Y. (2021). *The Saudi drive to lead the green revolution in the Middle East.* INSS Insight No. 1486. Retrieved December 8, 2021, from https://www.inss.org.il/publication/green-saudi-arabia/

Obeid, J. (2022). Energy governance: is the new meeting the old in Saudi Arabia's energy industries? In M. Thompson, & N. Quilliam (Eds.), *Governance and domestic policy-making in Saudi Arabia. Transforming society, economics, politics and culture* (pp. 169–196). I.B. Tauris.

PourMirza, A. (2017). Gas flaring status, trend and policy around the Persian Gulf, energy sources. *Economics, Planning, and Policy, 12*(3), 250–259.

Quaile, I. (2013, March 21). Green energy revolution in the Gulf? *Deutsche Welle.* https://www.dw.com/en/green-energy-revolution-in-the-gulf/a-16608352

Rahman, K. (2017). The Qatar national master plan. In Sillitoe, P. (Ed.), *Sustainable development. An appraisal of the Gulf region* (pp. 82–96). Berghahn Books.

Reuters. (2021, October 19). Qatar forms climate change ministry, appoints finance minister. *Reuters* https://www.reuters.com/world/middle-east/qatar-emir-appoints-al-kawari-finance-minister-government-reshuffle-2021-10-19/

Richer, R. (2009). *Conservation in Qatar: Impacts of increasing industrialization* (CIRS Occasional Paper No. 2). Retrieved December 13, 2021, from https://papers.ssrn.com/sol3/papers.cfm?abstract_id=2825865

Richer, R. (2014). Sustainable development in Qatar: Challenges and opportunities. *QScience Connect* (1), 2–14. https://doi.org/10.5339/connect.2014.22

Rizzo, A. (2017). Sustainable urban development and green megaprojects in the Arab states of the Gulf region: Limitations, covert aims, and unintended outcomes in Doha, Qatar. *International Planning Studies, 22*(2), 85–98. https://doi.org/10.1080/13563475.2016.1182896

Sachs, J, Kroll, C., Lafortune, G., Fuller, G., & Woelm, F. (2021). *Sustainable Development Report 2021.* Retrieved January 16, 2022, from https://dashboards.sdgindex.org/

Sim, L. (2022). *Renewable power policies in the Arab Gulf states.* Middle East Institute. Retrieved February 10, 2022, from https://www.mei.edu/publications/renewable-power-policies-arab-gulf-states

Spiess, A. (2008). Developing adaptive capacity for responding to environmental change in the Arab Gulf states: Uncertainties to linking ecosystem conservation, sustainable development and society in authoritarian rentier economies. *Global and Planetary Change, 64*(3–4), 244–252.

Stenslie, S. (2012). *Regime stability in Saudi Arabia*. Routledge.

Taher, N., & Hajjar, B. (2014). *Energy and environment in Saudi Arabia*. Springer.

Thompson, M. (2018). Saudi Arabia: Civil society and natural resource management. In I. Overland (Ed.), *Public brainpower. Civil society and natural resource management* (pp. 291–309). Springer

Valeri, M. (2017). *Oman: Politics and society in the Qaboos state*. Hurst & Co.

Wright, S. (2018). Qatar: The context of a hydrocarbon-funded social contract. In I. Overland (Ed.), *Public brainpower* (pp. 247–259). Springer.

Woertz, E. (2016). The Gulf monarchies and climate change: Abu Dhabi and Qatar in an era of natural unsustainability. *Journal of Arabian Studies, 6*(1), 121–123. https://doi.org/10.1080/21534764.2016.1195128

Wogan, D., al-Mubarak, I., al-Badi, A., & Pradhan, S. (2019). Overview of energy supply and demand in the GCC. In H. Akhonbay (Ed.), *The economics of renewable energy in the Gulf* (pp. 10–40). Routledge

Young, K. (2019). Prioritizing renewable energy in the time of fiscal austerity. In H. Akhonbay (Ed.), *The economics of renewable energy in the Gulf* (pp. 77–99). Routledge.

Youngs, R. (2012). The Gulf in the new world order: A forgotten emerging power? In R. Youngs (Ed.), *The GCC in the global economy* (pp. 5–22). Gerlach Press.

Zumbraegel, T. (2019). Being green or being seen green? Strategies of eco regime resilience in Qatar. In H. Pouran, & H. Hakimian (Eds.), *Environmental challenges in the MENA region. The long road from conflict to cooperation* (pp. 49–71). The Gingko Library.

Zumbraegel, T. (2020). Beyond greenwashing: Sustaining power through sustainability in the Arab Gulf monarchies. *Orient, 61*(1), 28–35.

CHAPTER 5

Green Business Is Good Business: Environmental Sustainability and 'Adaptative State Capitalism'

Environmental Sustainability and the Market: A New Opportunity for Networked Policymaking and Capital Flows

Sustainability is closely linked to economic diversification and hence efforts towards it imply economic reorganization. As Gulf Arab monarchies have attempted to diversify their economies away from oil over the last few decades, entrepreneurship programmes and privatization have played a leading role. This was already outlined in the strategic long-term development plans (*visions*). Over the last few years, discussions of environmental sustainability and the green energy transition have also increased, as this field provides new business opportunities and monetary incentives. However, these commercial interests focus almost exclusively on innovation, technology and energy, leaving out environmental concerns (Gray, 2019).

It is often argued that the energy sector plays a very promising role in private sector growth and job creation. For instance, as renewable generation, particularly wind and solar PV, is more labour intensive than traditional energy sources (measured per unit of energy produced), Sylvain Côté points out that a green energy transition will inevitably create more jobs because of a wide spectrum of working fields and the many

T. Zumbraegel, *Political Power and Environmental Sustainability in Gulf Monarchies*, Contemporary Gulf Studies,
https://doi.org/10.1007/978-981-19-4431-4_5

operational steps involved. For instance, regarding solar PV the workforce includes at least the following steps of "project planning and management; manufacture of technology and procurement; transport; installation and/or plant construction; operations and maintenance; and eventually plant decommissioning" (Côté, 2019, 197). Adam Hanieh divides various form of capital accumulation along the value chain that can also be adapted to the field of environmental sustainability. These areas include the provision of services such as energy and water (*infrastructure*), the production and manufacturing of sustainability-related products and/or raw materials (e.g. solar cells) (*industry*) as well as the construction, contracting and development of green buildings or sustainability-focused constructions (*built environment*) (Hanieh, 2019).

As Jessica Obeid has discovered through the example of Saudi Arabia, the renewable energy industry has several benefits over the traditional oil industry in terms of business activities. This includes the acceptance of foreign investments, a potentially weak monopoly and more or less clearly defined award criteria and contract award mechanisms (Obeid, 2022). Several amendments to existing laws, privatization reforms and increased implementation of public–private partnership (PPP) models in the water and energy sectors over the last decade in the GCC underscores this development (IRENA, 2019, 38; Valeri, 2013; Young, 2019, 87–91). This has raised hopes among some scholars and pundits for a radical economic change or even reorganization of the old capitalist-driven economic model in the GCC. For instance, in the words of Eckart Woertz:

> The decentralized features of renewables have prompted hopes that energy transitions could strengthen political participation, enabling local ownership of energy resources by communities and 'prosumers'. (Woertz, 2021)

This can be observed in Dubai, where the government has undertaken measures to promote decentralized renewable power generation (Hertog & Luciani, 2012). One of them is the net-metering regulation Shams Dubai. In 2015, the Dubai Electricity and Water Authority (DEWA) launched a program to support customers in installing solar panels for their own use and provide compensation for any surplus that is fed back into the grid (Griffiths & Orkoubi, 2019; IRENA,

2019). Although DEWA regulates the market by allowing only registered contractors and consultants to deploy small-scale solar-powered applications, this has benefitted many companies that are not capable of participating in traditional large-scale utility projects. This explains why there is a comparatively wide variety of companies in the UAE's solar industry. Examples of these small- and medium-sized independent power producers include, among others, Noor Solar Technology, Al Maden Solar, Solon, Enviromena Power Systems, AMEA Power, Siraj Power, Enerwhere, Utico and Yellow Door Energy (IRENA, 2019; Young, 2019). These companies often provide equipment for small- and medium-sized solar-driven projects and sometimes also operate outside of their registered office address.[1] Too often, those companies are linked to powerful merchant families, who enjoy the blessing of the ruling families (Sim, 2022).

Yet, Dubai is rather an exceptional example of a distributed solar energy system and other GCC economies remain largely state controlled (Mishrif, 2018, 5). There are a number of reasons why the decentralized and distributive power generation of rooftop and small-scale installations remains a niche market in the GCC economies: These include structural barriers such as funding gaps and financing, risk of high penalties for bankruptcy and high investment costs per unit of capacity for small-scale solar applications as well as further cultural and technical barriers of awanress and know how (Gelil, 2016; Young, 2019; Al-Sarihi & Mansouri, 2022).[2] Perhaps the greatest obstacle though is the lack of support by the

[1] Interview #62 and interview #63.

[2] Interview #62 and interview #65. Abu Dhabi, UAE, September 2021. Regarding funding schemes only bonds, so-called sukuks, are allowed as funding schemes under Islamic law. More recently, some green sukuks have been applied in the GCC. One example is the Saudi Electricity Company, more than 80% owned by the state through direct shares (around 75%) and Saudi Aramco (around 7%), which has used green bonds for developing new power plants. Yet, small-scale deployments have difficulties receiving these kinds of funding (Young, 2019). Another successful example is a $750 million "green" bond in 2021 by the Arab Petroleum Investment Corp (Husari, 2022).

state.[3] Despite economic liberalization and privatization attempts, globalization dynamics and a stronger integration into the world economy, leaderships have remained in control over the economy. The complex system of state ownership has been coined by Oliver Schlumberger as 'patrimonial capitalism'. For him, patrimonial capitalism is endemic in environments with high political control of the state "where informal modes of interaction between state and business dominate over formal rules and laws" (Schlumberger, 2008, 622–623).

So far, the clean energy transition is mainly based on grand projects and initiatives at utility scale. While the risks are too big for small and medium enterprises (SMEs) to develop these large-scale projects, SMEs are also often excluded from tendering processes (Almezaini, 2013). According to an interviewee, who subsumed the situation of SMEs in Kuwait:

> It is absolutely not clear whether they can survive, we saw it in the pandemic, they got all crushed, and very little of recovery money went to SMEs, one official said it is less than 10% and asked why we should care about them as they are not rebuilding our economy, so why we care about it at all?[4]

Instead, state-affiliated entities and constituencies are the main actors in this field leaving the politics of energy still predominately state-led (Al-Sarihi & Mansouri, 2022). In the economic sector, four major agents can be identified (Hanieh, 2011, 2019; Hedges, 2021) that can also be translated to the field of environmental sustainability. These include: (a) national oil and gas companies (NOCs) such as Saudi Aramco, Abu Dhabi National Oil Company (ADNOC); (b) state-owned enterprises (SOEs) and green fiefdoms such as the above-mentioned Qatar Foundation (QF); (c) Sovereign Wealth Funds (SWFs) and investment vehicles such as Abu Dhabi's Mubadala, Saudi-based Public Investment Fund (PIF) and the Qatar Investment Authority (QIA) and (d) privately or state-owned/dominated champions such as ACWA Power or the Abu Dhabi National Energy Company, TAQA (see further: Almezaini, 2013;

[3] Interview #55 and interview #58. For instance, there was a lack of financial support to support SMEs after the economic crisis caused by the COVID-19 pandemic, see virtual roundtable: GCC Hydrocarbon Economies and COVID: Old Trends, New Realities, organized by the Qatar University. Retrieved December 28, 2021 from https://www.youtube.com/watch?v=thJbNRYibLY.

[4] Interview #77; further: Interview #55.

Mishrif, 2017; Young, 2019). Yet, it should be mentioned that it is often challenging to clearly delineate the blurry lines between private and public sector as both spheres are so entangled (Almezaini, 2013). Oftentimes, 'managerial networks' within the public sector are deeply intertwined with private 'business networks' through various mechanisms. In some cases, state-led fiefdoms create their own companies to develop and operationalize renewable energy sources and more energy efficient solutions. In other cases, state-led funds nurture privately owned national champions turning them into parastatal local companies. In addition to that, exclusive government contracts and licences are allocated to traditional segments of the business elite and powerful royal capitalists. Typical finance structure for private companies to engage with the public sector includes PPP-related mechanisms such as joint venture arrangements, engineering, procurement and construction (EPC) or build-operate-transfer (BOT) (Mishrif, 2017).[5] Public auctions in the energy market are tendered in the form of independent power producers (IPP) and/or and independent water and power producers (IWPPs), models that result in long-term power purchase agreements (PPA) with the selective company (see overviews: IRENA, 2019, 52–53; Young, 2019, 87–88). This growing entanglement between the public and private sectors underscores Adam Hanieh's and others' argument, that the lines between the state and capital are blurry. In this regard, he proposes to "avoid an overly sharp conceptual division" and instead emphasize the interplay between the state, the ruling families and private business elites (Hanieh, 2019, 66; also Almezaini, 2013).

Given this complex field of private and public entanglements, pundits are often puzzled as to how to classify the unique economic patterns and political economy of the hydrocarbon-wealthy Gulf monarchies. On the one hand, high personalization, the development of a bloated public sector as key part of the social contract as well as omnipresence of state-owned and parastatal enterprises, particularly in the hydrocarbon sector, clearly point towards state capitalist–driven economies. On the other hand, the Gulf monarchies differ considerably from the economic nationalization attempts by populist leaders that characterized state capitalist structures after World War II. Over the last three decades, these states

[5] EPC and BOT are schemes for attraction of private investment and a certain type of a PPP, in which private companies ***build***, ***operate*** and sometimes also ***own*** a certain facility over a specific period of time before ***transferring*** it back to the government.

have gradually restructured their economies "around core precepts of neoliberalism" (Hanieh, 2019, 9). Considering both aspects, it appears valid to speak of a "very dynamic form of state capitalism" (Gray, 2019, viii) or a "Gulf-specific model of state capitalism" (Coates Ulrichsen, 2017, 61).

This 'adaptative state capitalism' includes several patterns and characteristics. It requires an 'updated version' of the traditional concept of rentierism, so 'late rentierism' or 'post rentierism' (see Chapter 2) (Gray, 2011), where the allocation state adopts characteristics of a production state (e.g. taxation, decline of the distributional capacity, focus on profit-oriented marketing and human capital) (Hamedi, 2014; Krane, 2019; Yamada, 2020). Yet, favoritism and neopatrimonial practices are still in place, which becomes most apparent in the public–private assemblage in the absolutist Gulf monarchies. Concretely, the 'dynastic enterprises' exercise traditional unlimited authority through a web of cross-cutting coalitions to assure support and limit oppositional forces. In this way, some have also spoken of a "tribal capitalism", "patrimonial capitalism" (Davidson, 2009, 111; Schlumberger, 2008) or, in the specific case of Saudi Arabia, a Najdi-based *ʿasabiyya* capitalism (Daryl, 2003; Niblock, 2006, 56; Thompson, 2018). Since especially elites across the economic and political sectors benefit from this, one can also speak of a form of "inclusionary co-optation" that forms the basis of this interpersonal mechanism (Albrecht & Schlumberger, 2004, 383). Lastly, the Gulf monarchies' deep involvement in the global economy can be subsumed into what has been called 'economic statecraft'. Matthew Gray understands the close interlinkage of economic and diplomatic goals with this term (Gray, 2019, 5), or, according to Karen Young, economic statecraft is "using economic means to achieve foreign policy goals" (Young, 2020, 2). Both highlight the fact that a sustainable transformation relates to dynamics of a globalized world and the close entanglement of politics and economics. Here, environmental sustainability opens up new inward- and outward-oriented investment flows. As the following chapter will make explicit: Gulf monarchies are highly dependent on external investments, not so much because of capital injection but rather because of importing technology, know-how and expertise to diversify their economies and pursue an environmental sustainability agenda. In order to better assess this unique economic model, one needs to take a closer look at the role of specific stakeholders involved in sustainability policymaking, before turning more to the external level in the subsequent chapter.

Greening the Black Gold: The (Still Dominant) Role of the Hydrocarbon Sector

During the 1970s, the control of global oil shifted from big Western oil companies, known as the Seven Sisters,[6] to national oil companies (NOCs) within the Arab region. These state-controlled enterprises dominate more than 90% of the global oil market with the Gulf monarchies as epicentre. The oil and gas supply chain, with its divisions of upstream (exploration and production), midstream (processing and movement) and downstream (refining, marketing and distribution) businesses (Wald, 2018) is traditionally very emission intensive (see further: Gordon & Feldman, 2016). However, as the energy industry shifts from fossil fuels to renewable energy and low-carbon fuels—particularly in the transport and power generation sectors—in the medium to long-term oil in particular will face significant loss of value. Also, NOCs are experiencing increasing pressure from shareholders and climate advocates to lower their emissions and align their activities with the goals of the Paris Agreement (Dourian, 2019, 2021). Hence, it may not come as a big surprise that the hydrocarbon sector is highly engaged in the sustainable transformation.

However, that it has often played *the* decisive role in the early days is perhaps surprising. Formerly known as oil and gas majors, NOCs in the Gulf such as Saudi Aramco, ADNOC, Qatar Petroleum (nowadays Qatar Energy) and the Kuwait Petroleum Corporation (KPC) have restructured their operations to meet the current challenges. Their low-cost assets put them in a strategic position vis-à-vis other oil and gas companies in terms of capacities to develop low-carbon megaprojects and purchase the latest green technologies (Dourian, 2021; Krane, 2021). In other words, and somehow paradoxically at first glance, high oil prices and the influx of revenues have fueled efforts towards energy transition. Especially, during the time of the oil boom and high revenues (2006 to mid-2014) one could see NOCs taking first steps towards deploying early large-scale low-carbon technologies and projects to 'green' their images and maintain the competitive advantage of their energy monopoly status.[7] Moreover,

[6] They included Shell, the Anglo-Persian companies (now BP), three companies that are now part of Chevron (i.e. Gulf Oil, Texaco and Standard Oil of California) and two companies that have merged into ExxonMobil (i.e. Standard Oil Company of New York and Standard Oil Company of New Jersey), see also Krane (2019).

[7] Interview #61 and interview #77.

NOCs are one of the few market players capable of building, owning, operating and transferring large-scale renewable energy projects.

Saudi Arabia has immense amounts of oil but faces stronger pressure, due to its demographic size, in terms of energy security. Therefore, the kingdom's most valuable "island of efficiency" started comparatively early to look out for sustainable options (Hertog, 2010, 5). As described in Chapter 4, Aramco was involved in sustainability research activities from early on, by overseeing the green fiefdoms KAUST and KAPSARC (Coates Ulrichsen, 2017). In 2006, Saudi Aramco hosted an international conference to discuss the obstacles and pitfalls of better carbon management through CO_2 capture and sequestration (Hashmi & Al-Habib, 2013). However, the company's sustainability activities were not limited to research and technology transfer. In the light of growing 'turf wars' between already established and newly created fiefdoms (see Chapter 4), which were often not able to compete with the powerful oil major, Saudi Aramco started to take the lead in the kingdom's sustainability transformation. Already in 2010, Saudi Aramco commissioned, inter alia, a subsidiary of the local AlAbdulKarim Holding to install PV testing fields on its headquarters. In 2012, the company created Saudi Aramco Energy Ventures to focus on investing in renewable energy projects (Coates Ulrichsen, 2017). In the same year, in a joint venture with a German company, Saudi Aramco commissioned a 10.5 MW solar power–generating parking lot at its headquarters in Dharan. In December that same year, then Saudi Aramco President and CEO Khalid al-Falih celebrated the completion of the first phase of a bigger solar project at KAPSARC with an open land solar installation designed to produce approximately 3.5 MW (Bachellerie, 2012). The project was executed by a joint venture of Chinese and German companies and had been expanded to 5.3 MW in the scope of the second phase in 2014. During 2013, Saudi Aramco further developed a 1 MW solar energy source at its Tabul Bulk Plant. The pilot project of concentrating photovoltaic technology was established with the local investment company Khaled Juffali Company and a German solar company. Another initiative was a large solar thermal plant (around 17 MW) at the Princess Noura University for Women, near Riyadh, that was inaugurated in 2014 (Ferroukhi et al., 2016; Ramady, 2018).

Also, Qatar's gas major Qatar Petroleum began to advocate environmental sustainability by the late 2000s. A major focus included the reduction of gas flaring, more efficient LNG technology, sustainable water usage and more R&D towards carbon storage and utilization. In 2007, the company inaugurated the al-Shaheen oilfield as the region's first and largest carbon reduction project (Zumbraegel, 2019). Among other early initiatives was the previously mentioned research collaboration with Imperial College London and the Qatar Science and Technology Park to create the Qatar Carbonates and Carbon Storage Research Centre in 2008. Additionally, the company initiated a research facility, Qatar Petroleum's Research & Technology Centre, with a budget of around $75 million to focus on upstream oil and gas operations but also topics of environmental impact of the hydrocarbon sector, effects of climate change and energy efficiency were part of the centre's portfolio (Luomi, 2012, 190–192; Meltzer et al., 2014). Also, Qatar's renewable energy strategy was delegated to a department affiliated with Qatar Petroleum between 2010 and 2011 (Luomi, 2012). In the context of the climate summit in 2012, the company primarily attracted attention through greening activities that protected the natural Qatari habitat. Mostly in collaboration with the Ministry of Environment, Qatar Petroleum—also through subsidiaries such as Qatargas—launched programmes to preserve marine flora and fauna with a special focus on protecting local species like dugongs, sea turtles, whale sharks or mangroves. Additionally, Qatargas introduced a technique to reduce the dosing of chlorination chemicals pumped into industrial cooling seawater, aimed at minimizing the fouling of mussels and oysters (Howard, 2017). In 2012, Qatar Petroleum further organized its first Environmental Fair, which was also held in the following two years but seemed to cease afterwards. More recently, QP launched its sustainability strategy, which, among others, seek to significantly reduce methan leakage by 2025 and completely eliminate gas flaring by 2030; installing around 4 GW of RES and advance technology of CCUS to be applied across the whole natural gas value chain are further aims.

Also in other Gulf states, NOCs started to diversify their energy portfolios. In Bahrain, the Bahrain Petroleum Company (BAPCO) launched an R&D initiative on renewable energy sources and experimented with small-scale wind and solar projects (Bachellerie, 2012). In 2014, it completed Bahrain's first 5 MW solar plant. Meanwhile in Oman, the Petroleum Development Oman (PDO), which is an exception to the other oil companies as other international shareholders hold around 40 percent of the company, has experimented with deploying solar thermal technology since 2010. In 2015, Oman's PDO in collaboration with its international partner, GlassPoint, announced the development of the Miraah solar thermal plant. Once completed, the plant should generate more than 1 GW solar power (Al-Sarihi & Mason, 2020; Al-Sulayman, 2021). In summer 2020, PDO announced that it will continue the development of its flagship project despite the fact that GlassPoint went into insolvency (White, 2020). Previously and comparatively early, PDO has also experimenting with RES by establishing their own pilot projects (Al-Sarihi & Mansouri, 2022). In Kuwait, things look different. During the climate summit in Doha in 2012, the Ministry of Electricity and Water announced an ambitious renewable energy project, the so-called Shagaya Renewable Energy Park. Developed by KISR and the ministry but fully owned by a subsidiary of the Kuwait Oil Company (KOC), the construction of the first phase started in 2014 and was finished four years later. The plant produces around 70 MW (that is, 50 MW solar thermal, 10 MW wind and 10 MW solar PV). In 2018, the oil company invited bids for an extension of the Shagaya complex of up to 1.5 GW et al.-Dibdibah, near the Saudi border (IRENA, 2019). Yet in summer 2020, in the light of budgetary constraints, the company announced the cancellation of these plans (Al-Sulayman, 2021).[8] Also a more recent solar project, in which Qatar Petroleum holds a 40% share, appears to have been shelved (IRENA, 2019). In addition to Shagaya's first phase, KOC only managed to finish another small 10 MW solar-driven power plant at the Umm Gudair oil field, which, however, was the country's first solar plant until then.

The above-mentioned examples of 'green hyperactivity' on behalf of NOCs was closely bound to a period of swift oil and gas prices that then gradually declined from mid-2014 onwards. Fiscal austerity measures caused by declining oil prices and, more lately, the economic shock of the COVID-19 pandemic, have stopped many projects for the time being. During the last five to seven years, we can also see a more politically driven dynamic within some of the leading NOCs. Although in the hands of the regimes, the oil and gas companies traditionally behaved as independent actors to preserve their assets, prosperity and dominant role in the GCC economies. In this sense, officials in the UAE described how "ADNOC resembles and behaves like a 'kingdom within a kingdom'" (cited from: Luomi, 2012, 76). Also, Saudi Aramco enjoyed relative autonomy. The same is true for Qatar, where an interview partner referred to Qatar

[8] Interview #53 and interview #58.

Petroleum as the absolute mainstay of the country's energy sector, which "has the final word, while the Ministry of Energy and Industry has no say at all".[9]

However, in the scope of a broader reorganization that coincided with lower oil revenues since mid-2014, along with major political restructuring, some oil companies experienced a loss of autonomy and stronger control of the regimes. This was particularly the case in Saudi Arabia and the UAE. Both examples reveal how the ruling families and in particular ambitious claimants to the throne have seized power of the lucrative energy business. In 2015, the government in Riyadh announced a new ten-member supreme council for Saudi Aramco with the kingdom's then deputy crown prince, Mohammed bin Salman at the top. With this step, Mohammed bin Salman was the key representative of Aramco's only shareholder by then, the Saudi government. In the scope of Vision 2030, it was declared that parts of Aramco's profits would be transferred to the national sovereign wealth fund, the Public Investment Fund (PIF), which is also under the control of Mohammed bin Salman. The initial public offering (IPO) of 5% of the oil giant in 2019, dedicated large sums to the PIF. It all helped to boost the crown prince's power consolidation as heir apparent (Roll, 2019). At the same time, Yasser al-Rumayyan, the governor of the PIF, was appointed as Aramco's new CEO. Different sources reported that a major reason for this reorganization was the failing of the previous CEO Khalid al-Falih to attract greater foreign investments as well as disagreements over Aramco's IPO (Mills, 2019; Munro, 2016). Having said that, it should also be seen as an attempt to prevent al-Falih becoming too powerful in his position of controlling the important energy portfolio.

In Abu Dhabi, a similar development took place within ADNOC. Under the umbrella of Abu Dhabi's Supreme Petroleum Council—that was effectively controlled by the former president and ruler of Abu Dhabi, Khalifa bin Zayed since 2004—his brother, the now president Mohamed bin Zayed, gradually took control of the oil sector from 2014 onwards. Between 2016 and 2020, he restructured the petroleum council, broadened his influence and placed new members and close affiliates such as two of his brothers, Hazza bin Zayed and Mansour bin Zayed, on the

[9] Interview #11 and interview #21.

board of the council. He also appointed his trusted fellow, Sultan al-Jaber, as new CEO of ADNOC (Munro, 2016). In his function as energy minister since 2014, his other close companion Suhail bin Muhammad al-Mazroui was already a member of ADNOC's board (Hedges, 2021). In late 2020, Mohamed bin Zayed transferred the competences of the Supreme Petroleum Council into a newly created Supreme Council for Financial and Economic Affairs. While the UAE's President Khalifa bin Zayed chairs the Supreme Council, the crown prince has the de facto power in the new entity that oversees all economic activities (Cahill, 2021). Several months later, Mohamed bin Zayed was officially named chairman of the board of directors of ADNOC. A more prominent role in the energy company was also dedicated to one of his sons, Khaled bin Mohamed bin Zayed (see also overview: Hedges, 2021, 114).

These institutional reorganizations reflected the modernization programmes and economic visions of their leaders, in which the oil companies also played a strategic role (Hedges, 2021). Consequently, the corporate strategy and operation policies of those companies also changed. The restructuring was mainly under the responsibility of the already introduced "trusted lieutenants" (Cahill, 2021, 3), Suhail al-Mazroui, Sultan al-Jaber (in the UAE), Khalid al-Falih and later Yasir al-Rumayyan (in Saudi Arabia); all like-minded and forward-thinking technocrats, who saw the need for a change of the hitherto hydrocarbon-dependency. In addition to a more efficient operation that went along with budgetary cuts and terminations, the more market-oriented approach also mirrored a shift and rebrand "from oil giant(s) to energy titan(s)" (Sim, 2012, 83). The recent relabeling of Qatar Petroleum to Qatar Energy is perhaps the most obvious example of this development. Two strategies are especially apparent here: On the one hand, one can see that the oil companies have invested in upstream and dramatically increased their oil and gas capacities. On the other hand, they have also diversified their supply away from these two key resources (Krane, 2019; Munro, 2016). Thus, the companies seek a strategy to adapt to new realities in a climate-stressed world but also continue to market oil assuming that hydrocarbons will be considered a continual valid option as 'transition fuels' in the short and medium term.

For instance, in the scope of the newly launched Saudi Vision 2030, Khalid al-Falih–led Saudi Aramco announced its own objective to develop more solar energy with the aim of becoming "nothing less than a solar powerhouse" (cited from: Ramady, 2018, 53). Additionally, during Abu

Dhabi Sustainability Week in 2020, ADNOC introduced its comprehensive 2030 Sustainability Agenda. The plan foresees decreasing the company's emissions by 25% by 2030 and drastically expanding its CCUS programme. It further plans to improve the local environment by reusing large amounts of the water consumption for cooling purposes as well as planting 10 million mangrove seedlings. Also in November 2021, the major regional oil industry event, the Abu Dhabi International Petroleum Exhibition and Conference, put a major focal point on topics such as climate change and clean energy. Shortly before this, Aramco announced its net-zero target and earlier the same year Qatar Energy (previously Qatar Petroleum) launched its first Sustainability Series. According to Mari Luomi: "The conventional wisdom has it that when the oil and gas sector in the GCC gets serious, things happen" (Luomi, 2021, n/a). However, this should not obscure the fact that all NOCs have maintained or expanded their oil and gas production capacity in the last years (AGSIW, 2021; Munro, 2016). This not only relates to the exploitation of oil and gas fields within their own territorial borders but also gaining new concessions in other regions, for instance in the eastern Mediterranean.

This apparent contradiction between building a green image and expanding oil and gas ratio appears to be consistent for all the companies. For them, it is rather about controlling emissions, which can be managed through CCUS. or other low-carbon technologies. Those "advantaged hydrocarbons" are perceived as having a crucial role in a net-zero world (AGSIW, 2021, 6). More recently, enthusiasm about hydrogen has also reached the shores of the Gulf. Oil Majors such as Aramco, Oman's PDO and ADNOC have announced large-scale hydrogen projects and invested billions of dollars in this technology, despite the fact that there is very little commercial demand so far. For them and their leaderships, the race to become the major supplier of (blue and green) hydrogen over the next decade has already begun (Chenevix, 2021; Ansari, 2022).[10]

[10] Simplified, depending on the energy source that is used to split water into hydrogen and oxygen, different colours are applied to describe the process. Green hydrogen, which currently makes less than 1% of global hydrogen, is produced by using zero-carbon electricity. So far, the large part of hydrogen is produced by using fossil fuels (grey hydrogen). If the process involves techniques of CCUS, it is labelled blue hydrogen.

A steadily decarbonized world constitutes a threat for oil and gas companies worldwide. However, it is expected that the major oil giants in the Gulf such as Saudi Aramco, ADNOC and Qatar Petroleum "are likely to prevail in a net-zero world" given their capacities in drastically lowering their carbon emissions (AGSIW, 2021, 2). That this is sorely needed is demonstrated by Jim Krane through the example of Saudi Aramco, which is "responsible for about 4.3% of current global GHG emissions and about 3.2% of historical GHG atmospheric accumulations" (Krane, 2020, 9). Despite some promising steps lately towards being more committed to environmental sustainability, oil and gas companies have chronically ignored environmental concerns over the imperative of protecting their business. Even though environmental regulations were in place, they often did not comply with national standards to protect the environment. Given the fact that the companies are controlled—and hence also protected—by the ruling families, until now they have not had to fear climate-related lawsuits or litigation.[11]

Public–Private Assemblage: The Role of Sovereign Wealth Funds and State-Owned Enterprises

The previous chapter already indicated that there is another dominant player in the arena, namely the nations' sovereign wealth funds (SWFs). SWFs are perceived as arguably the second most important element in the GCC economies behind NOCs (Davidson, 2021). Despite being a very diverse group, these investment funds share a number of similarities: SWFs are typically owned by the government, are based on surpluses (e.g. from exporting resources) and often have a diversified asset allocation (see: Bahgat, 2012). Gulf SWFs are further rather opaque, seemingly "discretionary tools of the respective rulers" for achieving their (economic) vision (Woertz, 2013/2019; Young, 2020). In the scope of economic diversification efforts over the last two decades, new players have entered the field. Particularly some SWFs in Saudi Arabia, Qatar and especially the UAE are very active in the field of environmental sustainability.[12] Notably, all can be divided into different types: (a) portfolio SWFs such as Qatar Investment Authority (i.e. QIA), (b) funds with a private equity

[11] Interview #20.

[12] Interview #43.

nature (i.e. Abu Dhabi's Mubadala), (c) domestic development funds (i.e. Saudi Arabia's PIF) and (d) state-owned companies (e.g. the Abu Dhabi National Energy Company, TAQA) (see: Coates Ulrichen, 2017; Woertz, 2013, 220). In some instances, these funds have further created their state-owned enterprises (SOEs) (e.g. UAE-based Masdar or Qatari-based Nebras Power) or nurtured privately owned champions (e.g. Saudi-based ACWA Power). In so doing, Gulf states unlock new lucrative sectors and localize green technology and innovation.

In the last few years, the regimes have actively started to create and/or exploit new economic sectors that can complement and ultimately even replace the hydrocarbon path dependency of many GCC states. Comparatively early, Steffen Hertog emphasized the role of these "rent-financed *public* industries" (...) as "pivotal for understanding the GCC diversification process" (Hertog, 2012, 115). As Ashraf Mishrif states: "Gulf SOEs are relatively modern, financially sound, technologically developed and their management is structured in line with international corporate practices" (Mishrif, 2018, 8). SOEs often expand into areas of intensive capital and profitability and take care to be viewed positively. In this regard, many SOEs have also put much attention towards promoting sustainable practices. What many SOEs share with institutional or bureaucratic fiefdoms, however, is that they also often act as "silos of clientelism" providing certain privileges to selected individuals, groups or other entities (Youngs, 2012, 21; also: Kamrava, 2018). This can be best observed when looking at the SOE's leadership level that is often selected by the ruling families. Oftentimes, family members occupy chair positions in the SOEs, while the appointment of the CEO mainly follows merit-based recruitment. This may include expats with international standard or local technocrats from the bureaucratic or business sectors (Hertog, 2012). All these partially or fully SOEs implement various showcase projects and initiatives that constitute important pillars of the national visions and development strategies.

In this regard, the UAE is at the forefront. While Dubai started very early on to embark on this SOE-based development, particularly in the real estate sector through enterprises such as Emaar or Nakhel, neighbouring Abu Dhabi has understood the potential of sustainability as strategic 'vanity niche'. As mentioned previously, the launch of the Abu Dhabi Future Energy Company or 'Masdar' in 2006 marked a turning point in the country's energy sector. Masdar is wholly owned by the state-led holding company and investment fund, the Mubadala Development Company.[13] Mubadala was created in 2002 and is chaired by the President Sheikh Mohamed bin Zayed. His brother, Mansour bin Zayed, is vice-president of the company (Davidson, 2021). Mubadala's CEO, in turn, is the Emirati entrepreneur, Khaldun al-Mubarak, whose family has close ties with the royal family (Almezaini, 2013; Hedges, 2021; Hertog & Luciani, 2012). In fact, Khaldun has been described as "one of the most powerful figures", the president's "go to man" and "one of the Al-Nahyan family's most trusted advisors" (cited from: Davidson, 2021, 123). With this institutional background, Masdar was quickly elevated into a main tool for renewable energy in Abu Dhabi. Moreover, Mubadala provided Masdar with the necessary financial capacities. In fact, the CEO of Masdar, Sultan Ahmed al-Jaber, was quoted in 2007 stressing that the initiatives had "an ultimate budget for renewable energy projects" (Luomi, 2012, 121). Hence, it is not surprising that Masdar's subsidiary, the energy company Masdar Power, was relatively quickly able to offer the most competitive price for solar prices worldwide, making the company attractive for buyers all over the world. Until now, the SOE has developed renewable energy projects in more than thirty countries and is sole or co-developer of the largest solar plants in the UAE. It was further able to successfully bid to headquarter the International Renewable Energy Agency (IRENA) at Masdar City, receiving backup from the World Wide Fund For Nature (WWF) and launching the World Future Energy Summit (also nicknamed the 'Davos of renewable energy') that has taken place every year since 2008. It has further collaborated with internationally renowned companies such as General Electric and Siemens, as well as prestigious research institutes such as the Massachusetts Institute of Technology, MIT. All of this has enhanced Abu Dhabi's brand as a green leader in the niche of renewable energy, despite the country's ecological footprint and the fact that Masdar has lagged greatly behind its over-ambitious goals (Cugurullo, 2013).

In addition to Masdar, the government-controlled Abu Dhabi National Energy Company (TAQA), is another leading SOE in the clean energy sector. Created in 2005 by a royal decree, as a publicly listed company it has expanded quickly and now operates in more than eleven countries.

[13] In 2017, the Mubadala Development Company merged with the International Petroleum Investment Company (est. in 1984) to become the Mubadala Investment Company and one of the world's biggest investment companies.

Since 2020, TAQA has been chaired by Muhammad Hassan al-Suwaidi, who has worked for Mubadala for more than a decade. He and other relatives have a very strong presence in Abu Dhabi's business and energy sector and all stem from the Sudan section of the Bani Yas tribe, from which also the ruling family, and its family branch Bani Fatima, has its origin (Almezaini, 2013; Hedges, 2021). Besides his position at TAQA, Muhammad Hassan al-Suwaidi serves as a board member of ADNOC along with another investment company, ADQ, which, in turn, is also a major shareholder of TAQA. According to its official website, the holding company ADQ is chaired by a brother of the crown prince, Sheikh Tahnoon bin Zayed Al Nahyan, who is also the UAE national security advisor. Lately, it was reported that TAQA and ADQ have entered into a joint venture to invest several billion dollars in green projects in Central Asia.[14] Meanwhile, a "strategic partnership" of TAQA and ADNOC—both shareholders of Mubadala's Masdar—was announced between these two state-led enterprises. The stated aim was to boost the UAE's renewable capacity to 50 GW by 2030 and build upon The Abu Dhabi Hydrogen Alliance, created in January 2021, that comprises Mubadala, ADNOC and ADQ (Khan, 2021, December 2). This institutional entanglement, but also the multiple positions held by certain individuals such as Sultan al-Jaber as ADNOC's CEO, minister of industry and advanced technology, special envoy of climate change and chairman of Masdar, reveals the opaque public–private assemblage. The recent reorganization and joint ventures further illustrate the growing centralization of the country's sustainable development, where previously different agents such as oil giant ADNOC, Masdar, investment funds such as Mubadala or ADQ, and the bureaucratic system, acted rather autonomously.

A similar development has occurred in Qatar, although its sustainable transformation focuses mainly on urban planning projects and initiatives. As in other GCC countries, these large-scale infrastructure projects are managed by a state-led sovereign wealth fund, QIA. The fund is managed by Sheikh Hamad bin Jassim Al Thani, former prime minister and an "archetypal state capitalist" or "political-cum-businessman" (see: Coates Ulrichsen, 2017, 70). Apparently emulating practices of the (back then) successful 'Dubai model' and acting on a desire to diversify Qatar's economy, the national wealth fund QIA created several investment arms.

[14] See official website of ADQ. Retrieved December 28, 2021 from https://adq.ae/.

Among these is Qatari Diar as one of the oldest and most powerful (Hanieh, 2019; Koch, 2014). The property investment company Qatari Diar was established in 2005 by then emir of Qatar, Hamad bin Khalifa Al Thani and is fully controlled by the QIA. It is overseen by the prime minister, Sheikh Khalid bin Khalifa Al Thani, as chairman and Abdullah bin Hamad al-Attiyah as CEO (Roberts, 2017).

By the end of 2005, Qatari Diar started its flagship project Lusail City. The sustainable urban development project included a whole city complex with residential housing for more than 200,000 people. For this purpose, Qatari Diar brought the Lusail Real Estate Development Company into being, as main operator. The futuristic Lusail City is composed of eco-villas and has been described as a "landmark project that will strengthen Qatar's reputation as a leading advocate of sustainable development" (Aguilar, 2015, February 23).[15] By 2013, another large-scale sustainable project was completed. The so-called Barwa City Project in Mesaimeer (Doha) encompassed a whole district of eco-friendly villas, which had been designed by a renowned global architecture firm (HKT Architects) to resemble the old Arabic tradition of formal gardening. The operator was the then privately acting Barwa Real Estate Group, which, however, announced in summer 2014 that its entire share capital has been sold to Labregah Real Estate Company, a wholly owned subsidiary of Qatari Diar (Hanieh, 2019; Kamrava, 2017). The selling of Barwa City, by then one of the largest listed real estate companies in the country, to the property arm of the country's sovereign wealth fund is a vivid example of fully owned SOEs consolidating their monopoly in specific sectors. Qatar's big success of being awarded the hosting rights to the 2022 FIFA World Cup has further facilitated mega infrastructure projects (Kamrava, 2015; Scharfenort, 2012). Since it was announced as the first carbon-neutral event ('Green Qatar 2022')—a crucial point that apparently convinced the FIFA committee—many of those urbanization initiatives have shown a strong commitment to sustainability (Scharfenort, 2012, 219). Despite the fact that Qatar has lately experienced fiscal imbalance in its state budget due to a drop in global gas prices and the blockade by neighbouring countries (2017–2021), some sustainability projects "have (...) acquired lives of their own and cannot be easily dismantled or reversed" (Kamrava, 2015, xxiii). This is mainly true for all initiatives included in

[15] Interview #13.

the planning and preparation of the 2022 World Cup, whose committee is chaired by a brother of the current emir (Kamrava, 2015). As one interviewee explained: "They kept major projects in the World Cup despite budgetary constraints and made the cuts somewhere else: For example, 40% of Qatar Foundation because it does not much serve Qataris, rather expats (...), let's cut".[16]

Another of Qatari Diar's flagship projects is the construction of a fully integrated urban transport network and the first integrated railway system in the GCC. The project started in 2009 when a joint venture called Qatar Railways Development Company was formed between the state-owned Qatari Diar (51%) and Deutsche Bahn International (49%). In 2011, the Qatar Railways Company (i.e. Qatar Rail) was established by royal decree and purchased all stakes in the joint venture from DB International, thus becoming the sole owner and operator of the project. In the period since, Qatar Rail, which nowadays oversees Doha Metro, Lusail Rail and the Long-Distance Passenger and Freight Rail, has partnered with several other subsidiaries of Qatari Diar. The biggest one is Vinci Construction Grands Projects, which in turn is a subsidiary of Qatari Diar Vinci Construction; a joint venture between Qatari Diar (51%) and French Vinci Construction Grands Projects (49%). Vinci employs around 6000 migrant workers on its construction sites and is, among other things, in charge of the construction of Lusail Rail and Doha's Metro Red Line South. Furthermore, Qatari Diar also established another subsidiary, the gulf Organisation for Research & Development, that aims at spearheading environmental sustainability across the MENA region (Luomi, 2012). Among other initiatives, the organization developed a Qatar-specific green building code (Silva, 2016). In addition to Qatari Diar as the leading real estate investment company, QIA is also directly involved in the country's sustainable transformation. Through its investment arm, Qatar Holding, and in collaboration with the Qatar Electricity and Water Company, it created Nebras Power in 2014. The company is Qatar's leading developer of alternative energy and has invested in numerous renewable energy projects in eight countries all over the globe (IRENA, 2019).

Furthermore, the above-mentioned Qatar Foundation (QF) launched the real estate development company Msheireb Properties in 2009. The

[16] Interview #24. Also: Interview #10.

project was initially known as Dohaland as also chaired by the emir's mother, Sheikha Moza (Hertog, 2017). One of their showcase projects for safeguarding the environment and historical culture is Msheireb Downtown Doha, which is presented as a masterpiece of energy efficient urban planning with the self-labelling of possesing the highest concentration of LEED certified buildings in the world (see: Alraouf & Clarke, 2017, 331).[17] The different construction phases of this billion-dollar project were awarded to different global and domestic consortia, again benefitting locally-based private sector developers overseen by members of the ruling families or other influential tribes, which will be discussed in the next section. Additionally, QF has also created its own subsidiary, the solar manufacturer Qatar Solar Technologies. The company was established as a joint venture by QF (70% share), the Qatar National Bank (1%) and the German company SolarWorld (29%). After the insolvency of SolarWorld, QF's fully owned holding company, Qatar Solar, has apparently acquired the shares. Overall, through their web of agents, the Al Thani ensure to remain the ultimate 'power bloc'. Members strategically occupy the most important positions in the country and control powerful fiefdoms like QF, QIA and their sub-entities (e.g. Qatari Diar, Msheireib Properties).

A last and more recent example of a public–private assemblage is the rise of the Public Investment Fund (PIF) in Saudi Arabia and its systematic nurturing of the local company ACWA Power as national champion in the deployment of renewable energy sources. In the light of the power transition of 2015 when King Salman ascended the throne, his son, Mohammed bin Salman (crown prince since 2017), became responsible for the kingdom's economic restructure. As a first step, various previous Supreme Councils were dissolved by royal decree and replaced by the newly established Council for Economic and Development Affairs (CEDA), headed by Mohammed bin Salman. This incident was accompanied by further developments. It not only promoted several technocrats, particularly from the private sector to governmental position, but also led to the emergence of new entities and sub-committees. Among them was the National Centre for Privatization and Public Private Partnership (Hanieh, 2019, 210). Under its supervision, many new large-scale sustainable projects like metro systems (e.g. in Mecca) or urban rail

[17] LEED stands for: Leadership in Energy and Environmental Design certification system developed by the US Green Building Council, see further: Silva (2016).

projects (e.g. in Jeddah, Medina and Dammam) were designed through a PPP. Furthermore, CEDA is also the responsible entity for overseeing Saudi Vision 2030 and guaranteeing its success. In this vein, it dedicated a crucial role to the PIF as the investment vehicle and operationalizing arm (Davidson, 2021). In short, trough the newly established mechanism of CEDA and the PIF acting as 'tool', the crown prince was able to control the economy in the Saudi kingdom (Bsheer, 2021).

At the same time, state-led companies were sold. For instance, while the IPO of Saudi Aramco gained the greatest attention, the government also aimed at privatizing further entities like the Saudi Electricity Company (SEC) or the Saline Water Conversion Company (SWCC) (Hanieh, 2019, 204–205). The selling of some of ACWA Power's shares in October 2021 attracted a phenomenal order volume and became the second biggest IPO after Aramco. The earnings from these sell-offs (of which several are still delayed) have been directed to the PIF and in so doing, the relatively small and unknown fund is set to become the largest SWF in the world. Notably, in 2015 the PIF moved from the Ministry of Finance to the CEDA and eventually fell under the control of Mohammed bin Salman. In the last years, one of the main goals of the PIF has been diversifying Saudi Arabia's energy sector with a special focus on renewable energy sources. One major example that attracted great attention was the announcement in spring 2018 of the Solar Plan 2030 between PIF and the Japanese company SoftBank. With an investment that was expected to exceed $200 billion by 2030, it was planned to generate 200 GW of solar energy by 2032. The deal far exceeded the domestic demand for electricity as well as the country's planned budget for alternative energy. This contrasted with the energy ministry's fine-grained approach of a smooth low-carbon transition domestically. Meanwhile, it was reported that the deal was primarily enforced by the PIF which took the Ministry of Energy by surprise, revealing an internal struggle between the minister, al-Falih, and PIF's head, Yasir al-Rumayyan (Mills, 2018). By the end of 2018, news reports indicated that the SoftBank deal had been abandoned with its current status remaining unclear (Mills, 2018).

Despite this failure, a reminder of the chronic misperception between green pledges and implementation, PIF's chair, Yasir al-Rumayyan, declared in early 2019 that "we will be the largest investor in renewable energy in solar panels and PVs (photo-voltaic)" (Saadi, 2019, February 13). Apparently, an alternative solution was already in place:

In 2018, PIF purchased a larger share in the Saudi national champion of renewable energy sources, the privately owned Arabian Company for Water and Power Development (ACWA Power). The company was founded in 2004 as a joint venture between the Abunayyan Family (50%) and Abdul Kadir Al Muhaidib and Sons Group (50%); both are very important business branches in the country.[18] Under the leadership of Mohammad bin Abdullah Abunayyan as chairman and the Indian expatriate, Paddy Padmanathan, as CEO, ACWA Power became a global leader in water desalination and power generation. By 2018, the company had around 9,500 employees, owned several conventional and non-conventional power and desalination plants and was the market leader in the region regarding CSP by offering one of the cheapest prices on solar cells (Al-Sulayman, 2021).[19] When the PIF purchased a larger share in the company, one interview partner described the state's involvement as "milking a fat cow".[20] The relationship between PIF and ACWA Powers goes back to 2013 when PIF's fully owned subsidiary Sanabil Direct Investments Company initially invested a small share in the privately owned company. By 2018, PIF made its first direct investment in ACWA Power, purchasing 33.36% of the company's stakes. In autumn 2020, it was announced that PIF increased its ownership stake to 50% making ACWA the most precious clean energy developer for the kingdom's energy transition (Sim, 2022). Interestingly, since then ACWA Power has been dedicated the role of the absolute mainstay in the kingdom's cleaner energy transition. Several of REPDO's public tendering of renewable energy projects such as the Sakaka Solar PV Plant have been awarded to PIF-owned ACWA Power as the country's leading developer, owner, operator and investor for power generation and water desalination plants. Since REPDO is only responsible for 30% of renewable energy projects that are tendered, the role of ACWA Power is even more apparent in the direct assignments of the PIF, which awards up to 70% low-carbon projects. As its first initiative, the PIF launched the 1.5 MW Sudair Solar Energy project located in Saudi Arabia's Sudair Industrial City that shall be developed by a consortium led by ACWA Power. In April 2022, it was reported that ACWA shall also take the lead in the second round of the

[18] Interview #46.

[19] Interview #30.

[20] Interview #46.

PIF's renewable energy programme. This second phase includes a 2 GW PV independent power producer (IPP) project in Shuaiba and a 300 MW PV IPP in Rabigh area and is a vivid example of how the PIF is nurturing its own subsidiary (Energy & Utilities, 2022, April 19). Against this backdrop, it might be no surprise that ACWA has lately announced to focus more on the development of renewable power and increase its share from 33% of its total portfolio to 50% by 2030 (Sim, 2022).

Case Study: Layla Solar Plant
By the end of the year 2018, it was announced that Saudi Arabia has completed the first phase of the country's first IPP project in the province of Al-Aflaj. The small-scale solar plant called Layla extends on an area of 720,000 square metres and is able to produce 10 MW, which, however, shall be increased to 40 MW. The plant is directly linked to the kingdom's electric grid. A joint venture of the SEC, KACST and Taqnia Energy (est. 2014) was responsible for the development with the assistance of the Spanish engineering firm Typsa. Taqnia Energy is a subsidiary of the Saudi Technology Development and Investment Company (Taqnia), which is owned by the PIF and can be seen as the operating arm of KACST.[21] The project was initiated without public tendering and has mostly been financed by research funds of KACST.[22] This example is only one among many that reveals the strong public–private assemblage in the Saudi context.

The (Semi) Private Sector: The Role of "Royal Capitalists"

In addition to (semi) state-owned operators, another group of actors in the sustainability 'business networks' include the old merchant families, new capitalists or entrepreneurs from the private sector. As the previous chapters have shown, although public industry plays a dominant role, the private sector also plays an increasingly important part in these networks, even though it remains largely dependent on the state-led allocation

[21] Interview #46.

[22] Interview #28.

system. In the light of the processes of state formation in the twentieth century, merchant families and powerful oligarchic conglomerates, or 'crony capitalists', have been the backbone of the private sector and of political power in the Gulf region.[23] From early onwards, they claimed their economic stake in the ruling bargain. Oftentimes, these notable family businesses directly benefit from the state through financing, land concessions, customs exemptions, subsidies and government contracts. As Kristian Coates Ulrichsen states, the assignment of agency rights has been the most important trajectory towards the 'state-business' elite networks. It ensured that local companies are prioritized in seeking business opportunities in various industries and sectors. Businessmen, who are very close to the ruling families, are granted the most lucrative concessions. In turn, the ruling families can rely on the loyalty of the influential business elites (Coates Ulrichsen, 2017, 105).

While most of these large-scale private enterprises have traditionally started their business in sectors such as trading, construction, contracting or manufacturing, they have nowadays become major conglomerates that occupy various economic sectors (Hanieh, 2020). Prominent examples, some of whom have already been mentioned in other contexts, include BinLaden, Olayan and Ali Reza in Saudi Arabia; Kuwait's merchant families al-Kharafi, al-Ghanim groups; al-Suwaidi and Mazroui groups in the UAE; al-Misnad, al-Muhanni, al-Fakhroo (Darwish), Nasser Bin Khaled and al-Mana groups in Qatar; Zayani Group in Bahrain; and al-Rahas, al-Zubair and Bahwan groups in Oman (Almezaini, 2013; Hanieh, 2011; Kamrava, 2017; Valeri, 2017). With some other families, they have a major share of capital accumulation in the Gulf monarchies (Ahmad & El Agami, 2021). More recently, this also includes the field of 'ecopreneurship' and low-carbon development. Large Gulf-based companies, which have developed extravagant and unsustainable urban planning projects over the past few decades are now turning to environmentally sustainable architecture. In fact, many of them have benefitted from the economic diversification strategies in terms of economic reforms towards privatization or the exploitation of new green-related business opportunities (Valeri, 2013; Young, 2019). By now, these large merchant family-owned businesses are dominating much of the sustainability sector. In this regard, these family businesses fulfil numerous roles and have

[23] Interview #40.

a sizeable part in the 'green transition'. Mostly they take the role of so-called engineering–procurement–construction (EPC) companies, but some of them have seized positions across all segments of the value chain including equipment providers and manufacturers, financiers and even utility companies. Ultimately, the field of environmental sustainability, and the renewable energy market in particular, provides new opportunities and incentives for the 'oligarchic pact' and presents another example of the public–private assemblage (Valeri, 2017). Given the close long-term entanglement as well as the fact that chambers of commerce in the countries are often occupied by family members instead of business actors, it is ensured that the private sector's activities are aligned with the countries' overall vision on sustainable development (Moerenhout, 2016; Valeri, 2013).

Particularly, Kuwait and Qatar give us interesting insights since both states have a powerful merchant class tradition (Crystal, 1990). Both cases further highlight the close entanglement between the public and the 'private' sectors. In Qatar, which has focused mainly on sustainable urbanization projects as described previously, local business families have also benefitted tremendously from the 'green' construction boom caused by the preparation to host the FIFA World Cup in 2022. For instance, alongside international bidders, local companies such as Qatar Building Company (Mustafawi family), Galfar Al-Misnad Engineering (al-Misnad family), Al Darwish (al-Fakhroo) and HBK Contracting (in the hands of the Al Thani family) are all involved in developing the national urban transport system (Hanieh, 2011; Kamrava, 2017). Furthermore, Saad Ahmad al-Muhannadi was appointed as CEO of Qatar Rail. The tribe al-Muhannadi is one of the most influential families in Qatar through possessing its own business (i.e. al-Muhannadi Group) that provides different services in the sectors of industry, energy, manufacturing, design, transportation and information technology. Simultaneously, different members occupy leading positions in entities such as Barwa, Qatar Energy, Kahramaa, Qatar Natural Gas Transport Company (Nakilat) and are continually represented in the *shūrā* council (Kamrava, 2015; Luomi, 2012). Many of Qatar's local companies are also involved in the construction of the low-carbon stadia. For instance, the company HBK Contracting, owned by members of the ruling Al Thani family, is one partner in the construction of the Ras Abu Aboud and Lusail Iconic Stadium, whereas a subsidiary of the Al-Misnad Group is involved in building the Al Bayt Stadium/Al-Khor SC Stadium. While other domestic companies that are controlled by important families are involved, such as Al-Jaber Engineering (al-Jaber) and Al Balagh Trading (al-Kaabi), conglomerates of the al-Misnad group stands out. As Mehran Kamrava notes, the intermarriage of the daughter of one of al-Misnad's family elders, Moza bint Nasser al-Misnad, with the then heir apparent and later emir of Qatar, Sheikh Hamad bin Khalifa (ruled 1995–2013), boosted the business and investment ties between both families (Kamrava, 2017). Concretely, since Sheikh Moza (al-Misnad) became the chair of QF, "al-Misnad firms are among the most prominent contractors in the mammoth infrastructural development projects funded by Qatar Foundation" (Kamrava, 2017, 7).[24] The case of Qatar further reveals a practice that is very common in the Gulf but very difficult to investigate due to the widespread absence of a property register: Qatar's first inaugurated desalination plant powered by RES, inaugurated in 2016, is located at a farm that is owned by Ali Hussain Ali al-Sada, who has a strong presence in Qatar's business world and who is also a relative of the former minister of energy and industry.[25]

In Kuwait, the family al-Kharafi is the most powerful and important business family and Sunni tribe in Kuwait. The mainstay of the family's power is the Mohamed Abdulmohsin Al-Kharafi and Sons Company, which was founded in 1956. By now, the private company is involved in almost all commercial and economic sectors and has established a network of innumerable subsidiaries and other affiliations both inside and outside Kuwait. From the 1990s onwards, the company pioneered BOT schemes in Kuwait, making it indispensable. The company founder's son, Jassim Mohammad al-Kharafi, was a long-term speaker of the Kuwaiti National Assembly (1999–2011) and former minister of finance (Coates Ulrichsen, 2017, 107–108). His sons manage the conglomerate M. A. Kharafi & Sons. The family is known for its friendship with the former Emir Sabah. This close and personal bond to the ruling family al-Sabah is also strengthened through the intermarriage of the families (Alsharekh, 2017; Nosova, 2016). In cooperation with a Spanish company, Kharafi National—a subsidiary of Mohamed Abdulmohsin Al-Kharafi and Sons Company—won the bid to develop Kuwait's prestigious

[24] However, QF's Qatar Science and Technology Park (QSTP) was constructed by Al Darwish Engineering, controlled by the tribe Al Fakhroo (Kamrava 2017; Interview #9; interview #13 and interview #21).

[25] Interview #13.

renewable project, the Shagaya Renewable Energy Park. In a further tendering process to expand the large-scale utility project an international consortium led by the locally-based al-Ghanim International was awarded the contract to design, construct and operate the 10 MW wind park. As the company's name indicates, it belongs to the powerful al-Ghanim family in Kuwait.[26] The economic power of the old merchant family has even increased over the last years, when Marzouq al-Ghanim became speaker of the National Assembly and Ali al-Ghanim headed the Chamber of Commerce. Since Ali al-Ghanim is also a brother-in-law of the former minister of finance Jassim al-Kharafi, one can certainly speak of "the emergence of the Kharafi-Ghanim family as more powerful than some members of the Al Sabah family itself" (Alsharekh, 2017, 171). To some extent, this business bloc is involved in any large-scale project in Kuwait.[27] Both companies, Kharafi National and al-Ghanim International, were also shortlisted in another PPP venture, al- 'Abdaliya Integrated Solar Combined Cycle. While the Ministry of Electricity and Water as leading institution opened the tender in 2016, no progress can be seen so far. It reflects the overall trend that Kuwait has shelved many renewable energy projects (including a second phase of Shagaya) in the light of fiscal austerity caused by the COVID-19 pandemic and a further decline in oil price (Al-Sulayman, 2021).

Saudi Arabia is a particularly interesting case that reveals the fluidity of business networks and patronage under changing leaderships. Since the creation of the modern Kingdom of Saudi Arabia in 1932, The ruling elite has relied on major local business families, above all, the construction tycoon, the Binladin Group, that eventually became known as "the King's builder" (cited from: Wald, 2018, 47; see also: Bsheer, 2021). The mutual dependence and strong partnership goes back to a close friendship between the kingdom's founding father King Abdulaziz and the businessman and founder of the construction company, Mohammed bin Laden, but lasted until recently. Under late King Abdullah, the company had a strategic role in the country's sustainability transformation. For Instance, in 2011 the Binladin Group set up a laboratory for renewable and nuclear energy exploitation with a French company (Bachellerie,

[26] Interview #77.

[27] Interview #38; interview #39 and interview #73.

2012, 145). Additionally, in cooperation with other local and international companies it oversaw the construction of the Princess Noura University for Women with its large solar thermal plant (around 17 MW) (Hanieh, 2011). However, under the new leadership, the company came under increased criticism that ultimately culminated in the imprisonment of the firm's chairman Bakr bin Laden and other family members in the countrywide purge in November 2017 (Bsheer, 2021). Also, another construction giant, Saudi Oger (owned by the Lebanese/Saudi Harari family), which was responsible for constructing KAUST and parts of the Princess Noura University, appears to no longer play a dominant role.[28]

Apparently, the new leadership "has engendered new loyal elites, construction moguls and employees" by controlling the Arriyadh Development Authority for a long time, according to Rosie Bsheer (Bsheer, 2021, 214). For instance, under the auspices of the Arriyadh Development Authority, projects like an eco-friendlier public transport system (King Abdulaziz Project for Riyadh Public Transport, commissioned in 2011) as well as specific environmental initiatives under the Green Riyadh Project, one of the current four megaprojects launched in 2019, have been pushed forward.[29] With an overall estimated cost of $22.5 billion, it is seen as "the world's biggest civil-engineering contract" (Obeid, 2018) and another sign of how the Salman ruling branch benefits financially from the sustainable economic transition.

When the new leadership launched its ambitious clean energy targets framed under the King Salman Renewable Energy Initiative, in April 2017, it further boosted investment in this sector. This includes the representatives of the Abunayyan and Al Muhaidibi groups as well as their joint venture, ACWA Power, but also other business groups such as Al Rajhi, Abdul Latif Jameel and Olayan, which have diversified their operations towards energy and environmental services (Hanieh, 2011, 2019). One example of a profiteer is SIPCHEM (Saudi International Petrochemical Co.), which set up the kingdom's first ethylene vinyl acetate film plant to manufacture solar cells. The company is a joint venture between Saudi, Emirati and Kuwaiti investors, in which several of Saudi Arabia's most important families have stakes including Zamil Group (10%), Olayan

[28] Interview #46.

[29] See official homepage of the Royal Commission for Riyadh City. Retrieved December 28, 2021 from https://www.rcrc.gov.sa/en/projects/green-riyadh-project.

(7%) and Al Rajhi (3.3%) (Hanieh, 2011, 122). Meanwhile, the Al Rajhi Holding Group has also gained shares in ACWA Power. Other beneficiaries of the green turn include the Abdul Ali Al Ajmi Company, the Al Tamimi Group or the Al Jomaih Energy & Water Company. One interesting example worth looking more closely at is Nesma. In 2019, a subsidiary of the privately owned Saudi company was awarded the co-development of a large-scale solar project. Nesma was founded by Saleh Ali al-Turki, who was appointed Major of Jeddah in 2018 by the Salman leadership. The consortium, in which Nesma Renewable Energy plays a part, was commissioned by the PIF to construct a 300 MW solar power plant project near Jeddah.[30]

Conclusion

The clean energy transformation in the Gulf provides insights into the networked policymaking and deeply rooted entanglements between the public and the private sectors that plays a crucial role for processes of capital accumulation. It is often said that privatization is a key aspect of the Gulf countries' efforts towards economic diversification and sustainability. This is particularly important for the transformation of the energy sector. Instead of the longitudinal dominance of national oil companies (NOCs), small and medium enterprises (SMEs) could enter the market by providing new and cleaner energy solutions. For instance, renewable energy sources such as solar panels can easily be installed locally (e.g. on private rooftops). This provides incentives for smaller companies and a more decentralized power generation. And yet, despite this great potential the market remains mainly state dominated or controlled by privileged economic networks (Almezaini, 2013; Schlumberger, 2008). This can be mainly explained by rent-seeking behaviour of political and economic elites as well as enhanced methods of "inclusionary co-optation" by the state (Albrecht & Schlumberger, 2004, 383; Hedges, 2021). However, in order to do this, leaderships must also ensure that there are enough revenues and fund generation. Especially the transition from a hydrocarbon and emission-intensive economy towards a cleaner energy output constitutes a threat to this model. However, leaderships have been creative in order to favour the top-down and hyper-developmental 'business as

[30] See official homepage of Nesma. Retrieved December 28, 2021 from https://www.nesma.com/nesma-wins-utility-scale-pv-project.

usual' approach when it comes to sustainable development beyond oil. Hence, state authorities are heavily engaged in business and seek new business opportunities to increase capital. It resembles what Gray has called: "entrepreneurial state capitalism" (Gray, 2018, 32; also: Moritz, 2020). I have labelled this an 'adaptative state capitalism' model as it differs from a traditional form of state capitalism in some instances (see also: Gray, 2019; Hedges, 2021; Schlumberger, 2008). As previously seen in the state organization, also the economic models resemble a neopatrimonial approach, in which a core member of the ruling family, often a monarch himself but in Saudi Arabia and the UAE increasingly the second in line, is at the top of the pyramid with subordinate agencies creating a hierarchical, top-down web of networks.

Especially governmental or semi-governmental giants such as NOCs, SWFs and SOEs are dedicated an important role and control much of the green transformation process. Interestingly, the oil and gas sector has been the early mover and remains a dominant force in this low-carbon development. NOCs of all countries are involved in clean energy projects. While the NOCs' energy transitions differ in terms of speed and are linked to the individual scope conditions of their home countries, the overall direction towards a cleaner and less carbon-intensive supply chain is the same (Moerenhout, 2016). In this vein, they are often an early mover and key driving force to pushing new projects forward. At the same time, they also expand their oil and gas production dramatically and sell it, as long as it is economically viable. Their revenues provide financial backing for Gulf-based SWFs or SOEs, which also have a major stake in the countries' green transition. These enterprises are also often backed by a strong shareholding by a ruling family member and can act fairly autonomously from other government agencies. They not only develop new urban areas or whole cities, but also act as owners and regulators of these spaces. Examples include Qatar Foundation's control over Doha's Education City or Mubadala's Masdar city with all its subsidiaries (Hertog, 2017).

In many cases these SOEs either newly create or nurture (fully or partially) their own privately owned champions. This form of 'reproduced co-optation' explains why the number of SMEs is steadily growing without a fundamental shift in capital accumulation: If there are reports about successful SMEs it is often the case that they are another subsidiary of a SWF, larger conglomerate in the hands of royal families, or a small segment of influential Gulf-based business families (Hedges, 2021). In this vein, SWFs such as the PIF and Mubadala have recently created their own "fund of funds" to invest in non-oil SMEs (Davidson, 2021). This is a common practice as can be observed in other GCC contexts: For instance, allegedly independent power and water producers and developers in Qatar such as Siraj Power and Umm Al Houl Power are only joint ventures between big players such as the Qatar Electricity and Water Company, Qatar Energy (previously Qatar Petroleum) and the Qatar Foundation.[31] It all guarantees that the regimes meet their ambitious political objectives, but it also ensures their control over business activities. At the same time, other contexts such as Egypt have shown that SOEs have a comparatively higher ecological footprint than companies that compete in a free market model: Providing goods and services well below market value, based on excessive resource exploitation and overstaffing as a way of job creation; a focus on large-scale urban 'prestige projects' and autonomy from environmental regulations can all to act to the detriment of environmental sustainability (Sowers, 2013).

The state's involvement in the sustainability business sector is further expanded by nurturing privileged economic networks and the political-economic exchange between different elites. The market design in most GCC countries has long been dominated by a public–private assemblage that establishes power relations and interdependencies between public industry and the private sector, especially towards major business families or 'crony capitalists'. Wealthy and well-established family-run conglomerates have leveraged its power and influence in the sustainability sector. Concretely, governments involve the private sector, i.e. a few powerful large merchant family–owned businesses, by granting licences (e.g. construction, architecture), channelling financial assistance either through direct spending or indirectly through subsidized utilities as well as cheap and concessionary loans.[32] Especially apparent in the UAE, family business have established companies, which are specialized in developing small-scale solar power projects. Examples include firms such as Yellow Door, Siraj Power or AMEA Power (Sim, 2022). This discloses how the regime creates dependencies on the private sector. At the same time, due to the dual role of many powerful families in both business and politics, the ruling family can count on this loyal

[31] See official homepage of the Qatar Electricity and Water Company. Retrieved December 28, 2021 from https://www.qewc.com/qewc/en/subsidiaries/.

[32] Interview #11 and interview #22.

tribal and filial network in the process of policymaking.[33] Yet, the individual families are more or less balanced against each other to avoid one family becoming too powerful. In this vein, all these actors systematically benefit from exploiting sustainability politics without altering the state-centralized political economy characterized by nepotism, clientelism and favouritism (*wasṭa*). Ultimately, the field of environmental sustainability offers insights on the highly porous and complex boundaries between what is private, public or state-owned. This allows for completely new yet often highly under-researched forms of public–private assemblages that resemble neopatrimonial networks. It makes a case for how the economic context and various actors often operate as a prolonged 'arm of the state'.

[33] Interview #19.

References

AGSIW. (2021). *Petro diplomacy: Gulf countries in a net-zero world conference report* (AGSIW Event Report 2). Retrieved December 20, 2021 from https://agsiw.org/event-report-petro-diplomacy-gulf-countries-in-a-net-zero-world/

Aguilar, J. (2015, February 23). Minister leads EcoVilla stone-laying ceremony. *Gulf Times*. https://www.gulf-times.com/story/428318/Minister-leads-EcoVilla-stone-laying-ceremony

Ahmad, A., & El Agami, F. (2021). *Family businesses in the Gulf must not be left behind*. Atlantic Council. Retrieved December 28, 2021 from https://www.atlanticcouncil.org/blogs/menasource/family-businesses-in-the-gulf-must-not-be-left-behind/

Albrecht, H., & Schlumberger, O. (2004). "Waiting for Godot": Regime change without democratization in the Middle East. *International Political Science Review, 25*(4), 371–392.

Almezaini, K. (2013). Private sector actors in the UAE and their role in the process of economic and political reform. In S. Hertog, G. Luciani, & M. Valeri (Eds.), *Business politics in the Middle East* (pp. 43–66). Hurst & Co.

Alraouf, A., & Clarke, S. (2017). From pearling to skyscrapers: The predicament of sustainable architecture and urbanism in contemporary Gulf cities. In P. Sillitoe (Ed.), *Sustainable development: An appraisal of the Gulf region* (pp. 313–342). Berghahn Books.

Al-Sarihi, A., & Mansouri, N. (2022). Renewable energy development in the Gulf cooperation council countries: Status, barriers, and policy options. *Energies, 15*, 1923. https://doi.org/10.3390/en15051923

Al-Sarihi, A., & Mason, M. (2020). Challenges and opportunities for climate policy integration in oil-producing countries: The case of the UAE and Oman. *Climate Policy, 20*(10), 1226–1241. https://doi.org/10.1080/14693062.2020.1781036

Alsharekh, A. (2017). Youth, protest, and the new elite: Domestic security and dignity in Kuwait. In K. Coates Ulrichsen (Ed.), *The changing security dynamics of the Persian Gulf* (pp. 165–190). Oxford University Press.

Al-Sulayman, F. (2021). The rise of renewables in the Gulf states: Is the 'rentier effect' still holding back the energy transition? In R. Mills & L. Sim (Eds.), *Low carbon energy in the Middle East and North Africa* (pp. 93–120). Palgrave.

Ansari, D. (2022). *The hydrogen ambitions of the Gulf States. Achieving economic diversification while maintaining power*. SWP comment 44. Retrieved August 20, 2022 from https://www.swp-berlin.org/publikation/the-hydrogen-ambitions-of-the-gulf-states

Bachellerie, I. (2012). *Renewable energy in the GCC countries: Resources, potential, and prospects*. Gulf Research Center. Retrieved December 22,

2020 from https://gssd.mit.edu/search-gssd/site/renewable-energy-gcc-countries-resources-60069-tue-03-26-2013-0758

Bahgat, G. (2012). Sovereign wealth funds in the Gulf: An assessment. In D. Held & K. Coates Ulrichsen (Eds.), *The transformation of the Gulf: Politics, economics and the global order* (pp. 218–235). Routledge.

Bsheer, R. (2021). *Archive wars: The politics of history in Saudi Arabia*. Stanford University Press.

Cahill, B. (2021). *Everything at once: Transformation of Abu Dhabi's oil policy* (AGSIW Issue Paper 1). Retrieved December 17, 2021 from https://agsiw.org/everything-at-once-transformation-of-abu-dhabis-oil-policy/

Chenevix, M. (2021). *The Saudi-UAE race for hydrogen: A play for the renewables narrative, not profits*. AGSIW Blog Post. Retrieved December 20, 2021 from https://agsiw.org/the-saudi-uae-race-for-hydrogen-a-play-for-the-renewables-narrative-not-profits/

Coates Ulrichsen, K. (2017). *The Gulf states in international political economy*. Palgrave.

Côté, S. (2019). Renewable energy and its potential impact on GCC labor markets: Opportunities and constraints. In H. Akhonbay (Ed.), *The economics of renewable energy in the Gulf* (pp. 188–215). Routledge.

Crystal, J. (1990). *Oil and politics in the Gulf: Rulers and merchants in Kuwait and Qatar*. Cambridge University Press.

Cugurullo, F. (2013). How to build a sandcastle: An analysis of the genesis and development of Masdar City. *Journal of Urban Technology, 20*(1), 23–37. https://doi.org/10.1080/10630732.2012.735105

Daryl, C. (2003). *The paradoxical kingdom: Saudi Arabia and the momentum of reform*. Hurst & Co.

Davidson, C. (2009). *Abu Dhabi: Oil and beyond*. Oxford University Press.

Davidson, C. (2021). *From Sheikhs to Sultanism: Statecraft and authority in Saudi Arabia and the UAE*. Hurst & Co.

Dourian, K. (2019). *Challenges to the energy transition in the Gulf countries* (AGSIW Issue Paper 6). Retrieved December 15, 2021 from https://agsiw.org/challenges-to-the-energy-transition-in-the-gulf-countries/

Dourian, K. (2021). *Gulf countries gear up for a net-zero world* (AGSIW Issue Paper 5). Retrieved December 15, 2021 from https://agsiw.org/gulf-countries-gear-up-for-a-net-zero-world/

Energy & Utilities. (2022, April 19). *Developer working on proposals for 2.3GW Saudi solar projects*. Energy & Utilities. https://energy-utilities.com/developer-working-on-proposals-for-2-3gw-saudi-news117223.html

Ferroukhi, R., Khalid, A., Hawila, D., Nagpal, D., El-Katiri, L., Thenakis, V., & Al-Fara, A. (2016). *Renewable energy market analysis: The GCC region*.

IRENA Analysis. Retrieved December 10, 2021 from https://www.irena.org/publications/2016/Jan/Renewable-Energy-Market-Analysis-The-GCC-Region

Gelil, I. (2016). Barriers to greening the energy sector in the Gulf Cooperation Council. In M. Raouf & M. Luomi (Eds.), *The green economy in the Gulf* (pp. 25–52). Routledge.

Gordon, D., & Feldman, J. (2016). *Breaking down the barrel: Tracing GHG emissions through the oil supply chain.* Carnegie Endowment for International Peace. Retrieved December 15, 2021 from https://carnegieendowment.org/2016/02/09/breaking-down-barrel-tracing-ghg-emissions-through-oil-supply-chain-pub-62722

Gray, M. (2011). *A theory of "late rentierism" in the Arab states of the Gulf* (CIRS Occasional Paper 7). Retrieved October 29, 2021 from https://papers.ssrn.com/sol3/papers.cfm?abstract_id=2825905

Gray, M. (2018). Rentierism's siblings: On the linkages between rents, neopatrimonialism, and entrepreneurial state capitalism in the Persian Gulf monarchies. *Journal of Arabian Studies, 8*(Issue sup1), 29–45. https://doi.org/10.1080/21534764.2018.1546931

Gray, M. (2019). *The economy of the Gulf states.* Agenda publishing.

Griffiths, S., & Orkoubi, D. (2019). Energy and climate policies to stimulate renewables deployment in GCC countries. In H. Akhonbay (Ed.), *The economics of renewable energy in the Gulf* (pp. 139–166). Routledge.

Hamedi, Z. (2014). Energy transition in rentier states: A multi-level perspective. In G. Luciani & R. Ferroukhi (Eds.), *Political economy of energy reform: The clean energy-fossil fuel balance in the Gulf states* (pp. 85–118). Gerlach Press.

Hanieh, A. (2011). *Capitalism and class in the Gulf Arab states.* Palgrave.

Hanieh, A. (2019). *Money markets, and monarchies: The Gulf Cooperation Council and the political economy of the contemporary Middle East.* Cambridge University Press.

Hanieh, A. (2020). Rethinking class and state in the Gulf Cooperation Council. In J. Beinin, B. Haddad, & S. Seikaly (Eds.), *A critical political economy of the Middle East and North Africa* (pp. 105–122). Stanford University Press.

Hashmi, M., & Al-Habib, M. (2013). Sustainability and Carbon management practices in the Kingdom of Saudi Arabia. *Journal of Environmental Planning and Management, 56*(1), 140–157. https://doi.org/10.1080/09640568.2012.654849

Hedges, M. (2021). *Reinventing the sheikhdom: Clan, power and patronage in Mohammed bin Zayed's UAE.* Hurst & Co.

Hertog, S. (2010). *Princes, brokers, and bureaucrats: Oil and the state in Saudi Arabia.* Cornell University Press.

Hertog, S. (2012). Public industry as tool of rentier economy diversification: The GCC case. In G. Luciani (Ed.), *Resources blessed: Diversification and the Gulf development model* (pp. 115–138). Gerlach Press.

Hertog, S. (2017). *A quest for significance: Gulf oil monarchies' international 'soft power' strategies and their local urban dimensions* (LSE Kuwait Programme Paper Series 42). Retrieved December 28, 2021 from http://eprints.lse.ac.uk/69883/1/Hertog_42_2017.pdf

Hertog, S., & Luciani, G. (2012). Energy and sustainability policies in the Gulf states. In D. Held & K. Coates Ulrichsen (Eds.), *The transformation of the Gulf: Politics, economics and the global order* (pp. 236–257). Routledge.

Howard, J. (2017). Promoting sustainable development in marine regions. In P. Sillitoe (Ed.), *Sustainable development: An appraisal of the Gulf region* (pp. 270–290). Berghahn Books.

Husari, R. (2022). *For Gulf producers, decarbonization does not mean zero oil production*. Middle East Institute. Retrieved April 17, 2022 from https://www.mei.edu/publications/gulf-producers-decarbonization-does-not-mean-zero-oil-production

IRENA. (2019). *Renewable energy market analysis: GCC 2019*. Retrieved December 28, 2021 from https://www.irena.org/publications/2019/jan/renewable-energy-market-analysis-gcc-2019

Kamrava, M. (2015). *Qatar: Small state, big politics*. Cornell University Press.

Kamrava, M. (2017). State-business relations and clientelism in Qatar. *Journal of Arabian Studies, 7*(1), 1–27. https://doi.org/10.1080/21534764.2017.1288420

Kamrava, M. (2018). Oil and institutional stasis in the Persian Gulf. *Journal of Arabian Studies, 8*(supl), 1–12. https://doi.org/10.1080/21534764.2018.1546929

Khan, M. (2021, December 2). Adnoc and Taqa to become shareholders in Abu Dhabi's Masdar with Mubadala. *The National*. https://www.thenationalnews.com/business/energy/2021/12/01/adnoc-and-taqa-to-become-shareholders-in-abu-dhabis-masdar-with-mubadala/

Koch, N. (2014). "Building glass refrigerators in the desert": Discourses of urban sustainability and nation building in Qatar. *Urban Geography, 35*(8), 1118–1139. https://doi.org/10.1080/02723638.2014.952538

Krane, J. (2019). *Energy kingdoms: Oil and political survival in the Persian Gulf*. Columbia University Press.

Krane, J. (2020). Climate action versus inaction: Balancing the costs for Gulf energy exporters. *British Journal of Middle Eastern Studies, 47*(1), 117–135. https://doi.org/10.1080/13530194.2020.1714269

Krane, J. (2021). Pairing coal with solar: The UAE's fragmented electricity policy. In R. Mills & L. Sim (Eds.), *Low carbon energy in the Middle East and North Africa* (pp. 57–92). Palgrave.

Luomi, M. (2012). *The Gulf monarchies and climate change: Abu Dhabi and Qatar in an era of natural unsustainability*. Hurst & Co.

Luomi, M. (2021). From the year of climate ambition to action in the Gulf. *AGSIW blog post*. Retrieved January 15, 2022 from https://agsiw.org/from-the-year-of-climate-ambition-to-action-in-the-gulf/

Meltzer, J., Hultman, N., & Langley, C. (2014). *Low-carbon energy transitions in Qatar and the Gulf Cooperation Council region*. Brookings Papers on Economic Activity. Retrieved December 11, 2021 from: https://ssrn.com/abstract=2408743

Mills, R. (2018). *Saudi Arabia shelves softbank solar effort, reflecting challenges with megaprojects*. AGSIW Blog Post. Retrieved December 22, 2021 from https://agsiw.org/saudi-arabia-shelves-softbank-solar-effort-reflecting-challenges-with-megaprojects/

Mills, R. (2019). *Aramco, ministry reshuffle highlight role of oil giant in Saudi economic transformation*. AGSIW Blog Post. Retrieved December 17, 2021 from https://agsiw.org/aramco-ministry-reshuffle-highlight-role-of-oil-giant-in-saudi-economic-transformation/

Mishrif, A. (2017). Introduction to economic diversification in the GCC region. In M. Ashraf & Y. Al-Balushi (Eds.), *Economic diversification in the Gulf region Volume I: The private sector as an engine of growth* (pp. 1–26). Palgrave.

Mishrif, A. (2018). Challenges of economic diversification in the GCC countries. In A. Mishrif & Y. Al Balushi (Eds.), *Economic diversification in the Gulf region Volume II: Comparing global challenges* (pp. 1–20). Springer.

Moerenhout, T. (2016). Energy pricing reform and the green economy in the Gulf region. In M. Raouf & M. Luomi (Eds.), *The green economy in the Gulf* (pp. 53–76). Palgrave.

Moritz, J. (2020). Rentier political economy in the oil monarchies. In M. Kamrava (Ed.), *Routledge Handbook of Persian Gulf politics* (pp. 163–186). Routledge.

Munro, D. (2016). *ADNOC's CEO institutes seismic shift in corporate strategy*. AGSIW Blog Post. Retrieved December 17, 2021 from https://agsiw.org/adnocs-ceo-institutes-seismic-shift-in-corporate-strategy/

Niblock, T. (2006). *Saudi Arabia: Power, legitimacy and survival*. Routledge.

Nosova, A. (2016). *The merchant elite and parliamentary politics in Kuwait: The dynamics of business political participation in a rentier state*. PhD thesis, London School of Economics and Political Science. Retrieved December 28, 2021 from http://etheses.lse.ac.uk/3445/

Obeid, J. (2018). *Saudi Arabia is in a double bind on oil prices*. Chatham House. Retrieved December 28, 2021 from https://www.chathamhouse.org/expert/comment/saudi-arabia-double-bind-oil-prices

Obeid, J. (2022). Energy governance: Is the new meeting the old in Saudi Arabia's energy industries? In M. Thompson & N. Quilliam (Eds.), *Governance and domestic policy-making in Saudi Arabia: Transforming society, economics, politics and culture* (pp. 169–196). I.B. Tauris.

Ramady, M. (2018). *Saudi Aramco 2030: Post IPO challenges*. Springer.

Roberts, D. (2017). *Qatar: Securing the global ambitions of a city-state*. Hurst & Co.

Roll, S. (2019). *Aramco's IPO and Bin Salman's fiscal takeover*. Carnegie Brief. Retrieved December 17, 2021 from https://carnegieendowment.org/sada/80463

Saadi, D. (2019, February 13). Saudi sovereign fund to expand presence abroad. *The National*. https://www.pressreader.com/uae/the-national-news/20190214/281797105257401

Scharfenort, N. (2012). Urban development and social change in Qatar: The Qatar National Vision 2030 and the 2022 FIFA World Cup. *Journal of Arabian Studies, 2*(2), 209–230. https://doi.org/10.1080/21534764.2012.736204

Schlumberger, O. (2008). Structural reform, economic order, and development: Patrimonial capitalism. *Review of International Political Economy, 15*(4), 622–649. https://doi.org/10.1080/09692290802260670

Silva, C. (2016). Green buildings in the Arabian Gulf. In M. Abdel Raouf & M. Luomi (Eds.), *The green economy in the Gulf* (pp. 147–160). Routledge.

Sim, L. (2012). Re-branding Abu Dhabi: From oil giant to energy titan. *Place Branding and Public Diplomacy, 8*(1), 83–98.

Sim, L. (2022). *Renewable power policies in the Arab Gulf states*. Middle East Institute. Retrieved February 10, 2022 from https://www.mei.edu/publications/renewable-power-policies-arab-gulf-states

Sowers, J. (2013). *Environmental politics in Egypt: Activists, experts and the state*. Routledge.

Thompson, M. (2018). Saudi Arabia: Civil society and natural resource management. In I. Overland (Ed.), *Public brainpower: Civil society and natural resource management* (pp. 291–309). Springer.

Valeri, M. (2013). Oligarchy vs. oligarchy: Business and politics of reform in Bahrain and Oman. In S. Hertog, G. Luciani, & M. Valeri (Eds.), *Business politics in the Middle East* (pp. 17–42). Hurst & Co.

Valeri, M. (2017). Towards the end of the oligarchic pact? Business and politics in Abu Dhabi, Bahrain and Oman. In K. Coates Ulrichsen (Ed.), *The changing security dynamics of the Persian Gulf* (pp. 77–98). Oxford University Press.

Wald, C. (2018). *Saudi, Inc. The Arabian kingdom's pursuit of profit and power*. Pegasus Books.

White, B. (2020, May 18). *PDO says work on Miraah solar farm project will continue despite GlassPoint Solar liquidation*. ME Construction. https://meconstructionnews.com/41461/pdo-says-work-on-miraah-solar-farm-project-will-continue-despite-glasspoint-solar-liquidation

Woertz, E. (2013). *Oil for food: The global food crisis and the Middle East*. Oxford University Press.

Woertz, E. (2021). When "pariahs" go green: Energy transitions in the Middle East and the Biden administration. *Georgetown Journal of International Affairs*. Retrieved December 13, 2021 from https://gjia.georgetown.edu/2021/04/14/when-pariahs-go-green-energy-transitions-in-the-middle-east-and-the-biden-administration/

Yamada, M. (2020). Can a rentier state evolve to a production state? An 'institutional upgrading' approach. *British Journal of Middle Eastern Studies, 47*(1), 24–41. https://doi.org/10.1080/13530194.2020.1714867

Young, K. (2019). The Gulf's eastward turn: The logic of Gulf-China economic ties. *Journal of Arabian Studies, 9*(2), 236–252. https://doi.org/10.1080/21534764.2019.1768655

Young, K. (2020). Sovereign risk: Gulf sovereign wealth funds as engines of growth and political resource. *British Journal of Middle Eastern Studies, 47*(1), 1–21. https://doi.org/10.1080/13530194.2020.1714866

Youngs, R. (2012). The Gulf in the new world order: A forgotten emerging power? In R. Youngs (Ed.), *The GCC in the global economy* (pp. 5–22). Gerlach Press.

Zumbraegel, T. (2019). Being green or being seen green? Strategies of eco regime resilience in Qatar. In H. Pouran & H. Hakimian (Eds.), *Environmental challenges in the MENA region: The long road from conflict to cooperation* (pp. 49–71). The Gingko Library.

CHAPTER 6

Accommodating the Regional and International Ecosystems: Transnational Sustainability Governance

The GCC Between Environmental Coordination and Competition

Environmental Interdependence and Cooperation

Given the Gulf region's high degree of environmental insecurity, there is a growing understanding that climate security represents a key aspect to consider in any future security architecture (Coates Ulrichsen 2011; Soubrier, 2020). The combination of the increasing scale of climate change and high dependence on natural resources not only for survival and stability, but also for generation of revenues (as encapsulated by the water–energy nexus) makes the Gulf monarchies especially vulnerable. Political decision-makers across the GCC region have long been aware of this fact: Over the last decades, there have been several forms of regional coordination and integration schemes to counter and reduce this environmental insecurity (Raouf, 2014).

These include institution-building measures such as the creation of the Council of Arab Ministers Responsible for the Environment (CAMRE), the Committee on Climate Change of the members of the GCC or the Regional Organisation for the Protection of the Marine Environment (ROPME) (Al-Sarihi & Luomi, 2019, 5–6). They also include a number

T. Zumbraegel, *Political Power and Environmental Sustainability in Gulf Monarchies*, Contemporary Gulf Studies,
https://doi.org/10.1007/978-981-19-4431-4_6

of initiatives and plans mostly centred on environmental hazards, disasters, pollution and biodiversity protection (Al-Saidi, 2021, 3). As already described in Chapter 3, the 1995 launch of the General Regulations of Environment in the GCC States marked a watershed in regional environmental governance but remained rather a one-off instance of collective climate action during a time when the trauma of the Gulf war 1990–91 with its environmental consequences was still present. So far, the general output of regional climate action is rather modest (Al-Saidi, 2021; Raouf, 2014). One of the reasons is the non-binding character of many common laws. The implemented regional environmental regulations rather present models or guidelines, without obligations for the individual states. One example of this structural shortcoming includes the GCC United Water Strategy: Launched in 2016 as a sound, integrated and joint approach towards water management, it has not been adopted by the single states so far (Al-Saidi, 2021). Also, in other fields such as protecting the marine and terrestrial environments, as well as climate change adaptation, very little joint regional effort or collective commitment to limit these threats can be discerned. In fact, responses are almost exclusively made at a national level and have not been extended to the regional level (Al-Saidi, 2021; Al-Saidi et al., 2019; Sever et al., 2019; Zumbraegel, 2021).

The only field where substantial collective action has been put into practice is regional energy policy. Given the countries' energy abundance and the geopolitical importance of "energy chokepoints" such as the Bab al Mandab and Strait of Hormuz (Sim, 2020, 187), it is not surprising that regional energy cooperation is of urgent importance for all GCC states. The mainstay for regional energy integration and coordination is the electric transmission network operated by the Gulf Cooperation Council Interconnection Authority that is based in Dammam, Saudi Arabia. Since its inception in 2001, it has linked national energy grids into a unified GCC electricity grid, fostered coordination and adjustment of national utility companies and institutions as well as advanced energy efficiency measures (Moerenhout, 2016). The interconnected GCC grid, also known as "backbone" (Günel, 2018, 1), is mainly used for sharing available reserve capacity to bridge shortages. Until today, however, only a small amount of electricity (between 400 and 1200 MW) is exchanged between GCC countries due to a lack of a common trade and power market, varying domestic networks of electrical frequency as well as legal frameworks (e.g. on tariffing and national utility markets) (El-Katiri, 2011; IRENA, 2019).

While Laura El-Katiri has previously suggested that the grid has the potential "to become the backbone for systemic regional electricity market cooperation" and "a tool for the creation of a genuine regional market" (El-Katiri, 2011, 1), the opposite is the case so far: Some areas of the GCC frequently experience short power outages, indicating a fragile regional electricity infrastructure and failed marketization for trading electricity (Günel, 2018). As some experts have stressed, the exploitation of alternative and cleaner energy sources could overcome many of the GCC grid's shortcomings: Aligning ambitious large-scale alternative energy projects in some GCC countries with the regional level could expand its grid's power capacity, overcome the occasional energy vulnerability during the summer period, as well as the partial vulnerability in terms of power capacity more generally, improve R&D and renewable energy technology solutions, as well as foster economic integration in the GCC (Al-Ubaydli et al., 2019; Günel, 2019). However, this has not happened so far (Al-Saidi, 2021). There are only a few examples of bilateral collaboration.

In this vein, ACWA has various projects in Oman and one in Saudi Arabia's closest ally, Bahrain. Additionally, the company was shortlisted for low-carbon projects in Kuwait, but the country has struggled to get moving in light of a political stalemate and growing budget constraints. Masdar, in turn, is the leading company for the establishment of the first GCC wind park in Oman. According to an Omani journalist, the wind park in Oman developed by Abu Dhabi's company was one condition of reconciliation after the leak of an Omani spy cell operating in the office of Abu Dhabi's crown prince.[1] While Masdar and ACWA are competing economically, there is also a high degree of cooperation between their host countries, Saudi Arabia and Abu Dhabi. For instance, both companies have also developed numerous projects in the respective other country. Also, Abu Dhabi's other energy giant, TAQA, has been part of the development of many projects in Saudi Arabia and has lately announced that it will invest billions of dollars in further solar projects and power-saving desalination technologies in the kingdom.[2] This is all the manifestation of a new Saudi–Emirati axis that was institutionalized with

[1] Interview #74.

[2] See official websites of ACWA (https://www.acwapower.com/en/about-us/introduction/), Masdar (https://www.masdar.ae/en/About-Us) and TAQA (https://www.taqa.com/who-we-are/). Retrieved January 3, 2021.

the creation of a Saudi–Emirati Coordination Council in 2017 and that also expands to transnational sustainability governance (Hanieh, 2019, 110; further: Davidson, 2021).

Qatar, in contrast, has been left out, which is mostly explained by the recurring rifts in 2014 and from 2017 to 2021. Previously, more cooperation was detectable. For instance, a joint venture between Abu Dhabi-based Environmena, and the Qatari company, GreenGulf, was responsible for several small-scale solar energy grid projects around Doha. Most notably, the joint undertaking developed Qatar's first solar rooftop on the landmark project, the Qatar National Convention Centre in 2011, which was built for the upcoming climate conference (Luomi, 2012). Despite being part of one joint venture for a solar plant in Oman, Qatar's renewable energy developer, Nebras Power, has been rather side-lined in developing projects within the GCC, which can be explained by the dominance of the others' national champions.[3]

Yet, these projects and investments are isolated from each other and have no collective fundament in the scope of greater regional clean energy exchange and coordination. As Omar Al-Ubaydli and colleagues emphasize:

> While GCC countries have similar renewable goals and share similar challenges, a prevailing feature of current renewable energy efforts is that each country is operating unilaterally with, at best, minimal, and most frequently zero, collaboration and coordination with others. (Al-Ubaydli et al., 2019, 217)

The inadequate collective GCC response to environmental sustainability relates mostly to the structural shortcomings of limited accountability and weak institutions with little coordination both within and across entities (Al-Sarihi & Luomi, 2019). It, however, also points to a lack of political willingness and occasional friction between the member states. Here, Kuwait proves the exception to the rule. As already indicated in the chapter on environmental history in the region, Kuwait stands out as a country that has supported regional initiatives from early onwards. It was Kuwait that gave the impetus for creating the GCC as a subregional forum and became a strong defender of the organization, which can

[3] See official website of Nebras Power (https://nebras-power.com/). Retrieved January 3, 2021.

also be explained through the trauma of the Iraq invasion 1990/1991. Accordingly, “the psychological effects and physical destruction” of the war continue to have a deep impact on policymaking (Mishrif, 2017, 15). The systematic destruction of hundreds of oil wells across the country as well as the capsizing of many oil tankers alarmed environmentalists, scientists and ultimately, also policymakers. It all brought greater attention towards environmental awareness (Warner, 1991). This sensitive approach to the ecological system was not confined to the national level but also unfolded at the regional level. Comparatively early, Hamid A. Shuaib documented that Kuwait has been comparatively active in regional environmental activities and organizations (Shuaib, 1988). Apart from the foundation of ROPME as part of the Kuwait Action Plan Region in the late 1970s, Kuwait became a frontrunner in developing innovative firefighting methods and initiated numerous environment-related regulations and laws to its GCC counterparts during the 1990s. This was further flanked by multiple bilateral agreements and cooperations with other proximate countries (Al-Damkhi, 2007; Al-Damkhi et al., 2009; Haas, 2016). Additionally, as part of the Green Gulf Initiative in 2007, Kuwait created an Arab Regional Centre for Environmental Law (Sever et al., 2019) and initiated the creation of a Regional Emergency Management Center (formerly known as GCC Disaster Control Center) that was established in 2013 in Kuwait City. Furthermore, the emirate created the GCC environmental portal in 2014, which constitutes the central hub for monitoring and exchanging environmental information among its GCC fellows. This was followed up by the idea of launching a GCC e-gate on environment and an environmental portal to assert climate policies in the other states, but this plan has not been realized so far (Al-Saidi, 2021). Meanwhile, Kuwait also provided financial assistance to several regional environmental projects and organized a GCC–EU environment symposium on climate change and waste in 2011. Rhetorically, Kuwaiti leaders underlined the country’s role as regional “Arab environmental agency” and urged other GCC and Arab fellows to intensify their efforts to combat climate change (Emirates News Agency, 2017, October 20). It all indicates that the government in Kuwait City considers environmental sustainability as a major trajectory of a regional ecosystem and tends to take a proactive role as a regional environmental coordinator and mediator.[4]

More recently, other GCC countries have also pushed forward regional environmental initiatives and policies that overshadow previous attempts by Kuwait. In spring 2021, the leadership in Abu Dhabi gained attention by hosting its first Regional Climate Dialogue. Besides US climate envoy John Kerry, leaders from eleven other Arab countries convened to accelerate progress on climate action.[5] Discussions centred mostly on mitigation solutions such as deploying renewable energy sources and boosting decarbonization efforts. It all should result in a list of priorities and a roadmap for cooperation towards future global climate summits (Emirates News Agency, 2021, April 1). At the same time, Saudi Arabia's Crown Prince Mohammed bin Salman launched his 'Saudi Green Initiative' and 'Middle East Green Initiative'. In essence, Saudi's proposals emphasize the country's commitment of generating 50% renewable energy by 2030 and offsetting emissions by planting 10 billion trees in the kingdom and an additional 40 billion across the Middle East. During a specific event to promote the initiatives in October 2021, the Saudi government further announced the creation of several regional hubs and programmes. These include, for instance, regional centres for sustainable fishery, natural risks, cloud seeding and climate change, as well as a specific regional fund for clean energy investments (Al-Sarihi, 2021).

Both Saudi and Emirati initiatives have not translated into tangible measures of environmental cooperation so far and should rather be seen as two divergent approaches to showcasing regional leadership ambitions. There is some hope, however, that joint action to mitigate climate change and environmental degradation can also have a positive effect on regional cooperation. For instance, the Qatar blockade between 2017 and 2021 had its effect in hampering many efforts of environmental cooperation in the GCC (Al-Saidi, 2021). In light of Saudi Arabia's 'green initiatives' the Crown Prince, Mohammed bin Salman, called Qatar's Emir, Sheikh Tamim bin Hamad Al Thani, to discuss these pressing issues. It was reported as the first conversation between both decision-makers

[4] Interview #1; interview #39 and interview #77.

[5] The eleven countries that signed the final statement during the session included the UAE, Oman, Kuwait, Bahrain, Qatar, Egypt, Jordan, Morocco, Iraq, Sudan and the USA.

for years (Qarjouli, 2021, March 29). In this regard, the two countries have also resumed talks on a cross-border rail connection (*The Peninsula*, 2022, January 7).

A New Arena for Competition

What explains the lack of any truly regional initiatives and formalized multilateral approaches in terms of environmental sustainability? From a political perspective, such a stalemate can be best explained by a regional geopolitical setting that is dominated by fierce competition and a pursuit of hegemony. Intra-GCC competition, especially over strategic niches (e.g. aviation, sports, real estate, tourism, financial services, etc.), is an ever-present aspect of interaction. As one interview partner summarized: "There is a high competition within the GCC and they are always saying: We are the leader, we are better than the direct neighbor (...) one should not forget how important pride is within this region".[6] In terms of green energy solutions and technology, transfer of innovation is almost exclusively undertaken unilaterally with foreign nations or consultancy companies and not between GCC states.[7] Also, relying on Western consultancy is the dominant strategy rather than sharing experiences among the GCC peers (Davidson, 2021). Nations with an assertive and less risk-averse foreign policy such as Saudi Arabia and the UAE (plus Qatar until 2013) try to have a strategic advantage over others. In this vein, environmental sustainability is increasingly perceived as another field of soft power projection on the regional level. Basically, this intra-regional competition manifests itself mostly within two dimensions. First, Saudi Arabia's efforts to defend its self-described hegemonic aspirations towards the other GCC states and second, between the smaller GCC states and the question of who the second decisive power after Saudi Arabia is.[8]

Regarding the first dimension, despite a close Saudi Emirati alliance, this partnership indicates some fragility lately. As one interview partner summarized the 'special' relationship: "Especially between MBZ [Mohamed bin Zayed] and MBS [Mohammed bin Salman] there will come a time where both will clash and energy is one aspect of the

[6] Interview #12.

[7] Interview #28.

[8] Interview #2, interview #7 and interview #26.

struggle".[9] Here, the latest dispute within OPEC+ between both countries should be interpreted as a power game over who is to dominate oil production in the short to medium term, considering a climate-conscious and carbon-constrained world (see also: Guzansky et al., 2021). Alternative energy sources have also become another playground of competition. As Gawdat Bahgat quite early pointed out: "Watching the race for nuclear and renewable energy Saudi leaders do not want to fall behind other regional powers. Rather, they aspire to be at the forefront leading other countries in utilizing these important sources of energy" (Bahgat, 2013, 567). One interview partner declared that Saudi decision-makers agreed to go forward with a nuclear project despite the risks, because they were afraid of the UAE fast tracking on alternative energies.[10] As will be explained more in the upcoming chapter on hedging, ACWA Power and UAE-based Masdar Power are increasingly competing over market share. Additionally, Saudi Arabia's above-mentioned NEOM project could surpass the Emirates' Masdar city as a regional example of a zero-emissions urbanization project. Growing dissonance over the impact and seriousness of fighting the climate crisis between both partners were also apparent during the climate summit in Morocco in 2016 (Sever et al., 2019).

The competition between both ambitious leaderships also became apparent when the UAE invited the US special envoy on climate John Kerry and representatives from ten other Arab countries to a regional climate dialogue forum in Abu Dhabi in spring 2021. Saudi Arabia, however, did not participate. Instead, Riyadh collaborated with other nations to establish the so-called Net-Zero Producers Forum that excludes the UAE (Reuters, 2021, April 24). Also, the announcement of the 'Saudi Green Initiative' and the 'Middle East Green Initiative' at the same time should be seen as a sign that Saudi Arabia does not intend to join others but rather wants to lead the process. Another example was the recent pledge of individual zero-carbon targets by both countries shortly after one another. It was even reported that Saudi Arabia actively tries to hamper regional environmental projects which it is not a part of. In this vein, the Saudi government worked against a solar project between Israel

[9] Interview #44.

[10] Interview #29.

and Jordan under the Emirati leadership because it undermined the Saudi crown prince's 'Green Middle East' vision (Axios, 2021, November 24).

Also in other instances, Saudi Arabia underscores its hegemonic role. Traditionally, this has often happened in terms of energy security. In the past, Saudi Arabia has impeded the construction of pipelines and energy infrastructure projects that would undermine or question its (energy) authority and superiority (Zumbraegel, 2020b).[11] Nowadays, environmental sustainability has also been politicized. For instance, in 2015, the Saudi government decided to shut down the production of two joint Saudi–Kuwaiti oilfields, namely the onshore al-Wafra field and the offshore al-Khafji field. Riyadh cited environmental concerns and violations as reasons, but it became clear that this was rather a cover story to put economic pressure on the neighbouring country. According to one interviewee, the Saudi government used "lame excuses of environmentalism to close the oil fields".[12] Concretely, in a 2015 speech, King Salman's son and then deputy minister of petroleum and mineral resources, Prince Abdulaziz bin Salman, stressed that this decision will save up to 300,000 barrels of oil, which will have a considerable positive effect on the issue of global warming. In reality, however, Riyadh exerted pressure on Kuwait to comply with Saudi political interests, among these being the signing of a GCC security pact in 2015 (Zumbraegel, 2020b).[13] While it is unclear whether Kuwait ultimately backed down, the dispute was only solved by the end of 2019 and marked a major shake-up between the two GCC members (Mills, 2020).

As a second dimension, the competition between single GCC states is also apparent in the field of environmental sustainability. In this vein, the decision to host the climate summit 2012 in Doha was certainly a thorn in the side of Abu Dhabi, especially its self-given perception as climate leader that was mainly based on its Masdar initiative and the successful hosting of IRENA. During this time, one could perceive how both countries engaged in a contest over sustainability governance. For instance, Qatar, Dubai and Abu Dhabi have all established their own green certification systems for building (Hertog & Luciani, 2012; Luomi, 2012). This project was initially thought to be a collaborative initiative but has

[11] Interviews #37 and interview #56.

[12] Interview #39.

[13] Interview #39 and interview #40.

now become a subject of diverging interest, with every state promoting its own building code for use in other GCC states (Al-Saidi, 2021). Also, the creation of separate research institutions and green fiefdoms (see Chapter 4) and clean energy developers are further examples. As Li-Chen Sim further explains:

> It is noteworthy that the creation of Nebras in 2014 coincided with the intra-Gulf crisis over Qatar that year and was arguably an attempt to use clean energy diplomacy to emerge from the shadow of Saudi Arabia's traditional regional influence. (Sim, 2022)

The competition over exploiting environmental politics has mainly dwindled away over the blockade that created other priorities for Doha. However, other environmental-related problems also turned up. In spring 2020, Abu Dhabi completed its first commercial nuclear power station in the Arab region. With this reactor, Abu Dhabi seeks to lower its dependence on importing cheap gas from Qatar (Al-Saidi et al., 2019). Meanwhile, the development of the Barakah nuclear power plant, which is located closer to Qatar than Abu Dhabi's capital, added to the tensions between both countries. In this regard, it prompted Qatari policymakers to bring concerns over safety, the unclear ecological regulations of nuclear waste and the lack of cooperation to the International Atomic Energy Agency (IAEA).

Incorporating 'Green' into the Gulf States' Branding Strategies

In addition to regional dynamics that are related specifically to the GCC ecosystem, several GCC monarchies have made use of the rise of green topics around the globe to better position themselves in a forthcoming carbon and climate constrained world. One of these strategies relates to branding and the desire to foster regime popularity among the national and international community. Hereby, one can also notice how some Gulf leaders use the environmental and climate crisis by projecting itself as the sole legitimate steward of the environment.

It is academic wisdom that advocating environmental sustainability has great potential for image-polishing both domestically and internationally—at least if one is able to frame it right (Karlsson et al., 2012). Traditionally, the terminology of a brand stems from the economic marketplace. While it is often understood as the process of selling a specific product by advertising it to the customer, it can also become the product, i.e. a particular lifestyle choice or political philosophy. Here, it is the idea that is 'sold'. For instance, Germany is famous for luxurious cars, Italy for its food, France for its wine and so forth. Every process of branding constitutes part of the competition for gaining the highest reputation (van Ham, 2008; further: Jordan, 2014). For a long time, companies have integrated sustainability as part of their branding strategy "to appeal to clients that are concerned about sustainability, and thus, grant a competitive advantage" (Kumar & Christodoulopoulou, 2014: 9). This can also be applied to a broad range of agency such as the non-profit sector, the arts, governments and even supranational bodies (Koch, 2018). For instance, studies on the European Union show its attempts to portray itself as a legitimate green leader, revealing how the field of environmental sustainability offers opportunities for state branding (Gupta & Ringius, 2001; Kilian & Elgström, 2010). Some GCC states such as Dubai, Qatar and Abu Dhabi have a long-established reputation for branding (e.g. the 'Dubai model') in various niches (Hvidt, 2020; Peterson, 2006).[14] While their branding was for a long time characterized by a luxurious, ultramodern and unsustainable lifestyle based on the excessive exploitation of natural resources to the detriment of the environment, things changed slowly during the mid-2000s. As Luomi aptly demonstrates, negative resonance in media and low performance in international climate rankings and indices had a huge effect on the countries' "image conscious leaderships" (Luomi, 2012, 106). Particularly, the above-mentioned pioneers of branding increasingly aligned their national policies and hypermodern development models with broader branding strategies to banish their images as leading climate-polluters (Reiche, 2010, 8). As Natalie Koch pinpoints more accurately:

> Conspicuous sustainability can be useful in this regard, as it may deflect attention from a problematic, harmful, or at least contentious practice or industry. Its diversionary potential rests on the ability to guide the conversation in one direction, while potential problems or criticisms go unnamed. (Koch, 2018, 532)[15]

[14] Interview #11 and interview #26.

[15] Koch describes conspicuous sustainability as a practice "when a community or organization undertakes an initiative that gains much of its value from its visibility, iconicity

Yet, promoting environmental sustainability has further benefits to other globally popular 'vanity niches' such as sport, iconic architecture or arts. Since sustainable and energy efficient technology is perceived as the backbone of a prosperous development in future, "it will dovetail with existing industrial structures in the Gulf" (Hertog & Luciani, 2012, 249). Moreover, and following Li-Chem Sim, it can be argued that in general sustainability is considered a "'good' universal idea aimed at global betterment in today's social context" that is desirable, and those who are very active should be "rewarded for its goodness" (Sim, 2012, 87). In this vein, within an ecologically conscious world "'being green' is increasingly seen as a mark of progressive thinking" (Koch, 2018, 528).

Branding unfolds in many different arenas and its manifestations are sometimes an 'illusive by-product'. Aspects such as environmental diplomacy or environmental hedging that will be explained in the upcoming section can also be part of a broader green branding strategy (Zumbraegel, 2020a). Accordingly, branding can be part of a stronger environmental integration within the political body of the UNFCCC or through other diplomatic channels. Additionally, branding is important for attracting foreign investment. One need only think of investment vehicles and branding examples par excellence, such as Abu Dhabi's Masdar City or Saudi Arabia's NEOM initiative that have established transnational links to private and public sectors all over the world and attracted a lot of attention and other benefits (e.g. hosting IRENA or Siemens). With regard to Masdar, Hertog explains: "(…) it appears clear that Masdar's wider zero-carbon target was conceived before its commercial feasibility was assessed. Its purpose was symbolic and the audience international" (Hertog, 2017, 14).

Hertog's statement addresses the question of who the audience is, when it comes to branding. Both formalized environmental diplomacy and economic-oriented sustainability hedging strategies address a specific audience, for instance the global climate regime or international investors. In the following, I will rather focus on green branding as a general way to increase the state and leadership's reputation—in other words, for image-building. So far, much discussion on GCC branding has focused on the outside world (e.g. Kamrava, 2015; Roberts, 2017). These studies rely on van Ham's suggestion that it is particularly about constructing a specific

and symbolism (rather than from the environmental benefits it produces" (ibid., 2018, 532).

image to the outside world and not necessarily associated with a deep-rooted change in values and identity (van Ham, 2008, 128). Yet, as Paul Jordan reminds us, there is also an inward-oriented approach to nation branding (Jordan, 2014). Consequently, it can be argued that branding strategies might be primarily for gaining external attraction, but they are also closely interlinked with the national level and can fuel national sentiments (Zumbraegel, 2020a). Also, in the GCC, many sustainability projects are not exclusively implemented to impress the outside world and to attract positive press. Instead, they are often deeply imbued with national values. As Pernilla Ouis has demonstrated by using the example of the UAE's greening efforts: The idea of "'rolling back the desert', is promoted as a source and symbol of national pride" (Ouis, 2002, 337). This is not to equate nation branding with national identity building (*huwīya al-wataniyya*) (see: Jordan, 2014) but the former can certainly trigger domestic admiration and appreciation in the sense of national pride, a sense of belonging and perhaps a feeling of superiority to other nations. In short, it can constitute part of a nation's 'belief system' or one facet of a broader 'we-identity'. The methods of branding messages are both material (e.g. tangible outputs) and immaterial (e.g. narratives, sentimentality and rhetorical framing). This is often manifested through built structures like architectural monuments or landscapes as well as national and global events. The following sections discuss two aspects of 'belief systems' in the GCC, namely the elements of monarchism and personalism and how they are creatively connected to environmental sustainability.[16]

Monarchical Distinctiveness: The Neo-Traditional Brand and Ecological Modernization

Often described as anachronistic, Gulf monarchies have managed to preserve their traditional patterns of state formation and successfully embedded this political culture and 'belief system' into a modern design

[16] As Chapter 4 indicates, another factor is the strategic rhetorical branding of environmental sustainability. As Natalie Koch states: "Sustainability rhetoric is also especially flexible because it allows speakers to reference vague, global issues, and position ecological challenges as those facing all of humanity and having uncertain origins" (Koch, 2018, 532). This 'discourse power' is often applied by key elites and the state-controlled or state-affiliated media and encompasses various strategies of whitewashing, concealment and/or blame shifting.

of dynastical rule. This combination of traditional elements and cutting-edge modernization has also been described as 'neo-traditional' or 'post-traditional' (Peterson, 2005, 2) and constitutes an important lever for the political legitimacy of the monarchies. Many studies have emphasized how pre-modern elements have been carefully translated into a modern (nation) state. Most apparent is the preservation of traditional patterns of participation (*majlis*) and consultation (*shura*) as important formalized institutional settings (see Chapter 2). Environmental sustainability, however, also offers several entry points for marketing this specific idea or distinctive vision. On the one hand, monarchs might evoke traditional narratives of Islamic and/or national heritage and link these to environmental protection and conservation in order to cultivate a sense of 'we-identity' (Wilson, 2017). On the other hand, sustainability as a modern trend ensures the perception of a country as being at the vanguard of modernity, development and innovation. In this sense, they can continue their development of "high modernism" that has been taking place since the first oil boom (Kamrava, 2015, 14).

Firstly, many official documents and strategic long-term development plans of the Gulf monarchies are underpinned by an imperative to protect the environment. For instance, articles 29 and 33 of Qatar's constitution emphasize that the state shall preserve the given resources and natural wealth as well as "protect the environment and its natural balance" (Ministry of Development Planning & Statistics, 2018, 283). Similarly, Qatar's National Vision, 2030 reiterates the words of Sheikha Moza, who stresses: "We need to care for our natural environment for it was entrusted to us by God to use with responsibility and respect for the benefit of human kind. If we nurture our environment, it will nurture us" (General Secretariat for Development Planning, 2008, 30). In the Saudi Vision 2030, the first section on environmental sustainability belies a similar thought: "By preserving our environment and natural resources, we fulfil our Islamic, human and moral duties" (Saudi Vision 2030, 2018, 23). Here, conserving the environment can be equalized with conserving the nation state and religious beliefs. Thus, policymakers strategically intend to nurture a common sense ('belief system') among the citizens. In Kuwait, environmental sustainability is often linked to the country's young but turbulent history. When celebrating the annual International Day for Preventing the Exploitation of the Environment in War and Armed Conflict, for instance, state-led agencies such as the Kuwait Environment Public Authority (EPA) take those events as an opportunity not only to remember the catastrophe of 1991 but also to emphasize Kuwait's aspiration to be at the forefront of environmental protection based on past experiences.

Additionally, common undertakings generate a sense of belonging. This is best reflected by greening campaigns performed by the government or state-affiliated entities from the private sector. Examples include a 'no paper' day, the planting of a million trees, beach clean-up events, sponsoring green marathons and several awards for green best practices (Al Othman & Clarke, 2017). More symbolic events like Earth Hour, which has gained popularity among Gulf citizens in recent years, as well as an increasing number of environmental symposiums and exhibitions, further trigger a sense of 'we' through raising awareness for the surrounding environment. To some extent, topics of environmental awareness and protection have also been put under a religious banner to serve the values of the respective society. For instance, shortly before and during the climate conference, the Qatar Islamic Cultural Centre initiated a coordinated message about the environmental responsibility of every citizen. Around 150 mosques around Qatar took part in the campaign.[17] In some contexts, mainly intellectual circles, debates about the Islamic-based concept of *zohd*, roughly paraphrased as a sufficient lifestyle and the idea of degrowth, have evolved.[18]

Secondly, while environmental sustainability can act as a lever to preserve existing traditional values and contribute to a common belief system, it also perfectly fits into the Gulf monarchies' narrative of modernity. This approach of ecological modernization (Al-Saidi & Elagib, 2018) unfolds through a mix of greening well-established branding strategies such as hosting international events and showcasing a cutting-edge built environment. For instance, Gulf states garner attention by organizing meetings, incentives, conferences and exhibitions (MICE) on environmental sustainability. Over the last few years, numerous sustainability-coined events have been established across the Gulf to sketch out business opportunities and facilitate cooperation and partnerships. Certain annual events such as the Sustainability Week and World Future Summit in Abu Dhabi or the Kuwait Green Building Conference and Exhibition as well as occasional events such as Dubai's Solar Middle East Exhibition (2014),

[17] Interview #20 and interview #23.

[18] Interview #59.

Clean Energy Forum (2014), World Green Economy Summit or the MENA Climate Week 2022 help the Gulf states in greening their images (*Khaleeji Times*, 2021, July 3). At the same time, Gulf states can present their cutting-edge technology and innovation with regard to environmental sustainability. Part of this strategy is also the greening of global events such as the FIFA World Cup 2022 or Dubai's Green Expo 2020, presenting these as the 'greenest' such event ever to take place (Bianco, 2021; Koch, forthcoming; Sankar, 2021, June 22).[19]

In addition to this MICE strategy, iconic architecture and spectacular urban development have long constituted useful framings of these branding messages. One needs only to think of the number of record-breaking buildings in the UAE or Qatar. While Masdar City is a prime example of an inherently sustainable role model city, there are many other projects and initiatives that have a primarily different goal but act as "an effective 'demo" of environmental sustainability (Koch, 2018, 533). This includes Qatar Foundation's Education City, Saudi Arabia's new tourist and technology hub, NEOM, or many of the university campuses that have emerged over the last years as part of the striving towards a knowledge-based economy (Alraouf & Clarke, 2017; Zaidan & Abdulibdeh, 2021). In fact, since knowledge production is seen as one solution to the 'resource curse' and promises prosperity and wealth beyond oil and gas, new green laboratories, incubators and other R&D facilities often gleam in sustainable state-of-the-art buildings (Koch, 2018). Overall, there is much evidence that Gulf states now dissociate from the once admired 'Dubai Model' with its glass-fronted skyscrapers, poor insulation and heavy air conditioning. Instead, "urban sustainability" is the new "orthodoxy" (Koch 2014, 1118). Certainly, large areas of Gulf cities are still cluttered up with unsustainable buildings, but they are not promoted and marketed in the same way as their greener peers (Zaidan & Abdulibdeh, 2021). For instance, Qatar's approach to sustainable urban planning comprises spectacular projects such as the construction of eight (previously twelve) low-carbon stadia for the FIFA 2022.[20] Other urban megaprojects like the creation of a smart and green transportation system (the Doha Metro), as well as sustainable hubs such as Lusail City, Barwa

[19] Interview #67.

[20] The reduction of the number is based on late fiscal shortcomings but is not considered as a problem since the previous plan of twelve stadia had the capacity to accommodate the entire Qatari population twice, compare: Herb (2014, 134).

City and Msheireb Downtown, vividly illustrate how the state remains in control of green output and the marketing of it (Kamrava, 2015). In many cases, Western individuals and companies are involved in this "sustainability spectacle" that guarantees also global attention (Koch, forthcoming). As Natalie Koch notes by the example of Abu Dhabi's Masdar project that was developed by the British 'starchitect' Norman Foster and his architecture firm, Foster + Partners:

> Involving Foster was guaranteed to get Masdar spectacular treatment in the media. Foster is not famous just because of his sensational buildings, but because he relishes the limelight and is highly skilled at curating the spectacle around his work. (Koch, forthcoming)

Some icons are constructed in clear differentiation to this kind of Western-inspired architecture (Koch, 2018; Rizzo, 2013). For instance, spaces in Qatar such as Suq Waqif, the headquarters of the Qatar Foundation, as well as more recent projects like Katara and Msheireb, combine modern and old elements to represent local values and correspond with climatic conditions (Al-Nakib, 2020, 76; Rizzo, 2014). The campuses of Saudi Arabia's KAUST and Qatar University are explicitly designed to resemble traditional Arabian villages (Koch, 2018). In this vein, old Arab and Islamic patterns such as wide streets (*sikak*), external wooden panels (*mashrābīh*) or wind tower housing patterns (*bargīl*) have carefully recaptured traditional heritage and architecture (Alraouf & Clarke, 2017; Koch 2014). The development of these sustainable 'heritage villages' is part of a broader "heritage boom" (Abbot, 2020, 52). In this vein, urban centres in the Gulf try to manage the balancing act between being a cosmopolitan, open city and providing their residents with a feeling of cultural imprint that many gave up for lost in light of hegemonic globalization (Koch, 2018; Zaidan & Abdulibdeh, 2021). Populist celebrations of these icons include award ceremonies that further promote this 'own style', domestically and internationally. For instance, when Qatar's flagship project Msheireb Downtown Doha won a sustainable award in 2013, the acting CEO of Msheireb Properties told the press:

> We are extremely proud to be recognised for the pioneering work we are currently undertaking in the field of sustainability. We hope that the project will provide an inspiration to other cities around the world on how

> to blend innovative design that is inspired by the past with the latest in sustainable solutions. (*The Peninsula*, 2013, October 13)

The growing importance of marketing green aspirations through urban sustainability underscores the importance of cutting-edge architecture as branding strategy. According to Gardner: "Gulf cities are the trophy cases of a people and its leadership" (Gardner, 2017, 349), aiming at communicating a specific message of role model, both to its people and to a global audience. The new focus of combining a high-tech and "an imagined pre-modern, Bedouin-inspired environmentalism" (Luomi, 2012, 196) is just another facet of this neo-traditional aspect as described at the start of this chapter. Moreover, it must also be seen as a regional and international contest about who wins "the title of creating the 'greenest', 'eco-friendliest', or 'most sustainable' city" (Rizzo, 2017, 2). This branding of a distinctive model of sustainability and promotion of cultural superiority is another manifestation of the above-mentioned regional competition over certain niches.

Personal Branding: Climate Saviors

As already stated, the concepts of state and regime conflate in the highly personalist Gulf monarchies. Here, kings, emirs and sultans rule the state as their own personal property (Gause & Yom, 2012). Hence, individual monarchs and royals design their own vision of a national setting and gain legitimacy for their own claims to power by propagating this through specific framing and narratives that are closely associated with themselves. Monarchs foster 'cults of personality' or a "personalism-based legitimacy claim" (Soest & Grauvogel, 2017, 3) by portraying the people at the top of the state as enlightened "modernization managers", who care about their people (Derichs & Demmelhuber, 2014, 189). Patterns of sustainable development are constructed in relation to the head of states to highlight their charisma and paint them as 'strongman', 'father of the nation', 'conscientious monarch' and 'innovative dynastic enterprise', who also cares about the environment and global warming. Rephrased, ruling elites tailor environmental decisions and actions in order to foster personal image-building and glorify the leader's charisma. It resembles a point already made by Bailes in 1976. According to him, "Stalin's own name and reputation were more closely associated with the practice of technological legitimation than any other major leader during this period" (Bailes, 1976, 80).

One very commonly used practice is name recognition, whereby environmentally-friendly vanity projects are closely linked to the respective ruler at the top of the state.[21] For instance, already in 1987, Kuwait's Supreme Council for the Environment opened the Sabah Al-Ahmad Natural Reserve as the largest protected terrestrial ecosystem. In 2012, construction began of the Muhammed bin Rashid Al Maktoum Solar Park, Dubai's biggest solar-generated power plant. Since it bore his name, Muhammed bin Rashid Al Maktoum personally inaugurated the project with much fanfare. Manifold other prominent examples connecting sustainability and personal image-building can be found, particularly in Saudi Arabia. The fact that green entities such as KAUST, KAPSARC and K·A·CARE, as well as smaller initiatives (e.g. King Abdullah Initiative for solar water desalination, King Abdullah Center for Energy Efficiency) bear the name of the late King Abdullah, manifests a distinctive personification. Such an attempt to garner personal legitimacy through a green framing has also been continued by his successors, King Salman and his son. Examples include the proclamation of the King Salman Renewable Energy Initiative, a King Salman Park, the King Salman Environmental Awareness and Sustainable Development Program and the creation of the King Salman bin Abdulaziz Royal Natural Reserve and the Mohammed bin Salman Natural Reserve. Additionally, environmental forums and summits have taken place under the patronage of the Saudi leaders. This is not only confined to the domestic arena but also applies externally. Just recently, one of Africa's largest solar plants, the Mohamed bin Zayed complex, was inaugurated in Togo (*The National*, 2021, June 23).

However, grand prestigious sustainable projects do not always integrate the name of a specific ruler. In some instances, a strategic media framing of a certain project as personal concern of a ruler is already sufficient. In the words of Rizzo, mushrooming green projects are "invariably presented as the brainchild of a key figure in the ruling family (…) and portrayed as a grand gesture" (Rizzo, 2017, 10). Most recently, Saudi Arabia's superlative NEOM project cannot be disassociated from the Crown Prince, Mohammed bin Salman. Similarly, his Saudi and Middle East Green Initiatives are closely bound to his person. In Qatar, all

[21] Interview #25 and interview #45.

high-profile projects have been continually portrayed as 'seeds' of the emir's wisdom and vision (Koch, 2014). A special role is also dedicated to Sheikha Moza in this kind of personal image-building. As patron of QF, she is inevitably associated with the country's eco-friendly label. In the UAE, the sustainable transformation is mainly framed under the banner of preserving the environmental legacy of the founding father, Sheikh Zayed bin Sultan Al Nahyan, who is famous for his personal interest in preserving the ecological landscape and biodiversity (Davidson, 2009; Günel, 2019; Koch, forthcoming). His successors have not only maintained much of his legacy but continue to enhance the country's environmental sustainability. A well-known example is the generously endowed Zayed Sustainability Prize (formerly the Zayed Future Energy Prize), in honour of the founding father, which annually awards cutting-edge and innovative sustainable solutions across different categories. In 2021, award applications hit a new record with around 4000 entries from 151 countries, indicating the international appeal of the Zayed Prize. During the ceremony, Sultan al-Jaber commented: "Inspired by the legacy of the UAE's Founding Father, the late Sheikh Zayed bin Sultan Al Nahyan, the prize continues to demonstrate the UAE's commitment to promoting sustainability and humanitarianism" (*The National*, 2021, June 3).

Adorning a programme with the great popularity of late Sheikh Zayed can be useful, in particular for younger leaders, who are yet to garner their own personal legitimacy. Additionally, others, often second-tier royals, have established manifold ecological conservation and wildlife protection programmes. Royals in Saudi Arabia, Oman and the UAE have taken a vanguard role in wildlife preservation programmes that protect endangered species like the Arabian (white) oryx. As Jeannie Sowers rightly points out, the fact that these programmes are often run in cooperation with international organizations such as the World Wildlife Fund is not without a certain degree of irony, as it is the royals themselves who have had a substantial impact in decimating the natural landscape and biodiversity through unregulated hunting and illegal poaching (Sowers, 2018).

Global Environmental Governance and Environmental Diplomacy: A New International Stage for the Gulf Monarchies

The Global Climate Regime and Governance Processes

Environmental diplomacy can be narrowly described as negotiations over environmental issues by nation states. While environmental diplomacy dates back at least to the middle of the last century, its importance grew with the environmental institutionalization process of the United Nations (Al-Saidi et al., 2019). Since climate change is a collective challenge (Never, 2014), states have built coalitions, institutions and mechanisms to counter climate threats in the form of a global governance. Such a climate governance can be best described as "all purposeful measures aimed at steering social systems toward preventing, mitigating, or adapting to the risks posed by climate change" (Jagers & Stripple, 2003, 388). Although events such as the first climate summit in Stockholm in 1972 or the creation of UNEP in 1988 may be marked as the beginning of an international environmental policy, it was the United Nations Conference on Environment and Development in Rio de Janeiro 1992 which received much more attention and is labelled as a milestone for the global integration of environmental protection. Ultimately, it was the Rio summit that gave rise to the United Nations Framework Convention on Climate Change (UNFCCC); as the only international frame of reference with broad legitimacy so far, it has a key role to play. The body is divided into three different blocs, namely industrialized nations (Annex I parties), economies in transition (Annex II) and developing countries (non-Annex I parties). Under the framework of common but differentiated responsibilities, Annex I and II countries shall assist non-Annex I countries with financial or technical resources or other forms of capacity building.

The regular conference of the parties (COP) is the supreme decision-making body of the convention, where all states which have signed the treaty are represented and make decisions and arrangements. Ad Hoc Working Groups can be described as the main pillars for the conceptual and institutional evolution of the UNFCCC.

A well-known example for a binding commitment is the Kyoto Protocol which was adopted at the COP3 1997 in Japan but not put into practice until 2005. All states which have signed the ratification regularly meet at the Conference of the Parties of the Kyoto Protocol

(CMP), while those states which have not ratified participate as observers. The Kyoto Protocol sets out a steady decrease in GHG emissions by the participating countries that should occur in two stages: At least 5% below 1990 levels in the first commitment period (2008–2012) and at least 18% in the following period (2013–2020). Furthermore, it seeks the financial compensation of developing countries by developed countries, technology transfer and capacity building for making countries less vulnerable to climate change on a national level. However, despite the existence of a (theoretical) Kyoto Protocol penalty, a practical enforcement of the agreement was essentially non-existent: When a country has failed the targets of the Kyoto Protocol, it has had almost no consequences, because countries were allowed to set new targets or easily withdraw from the agreement. Consequently, during the COPs since Kyoto, questions have arisen about the main perpetrators, the principle of state sovereignty, the non-interference into a country's environmental capital[22] and the willingness for concessions that have led to a division between the party blocs (Annex and non-Annex countries). Vehicles to appease the different standpoints have been established through the Kyoto Protocol's Clean Development Mechanism (CDM), which is a kind of tradable certified emission system for Annex countries to support non-Annex countries, and Nationally Appropriate Mitigation Actions (NAMAs), which were created during the COP in Bali in 2007 with the aim of encouraging developing countries to reduce emissions and receive funding for it from the UNFCCC (Luomi, 2014; Magnani, 2012). According to Luomi, in contrast to the CDM, the more flexible character of NAMAs have made them to "become the de facto main vehicle" (Luomi, 2014, 7). Yet, the so-called firewall between clear commitments of industrialized nations and voluntary actions for developing nations appears difficult to overcome. As a consequence, the Paris Agreement of 2015 during the COP21 reinforced bottom-up initiatives by demanding that every member submit individual intended nationally determined contributions (INDCs) (Kinley, 2017, 10). Although there is still no official sanctioning mechanism if a country fails to do so, this provides a more nuanced approach of collective willingness instead of a strong division between industrialized and developing countries (Kinley, 2017, 11).

[22] Environmental capital means "the portion of a country's overall capital assets that directly relate to the environment—for example, forests, soil quality, and ground water" (Todaro & Smith, 2012, 476).

It would be misleading, however, to understand the international climate regime solely as a state actor issue within the UNFCCC: As Lisa Campbell and colleagues have pointed out, it is environmental governance which is produced by formal agreements and decisions at global environmental meetings. It must be noted in this context that governments do not determine the outcome and process in absolute isolation. The underlying scientific basis for what needs to be done in terms of climate change stems from the annual reports of the Intergovernmental Panel for Climate Change (IPCC). The IPCC's reports have a great influence on the discussion and understanding of climate threats and thus, in the end, have a huge impact on the policy decision-dynamics. Additionally, there is always an active audience including non-governmental and intergovernmental organizations, businesses and parts of civil society who observe these meetings and influence the outcomes (Campbell et al., 2014). These include non-state actors of environmental stewardship like Greenpeace or WWF as well as other global institutions such as World Bank, the International Renewable Energy Agency (IRENA), International Energy Agency (IEA), Global Environment Facility and Carbon Sequestration Leadership Forum. Additionally, a number of states are represented through different groups such as G77+ China, European Union, Association of Small Island States, OPEC and the like, which have a great impact on the global climate decision-making dynamics.

Despite their high income, the GCC monarchies are not categorized as Annex countries within the UNFCCC, which means that they do not have binding emission reduction targets. All six Gulf states were early members of the Convention, joining the UNFCC between 1994 and 1996 and ratified the Kyoto Protocol between 2005 and 2006. However, their impact has not been non-existent but rather defective. While the Arab League always had a weak role in the international climate regime, the environmental agenda shifted to the Organization of Arab Petroleum Exporting Countries (OAPEC). Due to a lack of competing voices, this organization had been constantly perceived as speaking for the whole Arab region with the consequence to advance the Gulf monarchies' interest over other countries (Althaus, 2012). Although Oman and Bahrain are not members of the OAPEC group, they have frequently seen their interests best represented by aligning with its most powerful member, Saudi Arabia. For a long time, Saudi Arabia "has been the only Arab state attending the UNFCCC meetings with well-prepared, vocal, and large delegations" outdoing other Arab nations and bolstering its position as dominant leader within the global climate regime (Luomi, 2012, 202). Also, within the GCC, all other states supported the Saudi position either because of foreign policy dependence (e.g. Bahrain) or a mix of interest alignment and conformity. Their roles were largely described as "generally invisible and quiet", echoing statements by the skilfully and rhetorically versed Saudi delegation.[23] Only on a few occasions have the UAE, Qatar and Oman deviated from the standpoint of their big neighbour and its minimal requirement policy (Luomi, 2012). In general, authorities across the Gulf feared that any international regulations on reducing GHG emissions might result in a decrease of its oil and gas exports (Al-Saidi et al., 2019). Moreover, regulations on behalf of the UNFCCC were perceived as an external interference in their environmental capital and thus a threat to their sovereignty.

In this vein, Saudi Arabia fiercely fought against the 1.5 °C target and opposed measures on decarbonization during international conferences such as the 2002 Johannesburg World Summit on Sustainable Development (Sever et al., 2019). Furthermore, as one of very few countries, the kingdom opposed any serious efforts to achieve comprehensive climate targets during the 2009 Copenhagen Conference (COP15) (Al-Saidi et al., 2019). The obstructionist policy of the kingdom received some scholarly attention (e.g. Aarts & Janssen, 2003; Luomi, 2009; Vrojilk, 2003). Joanna Depledge has described Saudi Arabia's tactics to impede the negotiations, which include (1) victimhood (demanding compensation for 'adverse effects'); (2) avoiding commitments (refusing, postponing or delaying the process of decision-making); and (3) seeking alliances with countries pursuing the same interests of preserving oil revenues to support former tactics (Depledge, 2008).

The question that remains is why countries such as Saudi Arabia enter forums like the UNFCCC? This is even more interesting since scholarship generally argues that autocratic states (like the GCC) are "less inclined to enter into legally binding forms of cooperation" (von Soest, 2015, 6). According to Depledge, Saudi Arabia and its GCC fellows joined the global climate regime to influence the proceedings and hamper it, wherever possible. With regard to the Kyoto Protocol, she assures a strategic behaviour of accession:

[23] Interview #51.

> It is interesting to note that eight OPEC members waited until there was certainty that the Kyoto Protocol would enter into force, and then acceded to it within a few months (the Protocol had been open for ratification for six years, receiving 128 ratifications, before that point). (Depledge, 2008, 12)

Similarly, in light of the 'firewall' between Annex and non-Annex countries, other scholars have raised the point that countries which had not been directly targeted by the Kyoto Protocol could obstruct the negotiations because a practical enforcement mechanism is essentially non-existent (Bodansky, 1999: 617). In this vein, Saudi Arabia managed to "slow [...] down the climate protection and reduction target negotiations, and thus protect the status of petroleum in the global energy industry" (Althaus, 2012, 2). In this sense, Saudi Arabia has changed its strategy from a cautious or obstructionist approach towards a progressive involvement (Sever et al., 2019). Indeed, the times when the Saudi delegation openly objected to a relationship between human activities and climate change as it did during the preparations for the climate accord in Copenhagen in 2009 might be over. This is not to say, however, that Saudi Arabia and other GCC states have developed a genuine interest towards climate change and carbon reduction. As has been noted, both Saudi Arabia and Kuwait joined the USA and Russia to counteract a measure to support the scientific findings of the latest report by the UN Intergovernmental Panel on Climate Change (IPCC) (Al-Saidi et al., 2019, 10). Prior to the latest climate summit in Glasgow in November 2021, leaked documents revealed that the Saudi kingdom (as well as other nations) tried to influence the negotiation process in their favour (Rowlatt & Gerken, 2021, October 21). This reflects a broader development of stronger environmental diplomacy and emancipation that has diffused among the GCC states.

From Reluctance Towards Setting and Shaping the Agenda

Over the last years, one can observe a policy shift within the Saudi-led GCC bloc towards the UNFCCC that is characterized by a more progressive participation (Luomi & Michaelowa, 2012). The latter has been described as primarily benefit-oriented and rent-seeking motivation to receive capacity building, technology transfer or financial compensation for their climate transition (Al-Sarihi & Mason, 2020). In this vein, the number of Designated National Authorities (DNA) to the UNFCCC increased significantly. DNA bodies intend to streamline national climate efforts that comply with international agreements and commitments. Furthermore, they are a precondition to registering for Clean Development Mechanism (CDM) projects through which they receive financial and/or technological assistance from the UNFCCC. Additionally, all GCC states have signed and ratified the Paris Climate Agreement and have prepared and communicated their Nationally Determined Contributions (NDCs) to the UNFCCC (Sever et al., 2019; Wogan et al., 2019).

This 'de-decarbonization policy 2.0' to proactively influence the course of action is also seen in other contexts. As Luomi observed: "The oil-exporting monarchies have monopolized regional climate policy at the level of declarations" (Luomi, 2012, 259). Examples include the Abu Dhabi Declaration on Environment and Energy (2003), the Arab Ministerial Declaration on Climate Change (2007) and the Statement on Climate Change issued by the Council of Arab Ministers Responsible for the Environment (2009). Conformity among the GCC is particularly apparent when it comes to core aspects of energy security and sovereignty. In this vein, greater willingness towards decarbonization can be noticed, in the form of 'throw in' strategies (Krane, 2021). Among these are already introduced measures such as carbon utilization and carbon capture and storage, enhanced oil recovery, CDM-certified projects and the management of gas flares. The new approach is also accelerated by more engagement in other multilateral treaties and programmes in an attempt to foster international linkages and leverage (Zumbraegel, 2019). As one very early example, Saudi Arabia and the UAE joined the Carbon Sequestration Leadership Forum, the only Arab countries to do so. During an OPEC summit in 2007, several GCC heads of states promised to invest $300 billion for research on energy, environment and climate change (Depledge, 2008). Qatar and UAE, in turn, facilitated partnerships by taking part in various organizations such as the Global Green Growth Forum and the Global Green Growth Institute (Luomi, 2015). In 2015, Saudi Arabia, the UAE and Oman joined the International Solar Alliance that was conceived as a joint effort by France and India in the scope of the COP21 in Paris that year.

A salient and early example of cooperation is the EU-GCC Clean Energy Technology Network. This multi-stakeholder platform was established in 2009 and jointly hosted the Gulf Research Center Foundation

(Geneva), the National Technical University of Athens and Masdar Institute of Science and Technology (Abu Dhabi). Bringing together hundreds of actors from different backgrounds, it has fostered the promotion of knowledge, technology and strengthening cooperation. One could say that the materialization of around sixty successful initiatives by 2016 is more than modest, even though the period from 2010 to 2014 was mainly focused on research cooperation (Sever et al., 2019). In light of the renewed focus on sustainability, a four-year EU-GCC Joint Action Programme, running from 2010 to 2013, was also established. In the aftermath of the Paris Agreement, the EU launched the 'EU-GCC Clean Energy Network II' project. As previously, it continues the inter-regional cooperation in terms of renewable energy and efficient use of electricity and water (Bianco, 2021; Luomi, 2015).[24]

The scale and speed of the individual states, however, differ dramatically. As Jim Krane has exemplified on the Saudi case, behaviour varies between strategies of "dig in" (i.e. defending hydrocarbons), "join in" (i.e. implementing low-carbon policies that "provide secondary benefits") and "throw in" (i.e. accepting climate damage) (Krane, 2021, 304). Against this backdrop, the UAE as 'green advocate' tends to increasingly align its domestic climate action with its global commitment to combat climate change. While this 'throw in' strategy of taking the lead is illustrated by the UAE being the first GCC country to ratify the Paris Agreement and the most ambitious one in terms of submitting NDCs (Sever et al., 2019), it does not mean that the country completely dismisses the other strategies.

Qatar, in turn, applies a mixed method of greater participation but also defending hydrocarbons, especially its abundance of less emission-intensive natural gas as transition fuel. In this vein, Qatar's energy minister lately declared that "gas is sort of in a Catholic marriage with renewables. They would need to stay together for a very long time for you to have the transition successfully" (cited from: Bianco, 2021). Both leaderships in Doha and Abu Dhabi also tend to take a robustly independent position from their big Saudi neighbour. Meanwhile, the resource-poorer countries such as Bahrain and Oman outweigh a more constructive position towards climate change mitigation and adaptation in favour of the traditional agenda of "compensation for response measures-related losses"

[24] Interview #63 and interview #65.

(Luomi, 2012, 206). This position between 'dig in' and 'join in' is most apparent in Kuwait: As least diversified economy and highly dependent on oil exports, the Kuwaiti government remains in a difficult position between its traditional obstructionist position and positive incentives such as funds and technology transfer through UNFCCC-related mechanisms such as the CDM. Currently, five CDMs are under review, and since Paris in 2015, Kuwait obviously became eager to sign more international treaties such as a UN-led agreement on avoiding ozone-depleting substances used in air conditioners (Sever et al., 2019).

Within this policy shift from "climate antagonists to low-carbon protagonists" (Luomi & Michaelowa, 2012, 1), it is useful to have a closer look at the three most active states, Saudi Arabia, Qatar and the UAE, which all have their very own ulterior political motives. For instance, Saudi Arabia engages in environmental diplomacy to underline its regional leadership and diversify its international linkages. In this vein, it was a founding member of the above-mentioned Like-Minded Group within the UNFCCC that consists of oil-producing and developing economies which primarily demand more financial compensation and emissions reductions from the developed world. The kingdom further joined the Global Methane Initiative in early 2014 and is a member of the Four Kingdoms Initiative (along with the United Kingdom, Netherlands and Norway) for carbon capture utilization and storage. In 2015, Saudi Arabia joined the Clean Energy Ministerial and Mission and co-founded Oil and Gas Climate Initiative, where a large number of CEOs from the oil industry seek to find climate-resilient solutions to minimize the GHG emissions of oil-exporting countries (Al-Sarihi, 2021). Environmental sustainability has also been explored by the Saudi leadership as a profitable field to boost its status as member of the Group of Twenty (G20). In its presidency of the G20 group, Saudi Arabia played a role as "climate crusader". During a G20 meeting in Naples, it was reported that the Saudi energy minister "played an uncharacteristic role in trying to bring dawdling polluters on board" (Cox, 2021, August 5). Furthermore, it was during this time that the Saudi King Salman announced the launch of a new decarbonization initiative, the so-called Circular Carbon Economy National Program (Bianco, 2021; Al Shehri et al., 2022).[25] Most recently, and perhaps to counterbalance Emirati efforts,

[25] Interview #50 and interview #55.

Saudi Arabia joined other industrialized oil and gas producers such as the USA, Canada, Norway, and Qatar in forming a new platform. The so-called Net Zero Producers Forum aims at finding solutions to implement the Paris Agreement on climate change (Reuters, 2021, April 24). Prior to the COP26 in Glasgow in 2021, Saudi Arabia announced a net-zero target by 2060 that foresees a drastic reduction of GHG emissions already by 2030 (Al-Sarihi, 2021).

Meanwhile, the UAE and Qatar gradually seized their own active roles on the global environmental stage to escape the Saudi sphere and showcase themselves as environmentally responsible countries (Al-Saidi et al., 2019). Both states tend to foster self-projections as 'global good citizens' with environmentally-conscious leaders, despite their unsustainable and environmentally questionable use of resources. A remarkable, and for many also surprising, example was the decision to host the climate summit COP18 in Doha in 2012. Despite huge criticism (see Chapter 3), Qatar managed to improve its bad climate image and used the opportunity to pursue its very own state interests (Zumbraegel, 2019). In fact, one could say that Doha managed to "steal the show" from other players like Saudi Arabia and the UAE, especially in determining policies and perceptions within the global climate regime (Luomi, 2012, 218). However, it did not last very long. Instead, the UAE continued its more incremental but target-oriented approach of translating its domestic sustainability governance efforts to the international audience and fleshing out its green profile within the community. In other words, quite early on policymakers in Abu Dhabi saw the political capital of the international dimension. The 2009 campaign to host IRENA—that out-triumphed Germany and Austria—marked the starting point of a new role perception. This was seen as a key message to the international community, that an oil-rich and developing country from the Global South understands its commitment towards a green transition (Luomi, 2012, 210). The successful hosting of IRENA also gave the impetus to create a collective unit for international environmental diplomacy under the auspices of the Foreign Ministry (Luomi, 2012, 211).

The robust and autonomous approach of the UAE, and Abu Dhabi in particular, resulted also in a more independent role in the UNFCCC. The UAE started to monopolize international climate policies. In 2010, the Emirati delegation at the COP in Copenhagen opposed the Saudi diplomats by supporting the controversial Copenhagen Accords (Luomi, 2012, 210). Also in the following years, the UAE proactively lobbied the UNFCCC to foster its own reputation and sustainable agenda in the international environmental community. As a party to the UNFCCC, the UAE issued its National Communications in the years 2007, 2010, 2013 and 2018 and is thus the only Arab country that managed to submit its second NDC in the default time frame of five years. Furthermore, the adoption of a comprehensive green growth strategy (i.e. green economy concept) during the 2012s Rio Earth Summit (Rio+ 20) was a major success and a further example of the Emirate's formal engagement (Al-Saidi, 2021; Luomi, 2015; Zaidan, 2019). It also takes an active part in the Cartagena Dialogue for Progressive Action that seeks collective global solutions to fight climate change. In November 2015, Dubai also hosted the 27th Meeting of the Parties to the Montreal Protocol of the Vienna Convention for the Protection of the Ozone Layer. Still, as with other GCC states, the UAE positively influenced processes of global environmental governance towards decarbonization measures such as CCUS technology to ensure the "lifetime of the UAE's oil fields" (Al-Sarihi & Mason, 2020, 12). Another high point was the announcement that the COP28 will be hosted in Abu Dhabi.

Sustainability Hedging: A New Playground for Enhancing Partnerships

In contrast to environmental diplomacy that happens multilaterally and through formalized mechanisms within the global climate regime, sustainability hedging is rather more informal and economically driven. Over the last years, one can notice the erosion of long-term patterns of alliance towards redefining new strategic partners. In this vein, "strategic hedging is a type of behaviour that helps second-tier states deal with certain kinds of uncertainty existing in unipolar systems" with the aim "to improve their economic and military capabilities as they compete against the hegemon, but can still free-ride the benefits which the great power provides to the unipolar system" (Chaziza, 2015, 442). In short, it is an "insurance policy" based on diversifying partnerships (Lake, 1996, 15) and can be located "between the two ends of the balancing-bandwagoning spectrum" (Cheng-Chwee, 2008, 165).

Over the last decade, one can notice how the Gulf monarchies have taken a more assertive foreign policy course and agenda that goes beyond the traditional US alliance (see Chapter 3). Asian countries, particularly China, India, Japan and the Republic of Korea, have not only become the most important trading partners for hydrocarbons from the Gulf, but further investment flows across many other sectors and branches continue to flourish resulting in a rebalancing with regard to Western countries. Certainly, this 'easternization' correlates also with the announced Belt and Road Initiative, which were presented by China in 2013. As Mordechai Chaziza states: This conceptual partnership is based on a strategic hedging calculus, of which one dominant factor is "a common (...) desire to seize economic opportunities, especially regarding energy security" (Chaziza, 2015, 443). In addition to policy coordination via the China-GCC Strategic Dialogue (since 2010) and ongoing negotiations towards a China-GCC free trade agreement (since 2004), Sino-Gulf cooperation builds mainly upon bilateral relationships, with the UAE and Saudi Arabia both having a special role. Both countries have agreed on 'comprehensive strategic partnerships' as highest level of bilateral ties with China, whereas other Gulf states fall into the second category of 'strategic partnerships' (Fulton, 2018). According to strategic documents such as 'China's Arab Policy Paper', there are three core dimensions of cooperation, namely (a) energy, (b) construction and infrastructure, trade and investment and (c) nuclear energy, aerospace and new energy.

Notably, while there are several different types of hedging, this section focuses on economic hedging (see further: Al Daffa, 2017; Koga, 2017). It is assumed that the approach of scouting and scoring new economic partnerships is especially apparent in the field of environmental sustainability, and particularly clean technology, as it offers a window of opportunity to bolster new political and economic (inter-)dependencies. As Kristian Coates Ulrichsen notes on the example of the UAE:

> Growing collaboration between local and global providers of renewable energy technology are intended to accelerate the transfer of technology and the creation of organic research clusters that will, in turn, form the cornerstone of economic diversification in the UAE. (Coates Ulrichsen, 2017, 116)

Hedging can be traced on the basis of foreign direct investment (FDI) that is understood as "the transfer of tangible or intangible assets from one country into another for the purpose of their use in that country to generate wealth" (cited from: Al Daffa, 2017, 118). Basically, hedging may have two underlying strategies that both aim at seeking new business and investment opportunities: On the one hand, an inward-oriented strategy seeks to bolster partnerships with industrialized and modern countries for the purpose of technological buy-in and knowledge transfer. On the other hand, an outward-oriented strategy involves the wealthy and modern Gulf countries' direct engagement with sustainability issues in other contexts.

The GCC as a Lucrative Market for Green Business

Gulf monarchies are highly dependent on external investments but not so much because of capital injection but rather because of importing technology, know-how and expertise to diversify their economies in order to achieve their announced sustainability goals (See also: Nosova, 2017, 38). As one interviewee summarized: "It is rather about knowledge and technology transfer than anything else. The plan is to invite people and to have their expertise and then do it by their own".[26]

Knowledge and technology transfer constitutes a major pillar in the collaboration between Gulf and European countries. Various investors and consultants are involved in the GCC's clean energy transition. For instance, Dubai's supposedly 'clean' coal plant (Hassayen) has been advised by a consortium of British firms (Ernst & Young plus CMS) as financial and legal advisers, as well as the Canadian consultant WSP for its technical expertise (Germany Trade & Invest, 2019). German companies such as Thyssenkrupp, Siemens and LTI Re Energy have also been desirable partners for their technical expertise in deploying large- and small-scale sustainable energy projects in the Gulf (Germany Trade & Invest, 2020). The oil- and gas-rich regimes primarily focus on receiving the best available technology through various cooperative ventures in order to accumulate a green expertise and pioneering role (Hertog & Luciani, 2012). Gulf states have designed basically two ways of bolstering economic opportunities through external cooperation and transfer (Gray, 2019, 128).

For instance, external companies can develop international joint ventures with local businesses, which hold the majority (at least 51%) of the venture. This reflects the tradition of agency rights to favour the local business elite where foreign companies need a local sponsor or agent to conduct business activities (Coates Ulrichsen, 2016; Hertog, 2017).

[26] Interview #4.

Examples of this practice include the above-mentioned cooperation with subsidiaries of Qatar's investment vehicle Qatari Diar and European companies such as Deutsche Bahn International and Vinci Construction. In both cases, the German and French companies held 49% of the shares (see Chapter 5). The importance of external buy-in is particularly apparent in the energy market and the development of large utility-scale renewable power plants. At the same time, it also shows that the GCC's location in the so-called Global Sunbelt makes it an attractive destination as it has some of the highest solar irradiances, providing high potential for solar energy. Here, the role of Western companies is apparent, which can be explained by the longstanding historical partnership with Western states (Hanieh, 2019, 61). One example is the US-Saudi solar partnership during the 1970 and 1980s that was a crucial component of Riyadh's diversification strategy (see Chapter 3 and further: Salam & Khan, 2017). Until recently, especially American, German, Spanish and French companies, as well as to a lesser degree Scandinavian companies, have dominated the market and developed renewable energy projects in the GCC (see Table 6.1). Not surprisingly due to their larger output, the UAE and Saudi Arabia have the most diversified number of foreign developers.

Over the last two decades, however, one can see a closer cooperation with Asian countries. For instance, the 350 MW Noor Abu Dhabi solar farm was awarded to a consortium of Japan's Marubeni Corp and China's JinkoSolar Holding. In neighbouring Saudi Arabia, the Farasan Island Solar Project was established as a joint venture between the Saudi Electricity Company and Japanese Showa Shell Sekiyu (Young, 2019). Previously, the Japanese company Hitachi Zosen helped the Saudi kingdom in its research on solar desalination plants (Salam & Khan, 2017). In 2018, the Riyadh announced a solar megaproject with the Japanese multinational conglomerate SoftBank that, however, did not materialize (Mills, 2018). Most recently, a number of Indian solar developers (e.g. Talettutayi Solar Project and TP Saurya) received bids for (co-) developing solar projects in Saudi Arabia with a total capacity of 1.5 GW (PV Magazine, 2021, September 1). At the same time, the first signs of a greater Sino-Gulf cooperation on renewable energy appear to be on the horizon (Fulton, 2018; Mogielnicki, 2021). China has overseen the construction of large-scale projects including Saudi Arabia's Yanbu Refinery and a high-speed rail line that connects Jeddah with Mecca and Medina. Clean energy is another element of increasing importance.

Table 6.1 Overview of Western companies' involvement in renewable energy projects in the GCC 2019

Country	*Foreign developer/ops*	*Country of origin*
UAE	First Solar Inc	USA
	SunPower	
	Chinook Sciences (also United Kingdom)	
	TSK	Spain
	Abengoa	
	Vestas	Denmark
	Total	France
Saudi Arabia	Belectric	Germany
	Conergy	
	Solar Frontier	
	EDF Renewables	France
	Soitec	
	General Electric	USA
	Canadian Solar Inc	Canada
	TSK	Spain
Kuwait	TSK	Spain
	Gestamp Solar	
Bahrain	Petra Solar	USA
Oman	GlassPoint Solar	USA
Qatar	Monsson Group	Sweden

See also IRENA (2019), Salam and Khan (2017), and Young (2019)[27]

Already in 2016, when the Chinese president visited Riyadh, both countries signed an MoU between the Silk Road Fund and Saudi Arabia's ACWA Power. The Saudi company evolved into a strategic asset of Sino-Saudi cooperation. In summer 2019, it was reported that China's Silk Road Fund had purchased 49% of ACWA Renewable Energy Holding (Calabrese, 2021). China's JinkoSolar Holding and the French energy giant EDF have also emerged as the leading bidders in Abu Dhabi's latest 2 GW solar tender that should be completed in mid-2022. Furthermore, the Silk Fund is a major investor in Dubai's Clean Energy Strategy 2050. In this vein, China's Shanghai Electric Group Co. was awarded two EPC contracts to co-develop a 700 MW CSP project and a 900 MW PV park in the emirate (Calabrese, 2021). Qatar has also hedged towards

[27] The list includes established projects but also projects being actively worked on or apparently remain stationary, sources.

China—this surged in light of the preparation for the FIFA World Cup in 2022 but ebbed by the time of Qatar's isolation in 2017. Following Emir Tamim's state visit to Beijing and the signing of the strategic partnership agreement in 2014, investments in infrastructure and development contracts with a volume of around $8 billion were agreed. This included the contracting of the 2022 World Cup's biggest venue, Lusail Stadium, to a joint venture between Beijing-based China Railway Construction Corporation Limited and the Qatari company HBK Contracting (Coates Ulrichsen, 2016, 227). Furthermore, in 2020, it was announced that Oman's plans for a 500 MW Ibri II solar plant will be built with the help of the Asian Infrastructure Investment Bank, where China holds a major share (Calabrese, 2021). The project was completed in January 2022.

The Asian continent has also become important for the Gulf states in their pursuit of harnessing nuclear energy that is labelled as an additional 'clean' energy option (Chaziza, 2020). While previously the USA and to a much lesser extent France had been attractive partners in terms of atomic energy, the centre of gravity has shifted to Asia. The most salient example so far is Abu Dhabi's first commercial nuclear power plant, Barakah, that was developed with the assistance of the Korea Electric Power Corporation. At the same time, the UAE also collaborated with the China National Nuclear Corporation (CNNC) and announced a platform for nuclear technology and finance cooperation in summer 2019 (Andrews-Speed & Lixia, 2022). As stated previously, Saudi Arabia has ambitions to rely on nuclear technology as part of its energy diversification plans (see Chapter 4). The fiefdom K·A·CARE, which was created under late King Abdullah and steadily marginalized after his death in 2015, was entrusted with the implementation of the national atomic policy and sought international support in pushing forward the Saudi atomic energy programme (Sim, 2021a). In so doing, it signed several memoranda of understanding, among others with Asian countries including South Korea, Russia and China. It seems that the talks with China are most advanced. Lately, it was also reported that China and Saudi Arabia have started to produce uranium yellowcake at a facility in the desert between Medina and Tabuk (Chaziza, 2020).

Overall, Gulf states benefit from this practice of creating joint ventures between local companies and external partners as they gain external expertise and technology while also protecting their domestic economies, as legal frameworks ensure that external companies acquire not more than 49% of a local company or joint venture. These formal regulations, in combination with informal practices such as systematically privileging certain business families, help the capitalist class to cement their monopolistic structures and make it difficult for both smaller and foreign companies to enter the market. At the same time, however, regulations that promote local sponsorships have curbed the appetite of foreign investors, which is why GCC states have consistently removed the entry barriers of domestic protectionist regulations in order to attract incoming investments. While the UAE was the first, other states have also followed (Mogielnicki, 2021). For instance, Saudi Arabia allowed foreign investors to buy initial public offerings in the kingdom from 2017 onwards, Kuwait facilitated legislative reforms on foreign investments in the same year, whereas Qatar abandoned the previous limit of 49% of foreign investment in many cases by 2018 (Nosova, 2017; Young, 2019).

In addition to structural barriers regarding ownership, there are also investment risks, including technology and liquidity risks (Poudineh et al., 2019; Young, 2019). This is succinctly shown by the example of Qatar's solar industry: In 2014, the joint venture Qatar Solar Energy launched a manufacturing company. Located in Ras Laffan, the company aimed at producing PV cells with a capacity of around 300 MW annually, which was mainly exported. There had been plans to expand to 1 GW alternative energy systems over the next decade, but with SolarWorld becoming insolvent, it seems that Qatar Solar Energy has also been stopped (IRENA, 2019; Luomi, 2014). Furthermore, there are several examples of solar panels manufactured in Germany not being capable of performing equally in a harsh climate like the Arabian Peninsula (Al-Ubaydli et al., 2019). Especially, sand and dust on the panels can lead to ineffective performance.[28] In order to circumvent some of these risks and provide more incentives to foreign companies, Gulf countries rely on another strategy.

Another strategy to boost economic prosperity by relying on external help includes the creation of several special economic free zones that shall help to facilitate attractiveness to foreign investors and circumvent some of the existing attractiveness restrictive protectionist policies in the Gulf. These spatial enclaves within national boundaries are often disconnected from other urban districts and apply "rules of business [that] are different from those that prevail in the national territory" (Mogielnicki, 2021, 5;

[28] Interview #30.

also: Keshavarzian, 2010). While there are no universal definitions of free zones, these have certain characteristics: (a) they assure 100% foreign ownership without the need to rely on local sponsors, (b) there are no or limited labour laws so that foreign companies can import expatriate workers without complying with national quotas or specific workforce regulations, and (c) free zones are mainly tax-free areas including specific exemptions of import/export income, corporate income taxes, custom duty and low costs of operations (Hertog, 2017; Keshavarzian, 2010; Mogielnicki, 2021). While free zones are a valid option to stimulate business, attract investment and receive revenues such as rental fees, all of this comes with trade-offs as it can impede labour reforms of nationalization and result in a loss of revenues due to the tax exemptions (Jensen, 2018). Those demarcated commercial areas with eased rules were first established in the UAE. Without a doubt, the UAE, and particularly Dubai, pioneered the practice of free zones. Dubai and other northern emirates created the first free zones in the 1980s while other GCC states followed later, around the 2000s. By today, dozens of areas with the characteristics of free zones have been created, but there are only a few that exclusively focus on environmental sustainability so far.

The earliest official free zone in neighbouring Abu Dhabi was Masdar City. Its free zone opened in 2006 with a clear and strategic focus on green technology. As Robert Mogielnicki describes, "Masdar Free Zone also carefully regulated which companies obtained free zone licenses, which impacted a given firm's ability to secure major contracts" (Mogielnicki, 2021, 60). Since its inception, many multinational and smaller companies have settled in Masdar to benefit from the city's services and 'green business environment'. However, so far its tenants have not fulfilled initial expectations (Hertog, 2017). This includes local solar companies such as Alsa Solar Systems LLC (Dubai), Shams Power Company (Abu Dhabi) as well as branches of foreign companies involved in clean technology such as Abengoa (Spain) Canadian Solar Inc. (Canada), Siemens and Belectric (Germany), CNIM (France) as well as Grundfos (Denmark).[29] All business-oriented enterprises work in close proximity to organizations such as IRENA and the Clean Energy Business Council, as well as branches of other international organizations such as the Seoul-based Global Green Growth Institute. Many other free zones

[29] See official website of Masdar Free Zone: https://masdarcityfreezone.com/en/.

were created during periods of political and/or economic shocks. Masdar is a succinct and early example of a creative mechanism to generate revenues in light of falling oil and gas prices (Mogielnicki, 2021).

In Saudi Arabia, the leadership transition in 2015 marked a new phase, in which free zones assumed a more important and strategic role in the country's development (Saudi Vision 2030). The announcement of the $500 billion NEOM project that stretches also into Egyptian and Jordanian territory marked the previous peak of this development. As with other newly-introduced features of Saudi Arabia's economic reform programme, it is presented as a brainchild of the Crown Prince, Mohammed bin Salman. NEOM certainly acts as another vehicle to consolidate his power and reputation both inside and outside the kingdom. In this vein, Mohammed bin Salman not only chairs the foundation board of NEOM but also controls the investment vehicle, the PIF, that is responsible for the megaproject. With this "megaproject-cum-free zone" (Mogielnicki, 2021, 17), Saudi Arabia aims to replicate the Masdar Initiative in many ways. For instance, it shall include a free-carbon city, act as technology and incubation hub and create its own subsidiaries and initiatives. One of them is the Red Sea Project. This large-scale tourism project aims to set new standards in environmental sustainability. PIF fully owns the executing arm, the Red Sea Development Company. In this vein, it has provided billions of 'green' loans for new hotels powered by renewable energy (Reuters, 2021, July 12).

However, despite repeated headline-grabbing announcements, not many global investors have actually agreed to open branches in NEOM. Instead, the first contracts awarded for NEOM included the creation of several royal palaces (Mogielnicki, 2021). It was only in summer 2020 when a joint venture between NEOM, ACWA Power and US-based Air Products (with technological assistance by German Thyssenkrupp and Danish Haldor Topsøe) was announced to create the largest green hydrogen and green ammonia plant worldwide. Oman pursues a similar strategy and has lately announced hydrogen projects in two free zones. Only a few months later, the Sultanate of Oman announced plans to build a green hydrogen plant that exceeds Saudi Arabia's initiative. Located in the Special Economic Zone at Duqm, the hydrogen project is supposed to produce around 15 GW green hydrogen. Construction will start by 2028 and is overseen by a consortium of Oman's local energy company OQ (previously Oman Oil Company), Hong Kong-based InterContinental Energy and Kuwait-based investor Enertech (Bianco, 2021). Another hydrogen scheme is planned in the economic zone of Sohar. The Sohar Port and Freezone collaborates with the Port of Rotterdam and uses technology from Germany to develop a large-scale production of hydrogen. For many, hydrogen is seen as the "holy grail of decarbonization" and "part of a long-term hedging strategy" for a time when it becomes more economically viable than oil and gas (Seznec & Mosis, 2020). In this vein, countries such as the USA, China, Germany and Singapore have already signalled major interest and MoUs on hydrogen partnerships have already been signed (Bianco, 2021; Sim, 2021b). For instance, Germany's energy partnerships with the Gulf are commissioned by the German Federal Ministry of Economic Affairs and Climate Action and implemented by the German Chambers of Commerce Abroad and the private company and consultancy Guidehouse Inc.

Qatar, in turn, has taken a different path. The creation of the sustainability-oriented Qatar Science and Technology Park (QSTP) on behalf of the Qatar Foundation (QF) has not so much focused on commercial but rather knowledge-based principles. It is therefore rather engaged with research and development, but also constitutes an important element of the country's economic diversification. Besides hosting major American and European companies, a number of Qatari enterprises are also headquartered at the QSTP. Fields of specialization include digitalization (e.g. Microsoft, SAP, Cisco), energy (e.g. Shell, General Electric, ExxonMobil) and defence and security (e.g. Barzan Holding, Rheinmetall Barzan), among others. Furthermore, QSTP sets a focus on innovation and incubation to support SMEs and entrepreneurship, with a special focus on tech start-ups. In contrast to many other free zones, it is the government in Qatar that is the primary investor in these (Mogielnicki, 2021). The state's involvement in QSTP has been apparent since its inception. QSTP was created in 2009 after the current emir, Tamim bin Hamad Al Thani, laid out the legal framework for the creation of the free zone in his then role of deputy prime minister. The fact that his mother, Sheikha Moza bin Nasser al-Misnad, oversees QSTP in her role as patron of the QF was certainly not a coincidence.[30]

As can be noticed, free zones constitute a key element of low-carbon development as they may generate non-hydrocarbon revenues. At the same time, they act as important platforms for hedging. Given the

[30] Interview #75.

GCC states' strategic geopolitical location, free zones make use of well-established business partnerships and capital flows to and from America, Europe and Asia but also benefit from newly established trading routes such China's Belt and Road Initiative. Examples include the presence of American and European companies across the Gulf but also more recent diplomatic developments. This includes Egyptian-Saudi collaboration over NEOM as well as the increasing presence of Turkish firms operating in Qatar and Israeli firms in the UAE. Furthermore, China has expanded its operation in the GCC free zones over its new trading routes (Mogielnicki, 2021). At the same time, it is crucial to note that free zones remain under the control of the ruling elites: Whether they are managed by trusted confidantes of political decision-makers (as in Abu Dhabi with representatives of al-Mubarak and al-Jaber) or in the direct hands of the ruling family (as in Qatar and Saudi Arabia), free zones are just another part of the broader neopatrimonial state structures that help to bolster the rule of a few individuals (Keshavarzian, 2010). Moreover, they help to shift Gulf capital in favour of the dynastic monarchies. As Mogielnicki rightly stresses:

> Free zones permit foreign businesspeople, an important segment of the region's business elite, to partner directly with governments, partially bypassing the historical role of local merchants as private sector intermediaries, agents, and sponsors. (Mogielnicki, 2021, 233)

Lastly, although many of the free zones' buildings comply with international environmental standards (e.g. LEED certification), they are a mirror of the Gulf states' hyper-development mantra that is highly resource-intensive. As demarcated enclaves, aspects such as "sustainability have little immediate relevance" (cited from: Hertog, 2017, 14). Moreover, in some cases established on artificial islands (Hvidt, 2020; see also Chapter 3), free zones have rather exacerbated the problem of human caused environmental degradation.

Despite GCC states' efforts to open up their economies in order to improve credit ratings as well as increase political and economic stability, foreign investments are comparatively low in the Gulf (Mogielnicki, 2021; Obeid & Moshashai, 2019). Especially, political and economic shocks like the financial crisis of 2007–2008, the Arab Upheavals of 2011, the downslide in oil price since mid-2014 and the outbreak of COVID-19 in 2020, as well as numerous leadership transitions, have all had a strong impact. But there are also other factors that explain the low performance of GCC states. For instance, external investors are often hesitant over structural constraints (e.g. undiversified stock-market listings or business infiltration by the political elite) and a damaged international reputation (e.g. human rights violations) or authoritarian resurgence (e.g. the murder of Saudi critic and journalist Jamal Khashoggi). This has all resulted in a downward trend of FDI since 2008. Additionally, large-scale megaprojects are often short-lived and fall short of expectations. This can be best seen in the case of Qatar, once labelled "the most attractive FDI destination in the GCC" (Fernandez & Joseph, 2016, 175). After a short boost in 2009, in light of being awarded the right to host the 2022 FIFA World Cup that went along with the announcement of many (sustainable) infrastructure projects like the Qatar Railways Project and Lusail City, the emirate experienced a downturn in receiving outward investments.

The Dual Role of Gulf States as Global Investors and Aid Providers

Investment flows are, however, not only inward-oriented but also outward-oriented. Over the past decade, various studies have also stressed the internationalization of Gulf capitalism or Gulf finance (Coates Ulrichsen, 2016; Hanieh, 2019). Interestingly, these outward-oriented hedging strategies are not only important for enhancing partnerships and safeguarding a "Khaleeji capitalism" (Hanieh, 2011, 103), they are also increasingly conflated with dimensions of environmental development aid in some instances.

The Gulf states, particularly Kuwait, Saudi Arabia, the UAE and Qatar, have a long tradition as development providers to other Arab countries. Over the last fifty years, these four countries have accounted for the bulk of Arab aid and official development assistance disbursement. Much of this aid is provided in the form of soft loans and commodity aid. From time to time, Gulf states also provide also specific environmental aid, often after natural hazards as was observed in 2020 when Yemen was hit by torrential rain and flash floods (Al-Akwa & Zumbraegel, 2021). Particularly since 2015 and in the scope of adopting the sustainable development goals (SDGs), Arab donors have also agreed to promote sustainable development in developing country partners. For instance, by far the top three recipients of Saudi support for the SDGs between 2016 and 2021 were Yemen (where the Saudi kingdom is also involved in the ongoing war) as well as strategic allies such as Egypt and Pakistan (Hamid, 2022). Not surprisingly by now, most of this sustainability assistance is most apparent in the renewable energy sector. Through their national champions ACWA and Masdar, Saudi Arabia and the UAE have managed to become world leaders in renewable and alternative energyAlternative energy systems and technology. These companies invest in numerous projects worldwide with a special focus on solar power plants developed in close Arab allies, poorer Asian and (Eastern) African countries and Central Asia. Interestingly, in many instances, state authorities cover these strategic investments as development aid and assistance measures.

All GCC states have also agreed to participate in the Sovereign Wealth Funds Initiative of the One Planet Summit that encourages its members to invest in green companies (IRENA, 2019). Building on landmark agreements on climate financing such as the Doha Declaration on Financing for Development in 2008 and the Addis Ababa Action Agenda on Financing for Development in 2015, the matter of sustainable financing has gained greater attention among Arab donors, even if it is still in its infancy (Saab & Sadik, 2018). During this time, one can notice a shift from unconditional financing assistance towards conditional capacity development that also includes development projects in line with the SDGs. A major focus lies on climate-resilient mitigation strategies with a clear focus on renewable energy and exploring business opportunities.

The UAE has pioneered this practice. Particularly, Abu Dhabi has taken a lead and started to use green financial instruments to provide assistance for sustainable development projects in other Arab countries. While information is fragmented, it has been reported that the UAE dedicated around 12% of its general development assistance in 2013 as part of the Millennium Development Goals (a preceding initiative of the SDGs) to promote environmental sustainability. Assistance through sustainable energy is a key element. Also in 2013, the UAE assigned several million dollars to IRENA (Luomi, 2015). According to Sultan al-Jaber, the UAE spent around $700 million on developing the renewable energy sector in developing countries between 2009 and 2014 (Gulf News, 2015, January 17). In the subsequent period, the UAE took a more systematic approach to financing sustainable energy. In 2015, the Emirates' MOCCAE established a working group with several financial institutions and representatives of central banks. This resulted in the creation of the Dubai Declaration on Sustainable Finance in 2016. In the following year, the First Abu Dhabi Bank issued the first five-year Green Bond in the region, for $587 million.

A special focus of deploying renewable energy projects lies on Egypt and Jordan. For instance, between 2013 and 2016, the Abu Dhabi Fund for Development dispersed vast amounts of financial help to Jordan including the construction of the 100 MW solar PV plant et al. Quweira, valued at $150 million (IRENA, 2019). In addition to agencies such as the Abu Dhabi Fund for Development and the UAE's Ministry of Foreign Affairs and International Cooperation, the energy company Masdar has a key role as renewable energy project developer and implementing partner. Especially since 2013 when renewable energy became more attractive, Masdar has "been used by the Emirati government to engage in targeted development aid" (Al-Sulayman, 2021, 114). Receiving much of its funds from official (non-private) sources, it has established the first green revolving credit facility in the GCC: The Masdar Clean Tech Fund acts as a main vehicle to develop renewable energy projects in the Middle East and beyond (IRENA, 2019; Luomi, 2015). Masdar and other Emirati firms are especially active in allied countries such as Jordan and Egypt. For instance, Masdar already has two projects in Jordan and four in Egypt. In April 2022, it was reported that Masdar will develop green hydrogen production plants with a total capacity of around 4 GW (*Khaleeji Times*, 2022, April 25). Dubai's Amea Power, in turn, plans to develop two large-scale projects in Egypt, namely a 500 MW wind project in the Gulf of Suez and a 500 MW solar PV plant in Aswan governorate.

Meanwhile, Saudi Arabia's national champion ACWA has also increasingly implemented clean energy projects in these countries. It runs four renewable energy projects in Jordan (two PV solar plants and two wind farms) and has two other solar-powered projects in Egypt (Calabrese, 2021). The largest planned utility-scale solar plant so far, the 200 MW Kom Ombo solar plant in Egypt, was financed with the assistance of five global development banks and announced in 2021, when both countries signed a major deal to link their energy grids (Bianco, 2021; Calabrese, 2021). In Jordan, a third player is also increasingly active. Qatar has emerged as a small but strategic investor in clean energy for the Jordanian kingdom. Its above-mentioned company Nebras Power, a joint venture between Qatar Electricity and Water Company and a subsidiary of the Qatar Investment Authority, has two smaller PV solar projects in Jordan including a 24% stake in the 40 MW AM Solar project and a 35% stake in the 52 MW Shams Ma'an Power Generation project (IRENA, 2019).

Also in other areas of the Middle East and North Africa, Gulf states are increasingly competing for market share and a climate leadership role

(Liga, 2021). Only recently, both Saudi and Emirati companies have announced plans to develop renewable projects in Iraq (Mills, 2020). Already in 2019, ACWA had planned to build a 1 GW solar power facility. One year later, Masdar jumped in and signed agreements for several renewable energy projects that would also account for 1 GW clean energy in total. Yet, despite memoranda of understanding, not much progress has been made, given the numerous political and economic uncertainties in unstable Iraq (Mills, 2020).[31] During the year 2021, it was also announced that the UAE will invest in renewable energy sources in war-torn Syria along with the Iranian region of Khuzestan, which experienced protests over water scarcity during the same year (Al Arabiya, 2021, November 11; Press TV, 2021, December 2021).

The Maghreb has always been considered a key region with vast economic potential for the Gulf states. Especially, in terms of green energy, Morocco, Tunisia and to a lesser degree Algeria offer strategic destinations for promoting renewable and alternative energy (Sons, 2021). From all Maghreb states, Morocco stands out due to its economic stability and perhaps also a political system similar to the Gulf monarchies. Hence not surprisingly, the GCC leaderships have focused on the Moroccan kingdom for investing in clean energy projects. This includes ACWA Power's 75% stake in the 120 MW wind project Khalladi and 73% stake in the 170 MW solar NOOR project (Badr et al., 2018; IRENA, 2019). Especially, the latter is known as Morocco's landmark project in terms of clean energy transition. The launch of the NOOR PV I Programme by the Moroccan Agency for Sustainable Energy (Masen) in collaboration with ACWA Power and other global companies was signed during COP22 in Marrakech under a 20-year BOT scheme (Badr et al., 2018). Masdar, in turn, is part of a joint venture to develop the 800 MW solar project Noor Midelt Phase I. Additionally, Abu Dhabi's energy firm, TAQA, lately announced the expansion of its renewable energy products towards Morocco (Liga, 2021). Both Saudi Arabia and the UAE are also major financial donors to the Energy Development Fund in Morocco, allocating $500 million and $300 million, respectively, to energy efficient projects. Conversely, Qatar, which enjoys deep-rooted relations to the government in Tunis that it has fostered since 2011, is the biggest investor in Tunisia. Numerous agreements and MoUs signed throughout

[31] Interview #63.

2019 also included aspects of environmental protection and pollution control (*The Peninsula*, 2020, November 15).

In addition to strategic partnerships with Arab nations that are of economic and/or geopolitical interest, Israel has recently become a new diplomatic partner for many Gulf states. Especially, Abu Dhabi has built close ties with the government in Jerusalem that, besides security aspects, also includes commercial interests. This normalization agreement between Israel and the UAE under the auspices of the US government culminated in the so-called Abraham Accord that was also joined by Bahrain later.

The agreement foresees closer partnership in transnational environmental protection and conservation, but this has not been a key feature so far. Instead of fostering environmental cooperation, concerns of environmental degradation have proved more of an acid test to the new partnership. In summer 2021, Israel's Environmental Protection Ministry declared a halt on the Israel-UAE pipeline deal until a new and more adequate risk assessment had taken place. In so doing, the ministry responded to a petition filed by environmental organizations that criticized the potential destruction of coral reefs in the Gulf of Eilat and claimed that this would negatively impact tourism in the resort town of Eilat (Henderson, 2021). As a more positive and recent example, under the auspices of the UAE, Israel and Jordan concluded an agreement on a solar-water-exchange plan. This foresees the UAE funding a large-scale solar facility in Jordan (built by Masdar), whose energy will be transferred to Israel in exchange for Jordan receiving desalinated freshwater from Israel (Axios, 2021, November 24; Riedel & Sachs, 2021). Such a transboundary collaboration on environmental sustainability has been very rare in the Middle East until now, which furthermore helps to sharpen the UAE's profile as a regional climate leader. Although the Kingdom of Saudi Arabia has not officially established diplomatic relations with Israel, it seems more than realistic that both countries will also expand their non-public cooperation towards environmental sustainability in future. Here, the sustainable megaproject NEOM, that might have the capacity to gradually shift economic interests from the Gulf waterways to the Red Sea, would make stronger coordination in these fields indispensable.[32]

The GCC states are also proactive in other areas outside their geographical region, although not as much as in the near proximity. Since

[32] Interview #60 and interview #62.

transfer of technology and expertise are mainly channelled from Western countries—and increasingly also the Asian region—to the Gulf, foreign trade of clean energy on behalf of the Gulf states has rather focused on other markets. For instance, while Masdar Power is involved in a few wind parks in the USA and United Kingdom, it has a stronger presence in low- and middle-income Eastern Europe, with projects in Poland, Serbia and Montenegro. Further part of Masdar's portfolio is projects in the Caspian/Central Asia area, including in Azerbaijan, Uzbekistan, Armenia and Afghanistan. Other projects, often under the banner of development aid and funded by Masdar and/or IRENA, have been developed in small countries of the Global South including Cuba, Mauritania, Seychelles and islands in the South Pacific (Al-Sulayman, 2021; Luomi, 2015). More recently, it was also reported that the Abu Dhabi Fund for Development has financed a new large-scale solar project in Togo, which will also be one of the largest solar power plants in West Africa (*The National*, 2021, June 23). Interestingly, the Saudi competitor ACWA Power also considers vast potential in Central Asia and has started to develop projects in Azerbaijan and Uzbekistan. Further projects are located in Turkey, Vietnam, Ethiopia and South Africa. Once finished, the CSP solar project in South Africa will reportedly be Africa's biggest renewable project (Calabrese, 2021).

Conclusion

In addition to the internal dynamics of a public–private assemblage across the public and private sector that reveals a wide web of patron–client relations ultimately privileging the ruling elites, the external dimension provides insights on the transboundary character of environmental sustainability politics. In so doing, it has zoomed in on intra-regional dynamics and taken a foray into various concepts from the field of international relations such as branding, diplomacy and hedging to understand their linkages to environmental sustainability. In short, this has all shed light on the soft power projection of this policy field on various fronts:

First, the chapter has elucidated some of the main socio-political trajectories to explain why environmental cooperation, although highly relevant, is barely existent among the Gulf states. It shows how sustainability governance is politically instrumentalized in a geopolitical setting that is dominated by fierce competition and the pursuit of hegemony. For many countries not a top priority, it has particularly been Kuwait that has pursued a mediating role. This inclusive approach, however, has lately taken a backseat because of a struggle between the UAE and Saudi Arabia over environmental leadership dominance. The divergent approaches to showcasing regional leadership ambitions also unfold at the international level (Al-Saidi et al., 2019; Zumbraegel, 2021). In many ways, looking at the regional level and the example of environmental sustainability reveals the tendency of the largest and most powerful GCC country to ensure its status as self-described regional hegemon and counterbalance similar aspirations by smaller GCC countries.

Second, this politically driven approach becomes also apparent in the strategic marketization of environmental sustainability. In many cases, ecological conservation and biodiversity are frequently instrumentalized for reasons of reputation. What can on the one hand be labelled an eco-friendly 'neo-traditional' brand of monarchism can also underline a country's superiority to surrounding states. Environmental sustainability can help to foster this image in two ways: Either through distinctive sustainable constructions or by greening cutting-edge projects and initiatives. Applied patterns of inclusion and exclusion trigger national feelings and shape the 'we-identity' as a legitimizing factor. As Natalie Koch states: "National pride here is often derived from superiority to regional neighbours, who are then cast as "followers" of the exemplary path carved out" by the visions of Qatar, Dubai, Abu Dhabi or lately also Saudi Arabia via its crown prince (Koch, 2014, 1125). On the other hand, rulers portray themselves as green regional champions: Mushrooming green projects are "invariably presented as the brainchild of a key figure in the ruling family (...) and portrayed as a grand gesture" (Rizzo, 2017, 10). All high-profile projects have been continually presented as 'seeds' of the emir's wisdom and vision (Koch, 2014). Thus, advocating a green agenda perfectly fits into the Gulf states' meta-narrative of "making the impossible possible" that triggers a unifying sense of pride and acts as a copycat model (Derichs & Demmelhuber, 2014, 189).

Third, the Gulf states take a proactive role on the international environmental front to strengthen old and foster new partnerships. Traditionally disinterested in or reluctant towards global climate politics, the political capital of environmental diplomacy to improve their own position within the global community has been noticed over the last two decades (Luomi, 2014; Reiche, 2010, 8). While it is usually said that the autocratic shy away from multilateral agreements (von Soest, 2015, 6), one can notice how leaderships in Riyadh, Abu Dhabi and Doha have started to intentionally shape environmental diplomacy for pursuing their own political agendas. Ulterior motives for this policy shift include gaining external influence, showcasing a green leadership globally and fostering technology and knowledge transfer by diversifying international linkages. Rephrased, the global climate regime acts as a kind of 'trojan horse' for some ambitious Gulf states (Zumbraegel, 2021). What is interesting when looking at environmental diplomacy policies of the GCC is that single countries often fight for the same things (e.g. safeguarding their energy monopoly, 'Gulf capital' and political sovereignty, while improving their reputation and influence) but do this mainly independently from each other in order to gain the biggest advantage for themselves.

Here, the Gulf states pursue a parallel hedging policy between the West and the East. On the one hand, the Western and industrialized world is of utmost interest for the Gulf region, which can already be already seen in its openness to Westernized concepts such as the SDGs or the Paris Agreement (Zaidan, 2019). Above all, the USA has been the most important external patron for the Gulf states. For a long time, environmental sustainability between the USA and the Gulf Arab states was of no concern as it was not a priority for either of them. However, leadership changes in the US administration and policy shifts within the global climate regime underline how US climate policies have tangible impacts on the Gulf monarchies' approach to addressing climate change. This could be seen in 2015 when the Obama administration encouraged other countries to sign the Paris Agreement, as well as more recently with the Biden administration's return to the negotiation table of global climate politics after a four-year hiatus. As a response to the nomination of former Secretary of State John Kerry as new climate envoy, the Emirati and Bahraini governments also appointed new special climate envoys (Bianco, 2021). Both countries became increasingly active in the international climate arena following the approval of the European Green Deal and the climate-related focus of the new Biden administration (Bianco, 2021). Initiatives such as Abu Dhabi's GCC and MENA Regional Climate Dialogue in April 2021 and Saudi Arabia's Middle East Green Initiative summit in October 2021 were strategically planned and organized to show their commitments towards a close US-led climate cooperation and "cater to Western-defined 'liberal' international norms and tastes" (Hertog, 2017, 6). At the same time, Qatar's sustainable investments in light of hosting the climate summit in 2012 and preparing to host the FIFA World Cup in 2022 overlap "closely with the effort of the EU and its member states to promote such endeavours" (Millner and Al-Mansouri, 2016: 58).

On the other hand, the "Asianization" of the region, or the Gulf states' 'pivot to Asia', marks another important cornerstone in international affairs (Sim, 2020, 197). Here, one can notice a greater exchange with Asian countries, above all, Japan, India, South Korea and China. Especially, the cooperation between China and Gulf states such as Saudi Arabia, the UAE and Qatar appears to be experiencing a "honeymoon period" (Demmelhuber et al., 2022). This can be seen, for instance, in greater capital flows in clean energy investments (Calabrese, 2021) but also through close elite entanglements of the highest power circles in some instances (Gurol et al., 2022). The closer cooperation with China should also be seen in political terms: Here, it can be expected that economic activities with other authoritarian states such as China are not linked to aspects of good governance (e.g. political reforms, liberalization, human rights accountability, etc.) that often accompany dealings with Western trading partners. For instance, the killing of Saudi journalist Jamal Khashoggi led many high-profile CEOs from industrialized countries of the West to avoid attending the Future Investment Initiative conference in Riyadh in autumn 2018, where many green projects were expected to be finalized.[33] Moreover, if Saudi Arabia seeks to continue its current plans for greater Sino-Saudi cooperation in terms of nuclear energy, further questions arise as this form of power generation aptly serves the authoritarian, state-centralized and state-controlled political setting of the absolutist Gulf monarchies. According to Giacomo Luciani, the adaptation to nuclear "requires the least adaptation to the current model" and is "compatible with or even mutually supportive of the authoritarian nature" (Luciani, 2014, 17). Until today, Saudi Arabia has refused to sign the standard IAEA requirements, which has hampered the nuclear development and cooperation with the West. Additionally, some Western states, such as Germany, have strong concerns over harnessing nuclear energy as an ecologically viable source of electricity. China could fill this gap and provide all required materials of the industrial chain to construct commercial nuclear reactors for producing electricity. As Morchai Chaziza subsumes: "Civil nuclear cooperation is officially a part

[33] Interview #55 and interview #70.

of China's BRI, and combating climate change is central to China's pitch" (Chaziza, 2020).

Fourth, the chapter also shows the close interdependence and fluidity of national and international political interests and capital accumulation. On the one hand, Gulf states have the resources to gain the best available technology and innovation to bolster their status of great economic significance in the Arab region. Here, it is especially Western consultancy that brings knowledge, data and experience, but Asian countries are also increasingly part of this external buy-in strategy. This all contributes to the professionalization of policy processes and increasing trust in the efficiency of the government in terms of performance and economic superiority. On the other hand, Saudi Arabia, the UAE and Qatar have created important instruments of economic hedging. National champions of the states' investment vehicles such as ACWA Power (PIF), Masdar (Mubadala) and Nebras (Qatar Electricity and Water Company/Qatar Holding) invest regionally and internationally at great speed. This is based on commercial interests but also on ulterior political motives to increase influence and leverage, as the conflation of strategic investments and increasingly conditional development assistance in some countries of the Global South shows. Investment flows paired with development support often happen with relevant partners (e.g. Egypt for Saudi Arabia and the UAE, Tunisia for Qatar) or structurally similar countries (e.g. Morocco and Jordan) pointing towards a strategic motive behind this support. Channelled through technical capacity development for clean energy, Gulf states increase their leverage over weaker regimes in the region and make them more dependent on Gulf investments and buy-in (see also: Hanieh, 2019).

References

Aarts, P., & Janssen, D. (2003). Shades of opinion: The oil exporting countries and international climate politics. *The Review of International Affairs, 3*(2), 332–351.

Abbot, L. (2020). The states of the Persian Gulf: From protectorates to independent countries. In M. Kamrava (Ed.), *Routledge handbook of Persian Gulf politics* (pp. 48–54). Routledge.

Al-Akwa, K., & Zumbraegel, T. (2021). *The disaster of Yemen's flash floods: Impact of and local responses to the torrential rains and flooding in 2020.*

CARPO Policy Brief. Retrieved January 14, 2022 from https://carpo-bonn.org/en/carpo-sustainability-series/

Al Arabiya. (2021, November 11). Syria signs agreement with UAE firms to build 300 megawatt power station. *Al Arabiya*. https://english.alarabiya.net/News/middle-east/2021/11/11/Syria-signs-agreement-with-UAE-firms-to-build-300-megawatt-power-station

Al Daffa, A. (2017). Policy and regulatory frameworks for foreign direct investment in Saudi Arabia. In A. Mishrif & Y. al-Balushi (Eds.), *Economic diversification in the Gulf region. Volume I: The private sector as an engine of growth* (pp. 117–135). Palgrave.

Al-Damkhi, A. (2007). Planning to rescue Kuwait's oil wells: An environmental issue. *Disaster Prevention and Management: An International Journal, 16*(4), 513–521.

Al-Damkhi, M., Abdul-Wahab, A., & al-Khulaifi, N. (2009). Kuwait's 1991 environmental tragedy: Lessons learned. *Disaster Prevention and Management: An International Journal, 18*(3), 233–248.

Al-Nakib, F. (2020). Modernity and the Arab Gulf states: The politics of heritage, memory, and forgetting. In M. Kamrava (Ed.), *Routledge handbook of Persian Gulf politics* (pp. 57–82). Routledge.

Al Othman, W., & Clarke, S. (2017). Charting the emergence of environmental legislation in Qatar: A step in the right direction or too little too late? In P. Sillitoe (Ed.), *Sustainable development: An appraisal of the Gulf region* (pp. 116–132). Berghahn Books.

Alraouf, A., & Clarke, S. (2017). From pearling to skyscrapers: The predicament of sustainable architecture and urbanism in contemporary Gulf cities. In P. Sillitoe (Ed.), *Sustainable development: An appraisal of the Gulf region* (pp. 313–342). Berghahn Books

Al-Saidi, M. (2021). Cooperation or competition? State environmental relations and the SDGs agenda in the Gulf Cooperation Council (GCC) region. *Environmental Development, 37*. https://doi.org/10.1016/j.envdev.2020.100581

Al-Saidi, M., & Elagib, N. (2018). Ecological modernization and responses for a low-carbon future in the Gulf Cooperation Council countries. *Wires Climate Change, 9*(4). https://doi.org/10.1002/wcc.528

Al-Saidi, M., Zaidan, E., & Hammad, S. (2019). Participation modes and diplomacy of Gulf Cooperation Council (GCC) countries towards the global sustainability agenda. *Dev. Pract., 29*(5), 545–558. https://doi.org/10.1080/09614524.2019.1597017

Al-Sarihi, A. (2021). *Saudi Arabia and the Paris climate agreement*. KFCRIS Commentaries. Retrieved December 8, 2021, from https://kfcris.com/en/view/post/363

Al-Sarihi, A., & Luomi, M. (2019). *Climate change governance and cooperation in the Arab region*. Emirates Diplomatic Academy Insight. Retrieved December 31, 2021, from https://www.agda.ac.ae/research/energy-climate-change-and-sustainable-development

Al-Sarihi, A., & Mason, M. (2020). Challenges and opportunities for climate policy integration in oil-producing countries: The case of the UAE and Oman. *Climate Policy, 20*(10), 1226–1241. https://doi.org/10.1080/14693062.2020.1781036

Al-Sulayman, F. (2021). The rise of renewables in the Gulf states: Is the 'rentier effect' still holding back the energy transition? In R. Mills & L. Sim (Eds.), *Low carbon energy in the middle east and north Africa* (pp. 93–120). Palgrave.

Al-Ubaydli, O., Abdulla, G., & Yaseen, L. (2019). Forging a more centralized GCC renewable energy policy. In H. Akhonbay (Ed.), *The economics of renewable energy in the Gulf* (pp. 216–234). Routledge.

Al Shehri, T., Braun, J. F., Howarth, N., Lanza, A., & Luomi, M. (2022). Saudi Arabia's climate change policy and the circular carbon economy approach. *Climate Policy*, 1–17. https://doi.org/10.1080/14693062.2022.2070118

Althaus, J. (2012). *COP 18 in Qatar: Between »Fossil of the Day« and »Best Green Practice«*. FES Perspective. Retrieved April 17, 2022 from https://library.fes.de/pdf-files/iez/global/09502.pdf

Andrews-Speed, P., & Lixia, Y. (2022). China's evolving energy relations with the Middle East. In J. Fulton (Ed.), *Routledge handbook on China-middle east relations* (pp. 227–244). Routledge.

Axios. (2021, November 24). Scoop: Saudis tried to stop UAE-Israel-Jordan solar energy deal. *Axios*. https://www.axios.com/saudis-uae-solar-farm-israel-d836a165-b901-4cc7-a929-377555784ec6.html

Badr, A., El Guindy, R., Wiehler, L., & Rizk, R. (2018). Investing in sustainable energy. In N. Saab & A. Sadik (Eds.), *Financing sustainable development in Arab countries: Annual report of Arab Forum for Environment and Development* (pp. 131–146). Retrieved January 13, 2022, from http://www.afedonline.org/uploads/afed_reports/AFEDReport-financingSDinArabCountries2018-.pdf

Bahgat, G. (2013). The changing Saudi energy outlook: Strategic implications. *The Middle East Journal, 67*(4), 565–579.

Bailes, K. (1976). Technology and legitimacy: Soviet aviation and Stalinism in the 1930s. *Technol. Cult., 17*(1), 55–81.

Bianco, C. (2021). *Power play: Europe's climate diplomacy in the Gulf*. ECFR Policy Brief. Retrieved January 16, 2022, from https://ecfr.eu/publication/power-play-europes-climate-diplomacy-in-the-gulf/?__cf_chl_f_tk=rflpDCcaRYSvGWfot1.z5oCxNYdHGEHKBIIufaFRceo-1642438456-0-gaNycGzNCD0

Bodansky, D. (1999). The legitimacy of international governance: A coming challenge for international environmental law? *The American Journal of International Law, 93*(3), 596–624.

Calabrese, J. (2021). *Sustainable momentum? China and the Mideast solar market.* Middle East Institute. Retrieved January 13, 2022, from https://www.mei.edu/publications/sustainable-momentum-china-and-mideast-solar-market

Campbell, L., Corson, C., Gray, N., & MacDonald, K. (2014). Studying global environmental meetings to understand global environmental governance: Collaborative event ethnography at the tenth conference of the parties to the convention on biological diversity. *Global Environmental Politics, 14*(3), 1–20. https://doi.org/10.1162/GLEP_e_00236

Chaziza, M. (2015). Strategic hedging partnership: A new framework for analyzing Sino-Saudi relations. *Israel Journal of Foreign Affairs, 9*(3), 441–452.

Chaziza, M. (2020). *Saudi Arabia's nuclear program and China.* Middle East Institute. Retrieved August 24, 2022, from https://www.mei.edu/publications/saudi-arabias-nuclear-program-and-china

Cheng-Chwee, K. (2008). The essence of hedging: Malaysia and Singapore's response to a rising China. *Contemporary Southeast Asia, 30*(2), 159–185.

Coates Ulrichsen, K. (2011). *Insecure Gulf: The end of certainty and the transition to the post-oil era.* Hurst & Co.

Coates Ulrichsen, K. (2016). *The Gulf states in international political economy.* Palgrave.

Coates Ulrichsen, K. (2017). *The United Arab Emirates: Power, politics and policy-making.* Routledge.

Cox, R. (2021, August 5). Cox: Saudi may have a super-green future after all. *Reuters.* https://www.reuters.com/breakingviews/cox-saudi-may-have-super-green-future-after-all-2021-08-05/

Davidson, C. (2009). *Abu Dhabi: Oil and beyond.* Oxford University Press.

Davidson, C. (2021). *From Sheikhs to Sultanism: Statecraft and authority in Saudi Arabia and the UAE.* Hurst & Co.

Demmelhuber, T., Gurol, J., & Zumbraegel, T. (2022). The Corona temptation? Autocratic linkages in times of a global pandemic. In J. Völkel, L. Möller, & H. Zeina (Eds.), *Arab countries and the COVID-19 pandemic: Impact, implications, and future prospects* (pp. 19-35). Routledge.

Depledge, J. (2008). Striving for no: Saudi Arabia in the climate change regime. *Global Environmental Politics, 8*(4), 9–35.

Derichs, C., & Demmelhuber, T. (2014). Monarchies and republics, state and regime, durability and fragility in view of the Arab Spring. *Journal of Arabian Studies, 4*(2), 180–194. https://doi.org/10.1080/21534764.2014.974322

El-Katiri, L. (2011). *Interlinking the Arab Gulf: Opportunities and challenges of GCC electricity market cooperation*. OIES Analysis. Retrieved January 15, 2022, from https://www.oxfordenergy.org/wpcms/wp-content/uploads/2011/07/EL_82.pdf

Emirates News Agency. (2017, October 20). *Kuwait supports initiatives for unified Arab environmental approach*. Emirates News Agency. http://wam.ae/en/details/1395302640149

Emirates News Agency. (2021, April 1). *UAE to host GCC and MENA Regional Climate Dialogue with participation of US Special Presidential Envoy for Climate John Kerry*. Emirates News Agency. http://wam.ae/en/details/1395302923333

Fernandez, M., & Joseph, R. (2016). Qatar emerging as the most attractive FDI destination in the GCC. *International Journal of Economics and Finance, 8*(11), 175. https://doi.org/10.5539/ijef.v8n11p175

Fulton, J. (2018). *China's relations with the Gulf monarchies*. Routledge.

Gardner, A. (2017). How the city grows: Urban growth and challenges to sustainable development in Doha, Qatar. In P. Sillitoe (Ed.), *Sustainable development: An appraisal of the Gulf region* (pp. 343–366). Berghahn Books.

Gause, F., & Yom, S. (2012). Resilient royals: How Arab monarchies hang on. *J. Democr., 23*(4), 74–88.

General Secretariat For Development Planning. (2008). *Qatar National Vision 2030*. Planning and Statistics Authority, Government of Qatar. Retrieved January 15, 2022, from https://www.psa.gov.qa/en/qnv1/pages/default.aspx

Germany Trade & Invest. (2019). *Die VAE bauen weitere Meerwasserentsalzungsanlagen*. Retrieved January 13, 2022, from https://www.gtai.de/gtai-de/trade/branchen/branchenbericht/vereinigte-arabische-emirate/die-vae-bauen-weitere-meerwasserentsalzungsanlagen-117522

Germany Trade & Invest. (2020). *Solarenergie auf dem Vormarsch*. Retrieved January 12, 2022, from https://www.gtai.de/blueprint/servlet/gtai-de/trade/branchen/branche-kompakt/vereinigte-arabische-emirate/solarenergie-auf-dem-vormarsch-224150

Giordano, M., Voss, K., & Stroming, S. (2020). Groundwater resources: Supply, use and security implications in the Middle East and North Africa. In M. D. King (Ed.), *Water and conflict in the Middle East* (pp. 101–120). Hurst & Co.

Gray, M. (2019). *The economy of the Gulf states*. Agenda Publishing.

Gulf News. (2015, January 17). Al Jaber: The UAE has allocated more than US$700 million to support renewable energy in developing countries. *Gulf News*. https://gulfnews.com/uae/environment/uae-gives-over-700m-for-renewable-energy-1.1442588

Günel, G. (2018). The backbone: Construction of a regional electricity grid in the Arabian Peninsula. *Eng. Stud., 19*(2–3), 90–114. https://doi.org/10.1080/19378629.2018.1523176

Günel, G. (2019). *Spaceship in the desert: Energy, climate change, and urban design in Abu Dhabi*. Duke University Press.

Gupta, J., & Ringius, L. (2001). The EU's climate leadership: Reconciling ambition and reality. *International Environmental Agreements: Politics, Law and Economics, 1*, 281–299.

Gurol, J., Zumbraegel, T., & Demmelhuber, T. (2022). Elite networks and the transregional dimension of authoritarianism: Sino-Emirati relations in times of a global pandemic. *Journal of Contemporary China*. Online First: https://doi.org/10.1080/10670564.2022.2052444

Guzansky, Y., Fadlon, T., & Rakov, D. (2021). *Oil, economics, and geopolitics: Relations between Saudi Arabia and UAE* (INSS Insight No. 1499). Retrieved January 26, 2022, from https://www.inss.org.il/publication/saudi-arabia-uae/

Haas, P. (2016). Regional climate governance. In T. Börzel & T. Risse (Eds.), *The Oxford handbook of comparative regionalism* (pp. 430–456). Oxford University Press.

Hamid, M. (2022). *Why the world needs partnerships with Saudi Arabia: Saudi Arabia's global humanitarian and development aid*. KFCRIS Special Report. Retrieved January 13, 2022, from https://kfcris.com/pdf/c2a6d869685a22b236cafc6d8aaf275161d6c986b220f.pdf

Hanieh, A. (2011). *Capitalism and class in the Gulf Arab states*. Palgrave.

Hanieh, A. (2019). *Money markets, and monarchies: The Gulf Cooperation Council and the political economy of the contemporary Middle East*. Cambridge University Press.

Henderson, S. (2021). *Israel-UAE pipeline deal delayed by environmental concerns*. The Washington Institute for Near East Policy Analysis. Retrieved January 13, 2022, from https://www.washingtoninstitute.org/policy-analysis/israel-uae-pipeline-deal-delayed-environmental-concerns

Herb, M. (2014). *The wages of oil. Parliaments and economic development in Kuwait and the UAE*. Cornell University Press.

Hertog, S. (2017). *A Quest for significance: Gulf oil monarchies' international 'soft power' strategies and their local urban dimensions* (LSE Kuwait Programme Paper Series 42). Retrieved December 28, 2021, from http://eprints.lse.ac.uk/69883/1/Hertog_42_2017.pdf

Hertog, S., & Luciani, G. (2012). Energy and sustainability policies in the Gulf states. In D. Held & K. Coates Ulrichsen (Eds.), *The transformation of the Gulf: Politics, economics and the global order* (pp. 236–257). Routledge.

Hvidt, M. (2020). The emergence and spread of the "Dubai Model" in the GCC countries. In M. Kamrava (Ed.), *Routledge handbook of Persian Gulf politics* (pp. 203–215). Routledge.

IRENA. (2019). *Renewable energy market analysis: GCC 2019*. Retrieved December 28, 2021, from https://www.irena.org/publications/2019/jan/renewable-energy-market-analysis-gcc-2019

Jagers, S. C., & Stripple, J. (2003). Climate governance beyond the State. *Glob. Gov., 9*(3), 385–400.

Jensen, S. (2018). Policy implications of the UAE's economic diversification strategy: Prioritizing national objectives. In A. Mishrif & Y. al-Balushi (Eds.), *Economic diversification in the Gulf region: Comparing global challenges* (pp. 67–88). Palgrave.

Jordan, P. (2014). Nation branding: A tool for nationalism? *Journal of Baltic Studies, 45*(3), 283–303.

Kamrava, M. (2015). *Qatar: Small state, big politics*. Cornell University Press.

Karlsson, C., Hjerpe, M., Parker, C., & Linner, B. (2012). The legitimacy of leadership in international climate change negotiations. *Ambio, 41*, 46–55. https://doi.org/10.1007/s13280-011-0240-7

Keshavarzian, A. (2010). Geopolitics and the genealogy of free trade zones in the Persian Gulf. *Geopolitics, 15*(2), 263–289. https://doi.org/10.1080/14650040903486926

Khaleeji Times. (2021, July 3). Dubai WGES supports UAE's effort to find sustainable solutions for global challenges. *Khaleeji Times*. https://www.khaleejtimes.com/local-business/dubai-wges-supports-uaes-effort-to-find-sustainable-solutions-for-global-challenges

Khaleeji Times. (2022, April 25). Masdar to develop 4 GW-capacity green hydrogen plants in Egypt by 2030. *Khaleeji Times*. https://www.khaleejtimes.com/energy/masdar-to-develop-4-gw-capacity-green-hydrogen-plants-in-egypt-by-2030

Kilian, B., & Elgström, O. (2010). Still a green leader? The European Union's role in international climate negotiations. *Coop. Confl., 45*(3), 255–273.

Kinley, R. (2017). Climate change after Paris: From turning point to transformation. *Climate Policy, 17*(1), 9–15. https://doi.org/10.1080/14693062.2016.1191009

Koch, N. (2014). "Building glass refrigerators in the Desert": Discourses of urban Sustainability and nation building in Qatar. *Urban Geogr., 35*(8), 1118–1139. https://doi.org/10.1080/02723638.2014.952538

Koch, N. (2018). Green laboratories: University campuses as sustainability "exemplars" in the Arabian Peninsula. *Society & Natural Resources, 31*(5), 525–540. https://doi.org/10.1080/08941920.2017.1383546

Koch, N. (Forthcoming). Sustainability spectacle: Modernity and the contemporary imperative to be green. *Environmental Politics*, n/a.

Koga, K. (2017). The concept of "Hedging" revisited: The case of Japan's Foreign policy strategy in East Asia's power shift. *Int. Stud. Rev., 20*(4), 1–28.

Krane, J. (2021). Climate strategy for producer countries: The case of Saudi Arabia. In G. Luciani & T. Moerenhout (Eds.), *When can oil economies be deemed sustainable?* (pp. 101–128). Palgrave.

Kumar, V., & Christodoulopoulou, A. (2014). Sustainability and branding: An integrated perspective. *Ind. Mark. Manag., 43*(1), 6–15. https://doi.org/10.1016/j.indmarman.2013.06.008

Lake, D. (1996). Anarchy, hierarchy, and the variety of international relations. *Int. Organ., 50*(1), 1–33.

Liga, A. (2021). Managing climate change and mapping an energy transition in North Africa. In K. Mezran & A. Sanguini (Eds.), *North Africa 2030: What the future holds for the region.* ISPI/Atlantic Council. Retrieved January 12, 2022, from https://www.ispionline.it/it/pubblicazione/north-africa-2030-what-future-holds-region-32022

Luciani, G. (2014). The political economy of gulf energy reform. In G. Luciani & R. Ferroukhi (Eds.), *Political economy of energy reform: The clean energy-fossil fuel balance in the gulf states* (pp. 7–24). Gerlach Press.

Luomi, M. (2009). *Bargaining in the Saudi bazaar. Common grounds for a post-2012 climate agreement?* The Finish Institute of International Affairs. Retrieved January 16, 2022, from https://www.fiia.fi/wp-content/uploads/2017/01/upi_briefing_paper_48_2009.pdf

Luomi, M. (2012). *The Gulf monarchies and climate change: Abu Dhabi and Qatar in an era of natural unsustainability.* Hurst & Co.

Luomi, M. (2014). *Mainstreaming climate policy in the Gulf Cooperation Council States* (OIES Paper 7). Retrieved January 6, 2022, from https://www.oxfordenergy.org/authors/mari-luomi/

Luomi, M. (2015). *The international relations of the green economy in the Gulf: Lessons from the UAE's state-led energy transition* (OIES Paper 12). Retrieved January 10, 2021, from https://www.oxfordenergy.org/publications/the-international-relations-of-the-green-economy-in-the-gulf-lessons-from-the-uaes-state-led-energy-transition/

Luomi, M. (2021). *Pressure builds on Gulf countries to take climate action.* AGSIW Blog Post. Retrieved December 7, 2021, from https://agsiw.org/pressure-builds-on-gulf-countries-to-take-climate-action/

Luomi, M., & Michaelowa, A. (2012). *From Climate Antagonists to Low-Carbon Protagonists? The changing role of the Gulf OPEC States in the UNFCCC.* Fridtjof Nansens Institutt. Retrieved April 20, 2022, from https://www.fni.no/publications/from-climate-antagonists-to-low-carbon-protagonists-the-changing-role-of-the-gulf-opec-states-in-the-unfccc

Magnani, N. (2012). The green energy transition sustainable development or ecological modernization? *Sociologica, 2.* https://doi.org/10.2383/38270

Millner, R., & al-Mansouri, K. (2016). Qatar foreign policy engagement with the European Union: Evolving priorities of a small state in the contemporary era. *Comillas Journal of International Relations, 5*, 47–64.

Mills, R. (2018). *Saudi Arabia shelves softbank solar effort, reflecting challenges with megaprojects*. AGSIW Blog Post. Retrieved December 22, 2021, from https://agsiw.org/saudi-arabia-shelves-softbank-solar-effort-reflecting-challenges-with-megaprojects/

Mills, R. (2020). *Protracted negotiations yield solution to Saudi-Kuwaiti neutral zone dispute*. AGSIW Blog Post. Retrieved January 3, 2021, from https://agsiw.org/protracted-negotiations-yield-solution-to-saudi-kuwaiti-neutral-zone-dispute/

Mills, R. (2021). *UAE and Saudi Arabia cut renewables deals to improve Iraq relations*. AGSIW Blog Post. Retrieved January 12, 2022, from https://agsiw.org/uae-and-saudi-arabia-cut-renewables-deals-to-improve-iraq-relations/

Ministry of Development Planning and Statistics. (2018). *Qatar Second National Development Strategy 2018–2022*. Retrieved January 4, 2021, from https://www.psa.gov.qa/en/knowledge/Documents/NDS2Final.pdf

Mishrif, A. (2017). Introduction to economic diversification in the GCC region. In A. Mishrif & Y. al-Balushi (Eds.), *Economic diversification in the Gulf Region. Volume I: The private sector as an engine of growth* (pp. 1–26). Palgrave.

Moerenhout, T. (2016). Energy pricing reform and the green economy in the Gulf region. In M. Raouf & M. Luomi (Eds.), *The green economy in the Gulf* (pp. 53–76). Palgrave.

Mogielnicki, R. (2021). *A political economy of free zones in Gulf Arab states*. Palgrave.

Never, B. (2014). *Knowledge systems and change in climate governance: Comparing India and South Africa*. Routledge.

Nosova, A. (2017). Private sector and economic diversification in Kuwait. In A. Mishrif & Y. al-Balushi (Eds.), *Economic diversification in the Gulf region. Volume I: The private sector as an engine of growth* (pp. 27–48). Palgrave.

Obeid, J., & Moshashai, D. (2019). *Grand designs: Are Saudi Arabia's infrastructure plans too ambitious?* Castlereagh Study. Retrieved January 12, 2022, from https://castlereagh.net/grand-designs-are-saudi-arabias-infrastructure-plans-too-ambitious/?pdf=1377

Ouis, P. (2002). 'Greening the emirates': The modern construction of nature in the United Arab Emirates. *Cult. Geogr., 9*(3), 334–347.

Peterson, J. (2005). *The emergence of post-traditional Oman* (Durham Middle East Papers 78). Retrieved January 3, 2021, from https://www.semanticscholar.org/paper/The-emergence-of-post-traditional-Oman.-Peterson/ea08f53e39a531c549b0859c7cdd5a86524e87e7

Peterson, J. (2006). Qatar and the world: Branding for a micro-state. *Middle East Journal, 60*(4), 732–748.

Poudineh, R., Sen, A., & Fattouh, B. (2019). Policies to promote renewables in the Middle East and North Africa's resource rich economies. In H. Akhonbay (Ed.), *The economics of renewable energy in the Gulf* (pp. 120–138). Routledge.

Press TV. (2021, December 8). UAE to build 300 MW power projects in Iran's Khuzestan. *Press TV*. https://www.presstv.ir/Detail/2021/12/08/672236/Iran-renewables-power-plant-UAE-Khuzestan

PV Magazine. (2021, September 1). Winners of 1.5 GW solar park auction to get 'letter of award' today. *PV Magazine*. https://www.pv-magazine-india.com/2021/09/01/winners-of-1-5-gw-solar-park-auction-to-get-letter-of-award-today/

Qarjouli, A. (2021, March 29). Qatar's amir, Saudi Arabia's MBS discuss 'green initiatives' in phone call. *Doha News*. https://www.dohanews.co/qatars-amir-saudi-arabias-mbs-discuss-green-initiatives-in-phone-call/

Raouf, M. (2014). *Promoting GCC regional integration: An environmental perspective*. GRC Gulf Papers. Retrieved January 2, 2021, from https://www.files.ethz.ch/isn/183788/Gulf_Unity_paper_2952.pdf

Reiche, D. (2010). Energy policies of Gulf Cooperation Council (GCC) countries: Possibilities and limitations of ecological modernization in rentier states. *Energy Policy, 38*(5), 2395–23403.

Reuters. (2021, July 12). Saudi sovereign wealth fund scopes banks for ESG framework—Sources. *Reuters*. https://www.reuters.com/business/sustainable-business/saudi-sovereign-wealth-fund-scopes-banks-esg-framework-sources-2021-07-12/+

Reuters. (2021, April 24). Saudi Arabia to join new forum on climate change—State news agency. *Reuters*. https://www.reuters.com/world/middle-east/saudi-arabia-join-new-forum-climate-change-state-news-agency-2021-04-24/

Riedel, B., & Sachs, N. (2021). *Israel, Jordan, and the UAE'senergydealisgood-news*. Brookings. Retrieved January 12, 2022, from https://www.brookings.edu/blog/order-from-chaos/2021/11/23/israel-jordan-and-the-uaes-energy-deal-is-good-news/

Rizzo, A. (2013). Doha Metro. *Cities, 31*, 533–543.

Rizzo, A. (2014). Rapid urban development and national master planning in Arab Gulf countries: Qatar as a case study. *Cities, 39*, 50–57. https://doi.org/10.1016/j.cities.2014.02.005

Rizzo, A. (2017). Sustainable urban development and green megaprojects in the Arab States of the Gulf region: Limitations, covert aims, and unintended outcomes in Doha, Qatar. *Int. Plan. Stud., 22*(2), 85–98. https://doi.org/10.1080/13563475.2016.1182896

Roberts, D. (2017). *Qatar: Securing the global ambitions of a city-state*. Hurst & Co.

Rowlatt, J., & Gerken, T. (2021, October 21). COP26: Document leak reveals nations lobbying to change key climate report. *BCC News*. https://www.bbc.com/news/science-environment-58982445

Saab, N., & Sadik, A. (2018). Introduction. In N. Saab & A. Sadik (Eds.), *Financing sustainable development in Arab countries: Annual report of Arab Forum for Environment and Development* (pp. 7–16). Retrieved January 13, 2022, from http://www.afedonline.org/uploads/afed_reports/AFEDReport-financingSDinArabCountries2018-.pdf

Salam, M., & Khan, S. (2017). Transition towards sustainable energy production: A review of the progress for solar energy in Saudi Arabia. *Energy Exploration & Exploitation, 36*(1), 3–27. https://doi.org/10.1177%2F0144598717737442

Sankar, A. (2021, June 22). Dubai: The making of the greenest expo ever. *Khaleeji Times*. Retrieved January 12, 2022 from https://www.khaleejtimes.com/expo/dubai-the-making-of-the-greenest-expo-ever

Saudi Vision 2030. (2018). *Thriving economy open for business. Government of Saudi Arabia*. Retrieved January 14, 2022 from https://www.vision2030.gov.sa/media/rc0b5oy1/saudi_vision203.pdf

Sever, S., Tok, M. E., & D'Alessandro, C. (2019). Global environmental governance and the GCC: Setting the agenda for climate change and energy security. In L. Pal & M. Tok (Eds.), *Global governance and Muslim organizations* (pp. 197–228). Springer.

Seznec, J., & Mosis, S. (2020). *The ACWA power–air products joint venture for green hydrogen: A new Saudi Energy policy?* Atlantic Council. Retrieved January 12, 2022, from https://www.atlanticcouncil.org/blogs/energysource/the-acwa-power-air-products-joint-venture-for-green-hydrogen-a-new saudi-energy-policy/

Shuaib, H. (1988). Oil, development, and the environment in Kuwait. *Environment, 30*(6), 19–44.

Sim, L. (2012). Re-branding Abu Dhabi: From oil giant to energy Titan. *Place Brand. Public Dipl., 8*(1), 83–98. https://doi.org/10.1057/pb.2011.31

Sim, L. (2020). Global energy market and the Persian Gulf. In M. Kamrava (Ed.), *Routledge handbook of Persian Gulf politics* (pp. 187–202). Routledge.

Sim, L. (2021a). Powering the Middle East and North Africa with nuclear energy: Stakeholders and technopolitics. In R. Mills & L. Sim (Eds.), *Low carbon energy in the Middle East and North Africa* (pp. 263–298). Palgrave.

Sim, L. (2021b). *Singapore and the Gulf: Economic engagement beyond hydrocarbons*. Middle East Institute. Retrieved January 12, 2022, from https://www.mei.edu/publications/singapore-and-gulf-economic-engagement-beyond-hydrocarbons

Sim, L. (2022). *Renewable power policies in the Arab Gulf states*. Middle East Institute. Retrieved February 10, 2022, from https://www.mei.edu/publications/renewable-power-policies-arab-gulf-states

Soest, C., & Grauvogel, J. (2017). Identity, procedures and performance: How authoritarian regimes legitimize their rule. *Contemp. Polit., 23*(3), 287–305. https://doi.org/10.1080/13569775.2017.1304319

Sons, S. (2021). *A new "pivot to the Maghreb" or "more of the same"? The transformative shift of the Gulf engagement in North Africa*. KAS Analysis. Retrieved January 12, 2022, from https://www.kas.de/en/web/poldimed/single-title/-/content/a-new-pivot-to-the-maghreb-or-more-of-the-same

Soubrier, E. (2020). *Redefining Gulf security begins by including the human dimension* (AGSIW Issue Paper 9). Retrieved December 31, 2021, from https://agsiw.org/redefining-gulf-security-begins-by-including-the-human-dimension/

Sowers, J. (2018). Environmental activism in the Middle East and North Africa. In H. Verhoeven (Ed.), *Environmental politics in the Middle East* (pp. 27–52). Oxford University Press.

The National. (2021, June 3). Zayed Sustainability Prize: Record 4,000 entries from 151 countries. *The National*. https://www.thenationalnews.com/uae/zayed-sustainability-prize-record-4-000-entries-from-151-countries-1.1234576

The National. (2021, June 23). Huge solar plant named after Sheikh Mohamed bin Zayed opens in Africa. *The National*. https://www.thenationalnews.com/uae/huge-solar-plant-named-after-sheikh-mohamed-bin-zayed-opens-in-africa-1.1247450

The Peninsula. (2013, October 13). Msheireb Properties wins Sustainability award, n/a.

The Peninsula. (2020, November 15). Qatar, Tunisia enjoy close fraternal ties, common goals and aspirations. *The Peninsula*. https://thepeninsulaqatar.com/article/15/11/2020/Qatar,-Tunisia-enjoy-close-fraternal-ties,-common-goals-and-aspirations

The Peninsula. (2022, January 7). Transport ministers of Qatar and Saudi discuss linking two countries through rail. *The Peninsula*. https://m.thepeninsulaqatar.com/article/07/01/2022/transport-ministers-of-qatar-and-saudi-discuss-linking-two-countries-through-rail

Todaro, M., & Smith, S. (2012). *Economic development*. Addison-Wesley.

Van Ham, P. (2008). Place branding: The state of the art. *The ANNALS of the American Academy of Political and Social Science, 616*(1), 126–49. https://doi.org/10.1177%2F0002716207312274

von Soest, C. (2015). Democracy prevention: The international collaboration of authoritarian regimes. *European Journal of Political Research, 54*(4), 623–638. https://doi.org/10.1111/1475-6765.12100

Vrojilk, C. (2003). Climate governance in the GCC. In T. Najem & M. Hetherington (Eds.), *Good governance in the Middle East oil monarchies* (pp. 119–136). Routledge.

Warner, F. (1991). The environmental consequences of the Gulf war. *Environment, 33*(5), 6–26.

Wilson, R. (2017). Islam and sustainable economic development. In P. Sillitoe (Ed.), *Sustainable development: An appraisal of the Gulf region* (pp. 178–269). Berghahn Books.

Wogan, D., & al-Mubarak, I., al-Badi, A., & Pradhan, S. (2019). Overview of energy supply and demand in the GCC. In H. Akhonbay (Ed.), *The economics of renewable energy in the Gulf* (pp. 10–40). Routledge.

Young, K. (2019). Prioritizing renewable energy in the time of fiscal austerity. In H. Akhonbay (Ed.), *The economics of renewable energy in the Gulf* (pp. 77–99). Routledge.

Zaidan, E. (2019). Cultural-based challenges of the westernised approach to development in newly developed societies. *Development in Practice, 29*(5), 570–581. https://doi.org/10.1080/09614524.2019.1598935

Zaidan, E., & Abulibdeh, A. (2021). Master planning and the evolving urban model in the Gulf cities: Principles, policies, and practices for the transition to sustainable urbanism. *Planning Practice & Research, 36*(2), 193–215. https://doi.org/10.1080/02697459.2020.1829278

Zumbraegel, T. (2019). Being green or being seen green? Strategies of eco regime resilience in Qatar. In H. Pouran & H. Hakimian (Ed.), *Environmental challenges in the MENA region: The long road from conflict to cooperation* (pp. 49–71). The Gingko Library.

Zumbraegel, T. (2020a). Beyond greenwashing: Sustaining power through sustainability in the Arab Gulf monarchies. *Orient, 61*(1), 28–35.

Zumbraegel, T. (2020b). Kingdom of gravity: Autocratic promotion and diffusion in Saudi Arabia. In M. Kneuer & T. Demmelhuber (Eds.), *Authoritarian gravity centres: A cross-regional study of authoritarian promotion and diffusion* (pp. 55–88). Routledge.

Zumbraegel, T. (2021). Environmental cooperation in the Gulf region: Why it matters and why it is failing. In L. Narbone & A. Divsallar (Eds.), *Stepping away from the abyss: A gradual approach towards a new security system in the Persian Gulf* (pp. 175–188). MEDirections, Florence. Retrieved January 2022, from bit.ly/3hrA3sG

CHAPTER 7

Conclusion and Outlook: The Green Delusion

The Delusion Behind the Green Turn

The GCC states, regularly criticized for their high emissions and extravagant lifestyles, have recently taken a more sustainable path towards revamping their hitherto image as some of the world's worst polluters. However, these countries remain far away from their self-description as green advocates. Also, flattering appraisal from outside the region, that a "green revolution" is taking place in the Gulf, is also misleading (Noach & Guzansky, 2021; Quaile, 2013). Although over the last years the Gulf monarchies have implemented and promoted policies of environmental sustainability that clearly surpass any assumption of a perfunctory 'greenwash' (further: Zumbraegel, 2020), until today these are based on a weak notion of sustainability in order to sustain economic growth and the services that improve citizens' welfare.

All GCC states have raised their production of fossil fuels considerably in the last years through implementing current technologies to exploit new reserves or utilize old reserves more efficiently. Innovation has optimized the processing of hydrocarbons, be it in the upstream, midstream or downstream sectors and thus helped to keep the hydrocarbon business lucrative. In this vein, the Saudi Crown Prince Mohammed bin Salman is far away from giving up the kingdom's addiction to oil, which he publicly announced several years ago (Ottaway, 2021). Even fossil-poor Oman

T. Zumbraegel, *Political Power and Environmental Sustainability in Gulf Monarchies*, Contemporary Gulf Studies,
https://doi.org/10.1007/978-981-19-4431-4_7

has been able to restore its 'hydrocarbon reputation' and bolster foreign investments in this sector through new technology and innovation in the gas sector (Valeri, 2020). All these developments bolster Luciani's latest assumption that:

> It is therefore quite possible that hydrocarbons will retain economic value for decades to come, while their use evolves in ways that make it compatible with maintaining global warming within the limits mandated by the Paris Agreement and supported by climate science. (Luciani, 2021, 11)

Especially, the increasing focus on natural gas as a cleaner 'transition fuel' (i.e. lower carbon-to-energy ratio than oil) is seen as a valid option and potential 'exit strategy' for the Gulf states (Dourian, 2019; Wright, 2018). Combined-cycle gas turbines have low initial capital cost, fast construction times and small plant sizes. Concerning the expansion of the hydrocarbon portfolio, the regimes steadily exploit non-associated gas. In contrast to associated gas, which is a natural by-product of crude oil extraction, non-associated gas is found in other geological strata. With the support of new techniques, the gas can be more easily drilled (Krane, 2019). In a nutshell, in contrast to global low-carbon development, the oil-exporting GCC states still count on the abundance and competitiveness of their fossil fuels and consider it as a kind of 'last man standing' tactic (Tagliapietra, 2017). As Saudi energy minister Khalid al-Falih stated in November 2017: "I am certain the last barrel that gets produced globally is going to be here in Saudi Arabia" (Bloomberg, 2 November 2017). The following graphic illustrates, for instance, how the natural gas production among the Gulf states have been gradually increased or at least stagnated over the last decade; with the COVID-19 pandemic nearly not affecting the output. At the same time, the consumption of fossil fuels (oil and gas) has steadily grown in all GCC states (BP, 2021). While Qatar's gas production remained almost stable over the last decade, this might change in the near future due to the Russian invasion into the Ukraine. European countries such seek to lower their dependence of Russian gas and look for alternatives. Accordingly, Qatar has lately announced to nearly double its LNG production over the next years (Fig. 7.1).

As already stated, the Gulf states do not consider oil and gas as problematic in themselves, but rather the emissions associated with their processing. Energy efficient measures have been implemented at a large

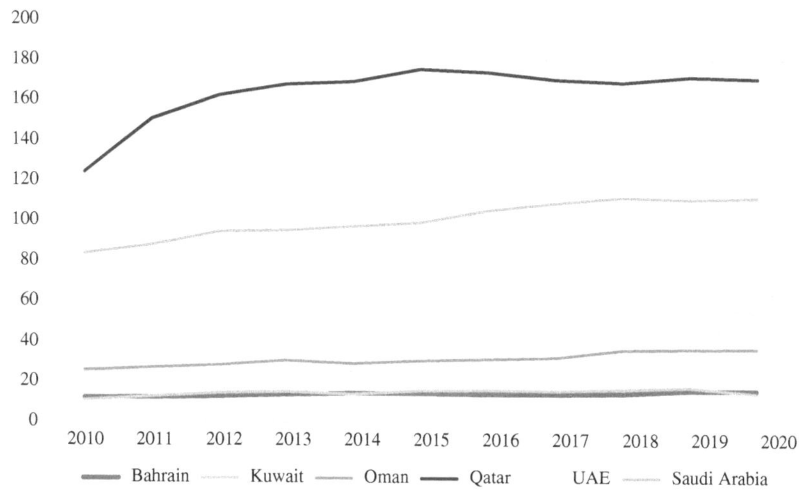

Fig. 7.1 Natural gas: Production in billion cubic metres 2010–2020 (BP, 2021)

scale. Here, techniques for reducing gas flaring and leaks during transport have been a success story over the last years. In other cases, the striving for efficiency has had rather absurd consequences, as the example of Dubai's idea of 'clean coal' explained in Chapter 4 has shown. Meanwhile, Gulf leaders aspire to develop new decarbonizing technologies such as carbon capture, utilization and storage (CCUS), because they want to secure future energy supply and reduce emissions (Raouf & Luomi, 2016, 12). This form of 'cleaning' fossil fuels is part of the net-zero ambitions of states such as Saudi Arabia, UAE and Bahrain. Several states also combine CCUS techniques with enhanced oil recovery to extract more oil. One example is the Rumaitha and Bab oilfields in the UAE. Carbon capture and sequestration is also perceived as a promising technology in terms of the growing demand for hydrogen. Here the Gulf monarchies are already positioning themselves and their oil and gas industries are playing a strategic role in experimenting with the production of blue hydrogen in large quantity. Still, as Fig. 7.2 shows, GHG emissions have been constantly rising or are remaining on a high plateau. The only exception includes the period of pandemic-related global lockdown measures such as travel bans and implementation of remote working policies during the year 2020. Even if the countries fasten their process of developing renewable energy sources and more energy-efficient solutions it is questionable whether the GHG emissions will drastically sink, or even plummet to zero, over the next years, since energy demand and consumption is steadily growing. As Florence Gaub and Clémentine Lienard subsumes in their latest report on *Arab Climate Futures*, commissioned by the European Union:

> While European states began to curb emissions from 1990 onwards, the region did the opposite: since the 1992 report warning of climate change, it has increased its CO2 emissions by more than double, approaching European Union levels. (Gaub & Lienard, 2021, 4)

Certainly, those comparisons are often misleading as the GCC countries have not nearly the same output as major European countries. In fact, their overall contribution of GHG emissions is relatively low. And still, they are among the top 25 in terms of CO_2 emissions per capita in the world.

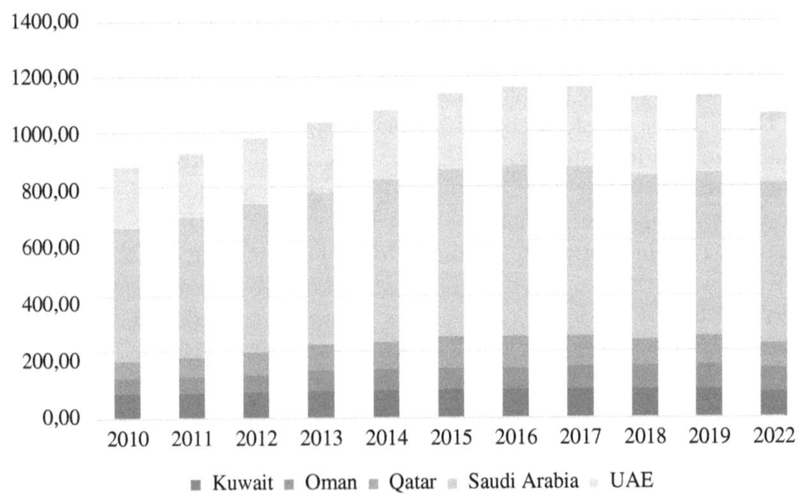

Fig. 7.2 Carbon dioxide emissions 2010–2020 (BP, 2021)[1]

[1] No data has been available for Bahrain.

Furthermore, in this equation of greening the 'black gold' environmental risks that accompany these mitigation measures are barely discussed: New gas drilling techniques also carry risks, such as the potential leakage of toxic substances like hydrogen sulphide (Krane, 2019). Carbon capture and storage projects are questionable as viable instruments for decarbonization as they consume additional energy, leading to more emissions (Krane, 2020; Theeyattuparampil et al., 2013). Especially, CCUS with enhanced oil recovery as practised in some of the GCC countries is detrimental to the environment, as this extracts more fossil fuels unleashing yet more emissions; perhaps not so much in terms of operation but in terms of refining and consumption. Further environmental concerns relate to toxicity, eutrophication, and acidification (Roefs et al., 2019). For instance, the amine-based solvents used at CO_2 capture facilities might leak into the natural environment and affect human health (Theeyattuparampil et al., 2013). Lastly, there are unknown risks associated with the global hydrogen transition. Leaked hydrogen, for instance during transportation, could react with hydroxyl radicals in the air and reduce their important role in cleaning smog and other atmospheric trace gases. According to some of the few studies on this, air contaminated with hydrogen could even substantially increase global warming (Pearman & Parther, 2020, August 9). Some estimates that hydrogen emissions (H2) could be "200 times that of carbon dioxide and larger than that of methane" (Ocko & Hamburg, 2022, 9350). Another barely discussed aspect is the fact that methane, several times more climate damaging than CO_2.

Yet, optimizing and transforming conventional energy sources cannot solve the whole problem. Thus, the Gulf states are also focusing on alternative energy systems (solar, wind and to a lesser extent nuclear power) to partially substitute their long-term primary energy sources of oil and gas. Again, the overall motive is to cut emissions, which explains why some countries are considering nuclear energy into their energy mix. Nuclear power is labelled as 'green', even though it comes with vast environmental and ecological risks. Disagreement among the GCC states concerning nuclear energy as a low-emission solution is obvious: While the UAE has already unveiled its first nuclear energy reactor, Saudi Arabia is actively purchasing this technology and plans around sixteen nuclear plants. In this vein, it has already signed various MoUs with the USA, France and South Korea as well as Russia and China "whose safeguards are decidedly more lax" (Jones, 2020, 198). Kuwait and Oman, in turn, gave up their own nuclear plans after the Fukushima nuclear disaster (Ahmad & Ramana, 2015).

Developing clean energy beyond oil and gas is generally seen by the GCC states as a new set of economic opportunities as well as a way to diversify their energy portfolios and become more energy resilient. For instance, it constitutes an additional source for satisfying the growing domestic energy demand so that oil and gas can be exported with higher returns. Surplus of renewable energy could also be exported to neighbouring states or used for green hydrogen and the European market, for instance. However, it is not only the clean energy products that can be sold profitably. Also, production technologies and investments in clean energy projects are seen as (new) pillars of economic diversification. So far, however, all of this seems more like daydreaming. Nuclear power has high initial investment costs, long construction phases and safety concerns. Wind and solar energy have become economically viable but still face the problem of intermittency and are currently not able to sufficiently support heavy industry and large-scale economic growth. Rising temperatures, sand dune movements and dust storms decrease the operability of solar panels. The almost daily cleaning of the panels to remove sand and dust storms further accelerate water scarcity in the region. Other options such as geothermal energy have rather been seen as niches so far, although there is still great potential for harnessing this renewable energy source (Sullivan, 2021). Also the new hype around green hydrogen, where especially Saudi Arabia and the UAE are currently taking the lead, has other negative side effects in the Gulf region: Besides the fact that it is energy-intensive and costly and far away of being a commercial commodity, so far, there are no public debates, where the large amounts of water shall come from that are needed to produce this form of energy. As previously discussed, relying more on environmentally unfriendly desalination technology is not a sustainable solution. Ultimately, the Gulf states have not nearly enough RES to justify their green hydrogen targets.

In fact, despite large and ambitions green pledges since the late 2000s, the deployment of renewable energy sources had been minimal until recently (Griffiths, 2017). In late 2018, the GCC region was far away from achieving these 'green dreams'. With a total of almost 150 GW of installed energy generation capacity, the share of renewable energy sources accounted for less than 1 GW (Alharbi & Csala, 2020). In the aftermath, renewable energy capacity increased significantly, especially in the UAE (Fig. 7.3).

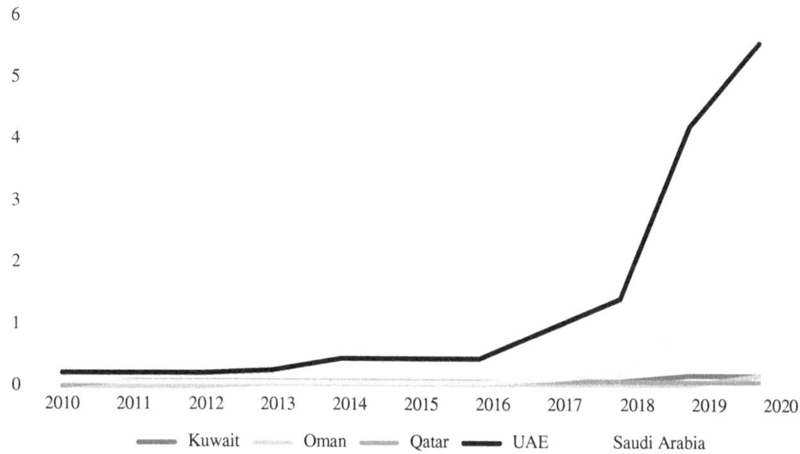

Fig. 7.3 Renewable power generation 2010–2020 (in terrawatt hours) (BP, 2021)[2]

Reasons for this lack are manifold and often arise from obstacles such as lack of data, know-how or financing, a lack of institutional capacity or need for bureaucratic reform, as well as further technical cultural barriers (Gelil, 2016; Al-Sarihi & Mansouri, 2022). Moreover, considering the fact that the demand for electricity within the GCC could double by 2030 (Alharbi & Csala, 2020) and that some countries have already announced large projects for exporting hydrogen, the energy diversification hype appears to be mostly unwarranted so far. As the national environmental and climate policies outlined in Chapter 4 show: The GCC countries must undertake extraordinary efforts within a short period of time if they want to meet their self-assigned clean energy and emission reduction targets. Even acknowledging that there are beneficial preconditions such as the falling cost of renewable energy sources, decades of experience, better technology as well as an autocratic, top-down, and fast-track policy approach, the scenarios seem unrealistic. As Marc Valeri stressed in the case of Oman: "The launch of these long-awaited renewable energy projects are welcome steps and should be applauded, however they remain a drop in the ocean of Oman's power demand" (Valeri, 2020, 168).

[2] No data has been available for Bahrain.

Moreover, Gulf states do not target the energy demand side in the same way that they target the supply side: A substantial alteration of the unsustainable political and economic structures in the Gulf is largely missing. Some of the implemented subsidy reforms have even been trashed for fear of growing societal discontent. Except for a cautious modification through price tariffs, other government policies like carbon taxes and restrictions, feed-in tariffs and emission trading systems have only been discussed but not implemented so far, mostly because rational policymakers fear delegitimizing repercussions. The following example may highlight this: People want their government to engage more actively in environmentalism but refuse to pay higher taxes or change their daily life habits. Yet, effective mitigation efforts must adequately address both the supply and demand side (Griffiths & Orkoubi, 2019, 143).

If the Gulf states' green transformation appears to be illusory in terms of energy sustainability, its record is even more disillusioning when looking to aspects of environmental protection and fighting climate change beyond emissions reduction. Although the Gulf states need comprehensive and integrated environmental and climate action if they want the region to remain livable in the second half of this century, very little has been done on this front. As the preceding chapters have shown, environmental agencies at the domestic level are mainly weak and undertakings have been rather cautious and cosmetic. As one interview notes: Ruling elites may understand the devastating role of water pollution but they are much more concerned about water scarcity, since reliable water supply is a prerequisite of social stability.[3] Regulative policies have been established in some instances for the sake of accountability over harsh environmental destruction but have barely been enforced as they are considered similarly unpopular as targeting the demand side, as discussed above. Besides the delegitimizing regulative character, another reason for this "command without control" practice (Kostka, 2015) simply relates to non-compliance: Powerful state-owned enterprises (SOEs) such as ARAMCO, QP and KOC frequently do not follow rules imposed by the weaker environmental agencies; especially if they lead to an economic loss. Here, pressure for environmental social governance comes rather from shareholders, insurers and lenders than state authorities.[4]

[3] Interview #76.

[4] Interview #20.

Instead of regulative policies of command and control, leaderships have rather concentrated on environmental policy tools of service and planning, which target the supply side, are distributive and enjoy greater societal support. This is particularly observable in the built environment. Urban megaprojects (either livable or theme cities) are planned as low carbon and/or carbon-neutral (Zaidan & Abulibdeh, 2021). Another succinct example is the long-held dream of 'greening the desert' (Ouis, 2002). Already in 2010, Sheikh Mohammad of the UAE launched the One Million Trees initiative as a means of greening the emirates and minimizing desertification. But the initiative failed dramatically, according to a project staff member: "100% of the trees have died and the initiative has failed completely" (Phelan, 2022, January 26). More recently, the Saudi crown prince announced a similar goal but details of how to achieve it have not been disclosed so far. This demonstrates the huge gap between headline-grabbing announcements and implementation, as touched upon in Chapter 4. Lastly, environmental information-sharing, which constitutes a crucial steering element of climate policy, barely exists in Gulf states' environmental policymaking. The lack of environmental reporting and consultancy, as well as environmental service provision to the public, refers not only to environmental hazards but also to political decision-making processes per se (Taher & Hajjar, 2014). In fact, leaderships appear not to feel pressure towards more inclusive environmental policymaking as there is (still) a general "irrelevance of societal input in the decision-making process on sustainability policies" (Atalay et al., 2016, 212). Also, the emergence of various environmental-oriented NGOs or GONGOs has not translated into higher public consciousness (Sowers, 2018).

To sum up, in terms of environmental sustainability oil- and gas-exporting countries focus on energy diversification and resilience but largely fail to address many other components of sustainability management. Rephrased, they focus mostly on promoting clean energy and a sustainable understanding of the built environment, leaving out significant aspects such as environmental conservation, protection of species, limiting soil and water pollution, or sustainable and responsible production and consumption. In fact, when looking at the environmental sustainability goals introduced in Chapter 1, GCC states are mainly focusing on only two of them (i.e. goals seven and eleven, and to a lesser extent goal six), which is also consistent with their economic development model. Even the case of energy sustainability is still in a nascent phase and the states are far from fulfiling their promises. In fact, the focus is mainly on greening the black gold that has ensured economic stability and welfare for such a long time. As one Gulf scholar and energy expert put it: The region has a tendency towards 'sustaining the unsustainable'.[5]

The way of sustainability management in the Gulf reveals a deeper understanding that is characterized by the absence of a genuine commitment to core values towards an ecological and social sustainable development. Instead, the idea of an 'environmental fix' prevails that those problems of emissions causing global warming, overaccumulation or resource depletion can be resolved or 'fixed' through progress, innovation and technology; in the Gulf states, it is mainly the main focus of reducing emissions as as 'green growth'. In this vein, the state present itself as an "anti-politics machine" (Ferguson, 1990), which can solve the world's climate crisis through the advancement of technologies and promising also new opportunities (e.g. green jobs) at the same time. It is this "green illusion" that "we can maintain our expanding patterns of energy consumption without consequence" (Zehner, 2012, 162) and that ultimately misdirect[s] our attention" and "sidetrack our most notable intentions" (Zehner, 2012, xvi). This, in its core very apolitical approach of an 'environmental fix' entails also—and this is the core argument of this book—a very central political calculus, namely the strategic element and key priority of power consolidation.

Making Power Sustainable

This book is guided by the overall thesis that not only do energy and economic considerations far outweigh sustainable environmental policies, but political factors and reasoning of power consolidation matter too. In addition to economic benefits, the field is strategically instrumentalized for the co-opting of various stakeholders from the political and economic spheres, bolstering the legitimation base of certain ruling elites and increasing external recognition and influence through linkages and leverage. Thereby, Chapter 2 discussed the manifold threats the Gulf Arab monarchies are facing currently. It indicated how the regime's political power base is threatened by a number of endogenous factors such as demographic trends, socioeconomic imbalance, weak institutionalization,

[5] Interview #77.

internal rivalry and mounting demands, as well as exogenous factors like climate change, fluctuation of oil price and low-carbon development. It thus sets the stage for the guiding key question of how leaderships in the Gulf—and especially those quite new in power—can adjust to these increasing risks and challenges by upholding their legitimacy base and maintaining authority and power.

Against this backdrop, Chapter 3 provided the broader historical context for a more nuanced understanding of the trajectories that have led to a rethinking since the 2000s. Such a history of environmentalism in the Gulf Arab monarchies has barely been set forth by scholars, with the notable exception of Toby Jones's seminal work on Saudi Arabia. Building on his argument about 'environmental power', the chapter also shows that the recent 'green hyperactivity' is not a radical reorientation of the Gulf monarchies but rather a revitalization of a 'green thought' that has deep roots throughout the twentieth century and has been an ever-present feature of Gulf politics. What can, however, be seen as a 'paradigm shift' is the realization by the oil- and gas-exporting countries, that they must fundamentally alter their hydrocarbon-based unsustainable path dependency in an increasingly climate- and carbon-constrained world. The challenges of sustaining economic growth and the welfare system needed to be harmonized with falling revenues from longstanding roller-coaster global oil prices and mounting pressure to address low-carbon, climate-resilient development. According to a Saudi businessman and member of one of the oligarchic families in Riyadh, it was "a time when everyone thinks that oil decline leads to confusion and panic, especially in the private sector and government". Consequently, it gave "the opportunity to revisit our programs and ways of spending".[6]

Hereby, recombinant leaderships across the Gulf have been smart and creative in addressing these core challenges and remain able "to clothe themselves in the mantle of legitimate authority" (Claude, 1988, 146). For instance, states such as Saudi Arabia have instrumentalized the threat of global warming and stronger demands for decarbonization as "convenient political cover" to start a cautious process of implementing regulative economic and financial instruments to attack the demand side of energy consumption (Krane, 2019, 151). Especially, the normative power of global climate commitments like the SDGs and the Paris

[6] Interview #3.

Agreement offers the 'perfect excuse' for rulers to enforce and defend unpopular austerity measures. According to an interviewee:

> We have tried before to cut subsidies, raise taxes but it did not work. Usually, the hearts of the kings are big, they are saying lots of money coming in, why bother people? But they did not listen to the professionals, who said that times will come where they have to save money.[7]

Despite a reconfiguration of the dialectical relationship between rulers and ruled, the field of environmental sustainability also offers deep insights as to how the Gulf countries are incrementally transforming from "allocative co-optation" towards "inclusionary co-optation" (Albrecht & Schlumberger, 2004, 383; Loewe et al., 2021, 10). This does not mean that the rentier-based allocation has been disregarded altogether, but rather that rulers are tending to put more effort than before towards inclusionary mechanisms of patronage as a means to consolidate their power base. Especially, Saudi Arabia, the UAE and Qatar as 'sustainable frontrunners' show how elites at the highest level of decision-making have positioned themselves to lead the countries' sustainable transformation. From the top of this 'sustainability governance pyramid' they create a patronage web of networks and co-opt politically relevant actors.

Especially, Chapter 4 shows how the field of environmental sustainability offers opportunities for this inclusionary co-optation. Members of the ruling families and major tribes and clans are an ever-present feature in this field. For instance, the Saudi crown prince's brother, Abdulaziz bin Salman, now oversees the energy transition in the kingdom. In Qatar, Sheikha Moza, the mother of the current emir, oversees all activities of the powerful state-related Qatar Foundation that develops and implements the bulk of sustainability projects in the country. While environmental authorities are filled with second-tier elites who have a rather minor impact, in Bahrain and Kuwait members of the ruling family are awarded a representative function in these institutions.[8] Additionally, other constituencies have been nurtured and closely tied to the regime. Close and loyal confidantes have been put into strategic positions aiming at increasing the ruler's support base through various stakeholders. These include technocrats such as Yasir al-Rumayyan and Khalid al-Falih in Saudi

[7] Interview #3.

[8] Interview #76.

Arabia, Suhail al-Mazroui and Sultan al-Jaber in the UAE. They all enjoy the personal blessing of the crown princes and de facto rulers of these countries. Those technocrats with long-term expertise in the respective field bring additional knowledge, experience and know-how that rationalizes governmental processes and increases the legitimation of policy processes. The creation of specific sustainable fiefdoms had the same goal but, as especially the Saudi case shows, these have rather remained siloed enclaves of broader co-optation.

While one can notice a certain degree of professionalization in sustainability management through these specialized technocrats, nepotism and favouritism remains strong in the political sector but even more apparent in the economic realm. Chapter 5 reveals the state-led and highly centralized capitalist system and the deep-rooted entanglements between the public and private sectors that plays a crucial role in processes of capital accumulation. Moreover, this public–private assemblage constitutes an integral part of power relations. One of the most vivid examples of this practice is the promotion of the formerly relatively less important Public Investment Fund (PIF) to the largest sovereign wealth fund. Grounded in the Vision 2030 and under the personal supervision of the Saudi crown prince, the PIF is strategically utilized as a political steering element of the Salman clique. Presumably, the Saudi Crown Prince learned from his counterpart in Abu Dhabi, where Mubadala holds a similar role. Besides the powerful Saudi Ministry of Energy, the PIF holds a crucial role in the kingdom's energy transition as it is responsible for around 70% of all developed renewable energy projects; the large portion of 'public tenders' are awarded to the PIF's protégé, the 'privately owned' energy company, ACWA Power. It indicates that ACWA's founders as well as other shareholders of the companies (e.g. the Al Rajhi family) are "generally on good terms with the court and Mohammad bin Salman".[9]

In Abu Dhabi, the leadership did not nurture its national champion but created it from scratch: The state-owned company Masdar Power, a subsidiary of the Masdar Initiative that is again overseen by the investment vehicle Mubadala, is the domestic clean energy leader. The involvement of the Qatari ruling family in the business sphere happens largely through its sovereign wealth fund and in terms of green urban planning projects. Further agents such as national oil and gas majors and

[9] Interview #47.

other state-owned enterprises complicate the picture and the ruling elite's grip on economic activities. They all form a web of 'reproduced co-optation' that also includes the powerful class of 'royal capitalists' whose appetite for capital gains and influence must be satisfied. This is particularly important in countries such as Kuwait, where the merchants also have substantial political power. Since the oil and gas business has remained state-controlled, the "embryonic Gulf capitalist class [have pursued] accumulation opportunities in other industries" (Hanieh, 2011, 69). This includes mostly service and construction works, which have prospered since local governments (but also international companies) have granted contracts to these sectors. This protective circuit mentality has continued through large-scale sustainable infrastructure projects including transport systems, low-carbon hubs and cities, sporting stadia and so on (Hanieh, 2011). Considering the endemic presence of clientelism, it is interesting that this is not only a tool for the patron to bind the client closer to him. In fact, it is a two-way relationship, because the patron is also dependent on the provision of services by the client. Rephrased, the ruler needs the services of the business sector (often mantled in an oligopoly) to achieve his visions of modernization and a hyper-developmentalist state.

In addition to cementing the power of the ruling elites and their associated elites, environmental sustainability is also used for strengthening the countries' linkages and leverage outside their own borders. Over the last years, Gulf states proactively engaged within the global climate regime and partially revised their previous image as climate laggards. Saudi Arabia, Qatar and especially the UAE made some constructive contributions during the last climate summits to present themselves as "legitimate leaders in the field of climate change" (Karlsson et al., 2012, 47). Sometimes more, sometimes less, all GCC countries also comply to internationally agreed climate commitments like submitting and updating their NDCs on a regular basis. They have also all engaged in numerous climate and environmental international networks and, in the case of Saudi Arabia and the UAE, also proposed their own regional climate plans and initiatives. However, leaked documents also reveal how some of the GCC countries, for instance Saudi Arabia and Kuwait, also tried to hamper the negotiation process at the 2021 climate summit in Glasgow. In short, climate diplomacy has been recognized as an important element for gaining influence and recognition. Not all Gulf states, however, are actively helping in the search for collective and global solutions to combat the severe effects of climate change. For some, it is rather a "façade to showcase" (Sever et al., 2019, 216). Especially Qatar's hosting of the COP18 in Doha in 2012 can be seen as one such example: After a short period of being energetically engaged in climate diplomacy prior, during and shortly after the summit, Qatari policymakers quickly lost interest later.

Another, probably more beneficial, tactic is to attract attention through eye-catching announcements and projects. Developing large-scale sustainable hubs like NEOM, Masdar City or putting a green label on projects like the FIFA World Cup 2022, infuses citizens with pride over their government's achievements, leading to more support and, ultimately, increasing the political legitimacy of the respective regimes and ruling families. As the case of Qatar shows, this sustainability spectacularism can be seen as an "integral component of the implicit contract between state and citizen" (Gardner, 2017, 353). It further underlines leadership qualities and attracts visitors, as well as diverting attention from other deficiencies.[10] Cutting-edge sustainability projects and initiatives are further underlined by a specific narrative: State officials and state-affiliated media outlets (over)emphasize the great achievements of the respective country, praising its leadership and fostering the construction of national affiliation and pride. Additionally, the regime avoids bad news coverage and hides government policymaking failures. Furthermore, incidents of environmental damage and destruction have regularly been covered up. Lastly, this form of ecological modernization also suits the political self-conception of the Gulf leaderships by accommodating the hierarchic, state-centralized autocratic patterns. For instance, large-scale clean energy projects implemented by governmental or semi-governmental entities support the above-described public–private assemblage and its neopatrimonial practices. Moreover, they are also often presented as grand ideas and gestures from a member of the ruling elite with the intention of creating an image of benevolence that demands gratitude by the populace.

Last but not least, environmental sustainability—and in particular the promotion of clean energy—is also used for (economic) hedging to diversify and increase political linkage and leverage across the geographical proximity and beyond. Since the first oil boom, Gulf states have made use of their energy abundance as a strategic tool of political leverage. In this

[10] Interview #44.

vein, they offer a new business destination, not only for traditional partners from the West but also increasingly for countries in the East, above all China. At the same time, the GCC monarchies invest in renewable energy projects in their close proximity and in economically underdeveloped regions to foster influence and create dependencies. In some instances, these investments are also covered as development assistance and part of 'clean energy diplomacy'.

The Bigger Picture

Until recently, environmental sustainability was largely perceived as a soft security issue with very low priority. Certainly, sustainability governance only represents one among many other policy fields. And yet, climate change mitigation, energy transition and energy security are no longer a soft but a hard policy field which demands immediate action by policymakers. In the light of the huge shift in focus and allocation of resources and capacities, one can deduce that the recent sustainable transformation in the region is more than just greenwashing (Zumbraegel, 2020).[11] Criticism of a mere green PR are often done by voices from the West that are in itself highly problematic "because it raises the question of who has the right to judge the green credentials of others" (Koch, forthcoming). Instead of assessing the performance of sustainability management, the more interesting aspect is a critical interrogation about its manifestation and effects as well as the underlying motives. In this vein, the book has shown that this 'green turn' should not be confused with a major policy shift that ultimately alters the GCC socioeconomic and political structures. Quite the opposite, this work has shown that it is rather seen as an instrument for *sustaining* the status quo as best as possible. Looking beyond discussions of a 'post-oil era' and focusing on the political dimension, the field provides several avenues for broader discussions.

First, the example of environmental sustainability underscores the adaptative capacity of and heterogeneity among the GCC states. It vividly illustrates how the long-lived traditional Gulf monarchies possess high adaptive capacities to adjust their policymaking to changing patterns and dynamics on the internal but also external level (i.e. both regionally and

[11] Interview #48.

internationally), if needed. New policy fields are adapted and exploited as a way of strategically and systematically responding to challenges these regimes face. The explicit example of environmental sustainability and the growing activity in policymaking offers some insights on how the state organization among the Gulf Arab monarchies functions and operates. Thus, the analysis clearly shows that the states act differently in their approach to sustainability governance, challenging the common perspective of considering the GCC as a monolithic bloc: All states strive towards a similar direction, but the speed and scale differ tremendously based on different scope conditions (Sim, 2022).

Second, environmental sustainability and its accompanying challenges reconfigures state–society relations. The citizens' needs and aspirations have rather cursorily been part of this investigation. The one-sided scholarly focus on key decision-makers' perceptions, preferences and choices—of which this work is no exception—is still a major caveat in scholarship. Especially in the light of the Arab mass uprisings in 2010 and 2011, which surprised many experts, some scholars have criticized the manifold top-down approaches and lack of critical voices in grassroots movements or in the public sphere. There are at least two aspects to consider here: On the one hand, environmental activism is expected to thrive in the Gulf and could express a new way of social contestation. On the other hand, and this is already now quite present, environmental sustainability measures touch upon the very nature of the social contract (Krane, 2018, 2019; Wright, 2018).

One fundamental aspect of this policy shift refers to the fact that the previous rentier regimes of the Gulf Arab monarchies are gradually turning from allocative towards an even stronger inclusionary power-based system. With fewer financial resources Gulf leaders are not able to sustain their full-fledged welfare programmes of free or highly subsidized utilities, services and well-paid jobs in the public sector. It resembles a development that Holger Albrecht and Oliver Schlumberger already noticed in the mid-2000s in other countries in the Arab world:

> During the rentier era that lasted until the late 1980s, co-optation was mainly based on the distribution of wealth. The regimes allocative power has structurally decreased over the past 15 years because rent income has shrunk, populations have grown, and economies have liberalized. This is especially true of semi-rentier states such as Egypt, Yemen, or Tunisia that have always been restricted by the modesty of their oil revenues, but is also

> true (though to a lesser extent) of some bigger oil and gas producers with large populations, such as Algeria and Iraq. (Albrecht & Schlumberger, 2004, 382–383)

The reorganization of the previously lucrative oil and gas industry will result in allocative or rentier states with limited allocative and patronage power. However, as the book and particularly the preceding chapter has indicated, this is not a stark caesura but a gradual process that also offers opportunities for the oil- and gas-exporting countries. A mix of optimization of the 'old' business model and the incorporation of new strategies such as partially outsourcing responsibilities to the 'private' sector, justifying spending cuts through the looming climate crisis or adding renewable energy sources into the energy portfolio should cushion the negative effects of fiscal austerity to a certain degree. So, it is basically the same old story of using environmental capital for consolidating power and asserting authority but changing the commodity/resources/capacities which are needed and used to pursue these goals.

Third, this work contributes to a better understanding of transnational dynamics. In general, the weak regional coordination and cooperation in the field of sustainability governance are puzzling in the light of the existence of institutional bodies and legal frameworks. The apparent high degree of regional competition, which is largely and primarily economically driven (Sever et al., 2019), has severe political repercussions: While the leadership role of Saudi Arabia is undisputed (albeit with some resentments) there is a socially-constructed struggle between the remaining GCC states. As one interviewee pinpoints: "The fact that number two is disputed gives more power to number one. Oman, Kuwait, Qatar, the UAE all have their own reasons to believe they are number two".[12] This intra-regional competition is also used for engendering national sentiments. The example of regional sustainability governance provides further insights on these dynamics. For instance, it shows the different approaches of individual states. During the last decade, especially Qatar and Abu Dhabi have been competing over their green branding strategies to underline the superiority of their model, whereas Kuwait has rather reinforced its idea of being a regional coordinator through environmental-related proposals and policies. The regional powerhouse Saudi Arabia came rather

[12] Interview #6.

late to the party but will soon trump the other pioneers on the basis of resources and scale.

When looking outside the GCC further questions arise. A significant but not much discussed question refers to environmental justice and responsibility in neighbouring war-torn Yemen that is experiencing a disastrous humanitarian and ecological crisis. Sustainability mismanagement, widespread pollution, environmental degradation and growing threats from climate change are exacerbating the catastrophic situation. As dominant external parties to the conflict, Saudi Arabia and the UAE both bear partial responsibility for Yemen's environmental suffering as both are accused of systematically destroying the natural environment and civilian infrastructure that is crucial for Yemen's human security (Zumbraegel, 2022). Beyond that, sustainability management further empowers alliance building between relevant actors within the Arab region and outside. It supports previous arguments for the GCC as gravity centre in the Arab region and its growing orientation towards Eastern countries without neglecting its traditional partnership with the West.

Outlook: A Long and Bumpy Road Ahead

Climate change and global warming are already imminent threats and accompanying environmental hazards are expected to grow over the next decades, making environmental sustainability a top priority. The analysis provided here shows how engaging in environmental sustainability is not only (or merely) advocated to tackle this problem of a looming climate collapse but—given its global importance and attention—also serves as a suitable field for increasing the power base of leaderships. However, despite the fact that the Gulf states have embarked on this journey and quite successfully weathered growing challenges, they still have a bumpy road ahead.

As Chapter 2 already stressed, so far the strong authoritarian setting in the region has resulted in a very low number of independent environmental NGOs, which "mostly rally around non-controversial, low-impact-high-visibility themes" such as beach cleaning or tree planting (Luomi, 2012, 72). Yet, there are indications that environmental activism and stronger consciousness about climate change is well on its way. For instance, in the case of Saudi Arabia, a 2017 survey reveals that two-thirds of the population share the view that the government is not putting enough effort into combating climate change. Even more importantly, around 45% claimed that nothing has changed during the last ten years (Saab, 2017, 27). It can be expected that such climate consciousness will steadily increase over the next years rather than decades, given the growing pressure of a global youth movement that demands stronger action by state leaders. Currently (early 2022), weekly 'Fridays for Future' demonstrations are held in the UAE as the only GCC country. Young citizens, who represent the vast majority of the public but frequently suffer unemployment, constitute a major pressure group. Moreover, the erosion of the rentier social contract will evoke stronger societal representation that may also translate into alleged soft policy fields like environmental protection and fighting climate change. Those demands by a well-educated and well-informed youth could be triggered by occasional environmental hazards like flash floods in Jeddah or incidents of pollution. When assuming greater environmental advocacy in the Gulf states, as is occurring elsewhere in the Middle East and North Africa (Sowers, 2018; Zumbraegel, 2020), then among the Arab states Kuwait appears to be best prepared to pass this severe test, due to its formalized input mechanisms of political participation and liberal approach with NGOs. However, also the UAE—though more autocratic than Kuwait—has implemented campaigns that facilitate greater dialogue with environmental stakeholders from civil society and Qatar is home to the Arab Climate Movement (Al Mubarak & Alam, 2012).

Whether social grievances and contestation over environmental degradation and climate change will lead to revolutionary fervour, as was seen in other cases (e.g. Turkey in 2013, Lebanon between 2015 and 2016 or the Iranian region Khuzestan during 2021), is also connected with the question of how the Gulf states will weather the socioeconomic transition of a changing social contract. Especially the outbreak of the COVID-19 pandemic in late 2019 also impacted the Gulf states' energy transition. Growing budgetary constraints and reduced energy demands have prompted governments to step back from their ambitious clean energy plans. Manal Shehabi foresees less environmental regulation and carbon reduction measures as the highest priority shifts to post-pandemic recovery and economic stimulus packages (Shehabi, 2020). For instance, as stated in Chapter 4, Kuwait shelved the expansion of its large solar project Shagaya as a means to balance the dual shock of falling oil prices and a pandemic-triggered decrease in economic activity. Scrapping renewable energy projects only distances the GCC states even more from the projected 80 GW renewable energy capacity (IRENA, 2019). Already now, it is expected that the role of SMEs and green entrepreneurship must substantially increase in this field as the very ambitious renewable energy targets cannot be met by national champions alone. Here, the economic sector must be fundamentally transformed from the above explained state-led centrality where some SOEs dominate (Woertz, 2021). Dubai's shams model could be an appealing example for others. Going beyond 'quick cash', more incentivized cooperation between venture capital, entrepreneurs and academics must be facilitated in order to create triple-win situations.[13]

Whether this will happen is not clear. While the COVID-19 pandemic increased talks about the potential of a green recovery in the Gulf (Al-Sarihi, 2021), the recent war in Ukraine and its political and economic implications have changed such an optimic outlook. The price of a barrel oil has soared and European leaders are looking towards the Gulf as their (new) energy insurance. Instead of fundamentally altering economic structures, new 'environmental technological fixes' such as blue and green hydrogen are presented. Despite the fact that hydrogen is very energy-intensive and years away of becoming a global commodity, the Gulf states are already position themselves. Key state players and national champions (ACWA Power, ADNOC, NEOM, Mubadala Investment Co. etc.) are taking over this business niche, helping to maintain a system of interlocking privileges of neopatrimonialism and state-led capital accumulation. The economic opportunities of hydrogen are also related to shifting aspects of a global market. While Europe seems a good market for green hydrogen, the Gulf states' increasing orientation towards the Asian market will probably be prioritized. Already closer to the Asian region than other Arab countries, especially China and India will become the major partners in the future. In the field of environmental sustainability, this might include (blue) hydrogen but also other utilities. Particularly, the solar business is expected to further thrive.

As the analysis has further indicated, the relationship among key regional actors might also shift. While there were recent tendencies towards rapprochement between previously adversarial countries that erupted since 2011, it remains to be seen whether there will be greater coordination and cooperation between countries such as Turkey, Egypt, Qatar, Iran, Saudi Arabia, and the UAE. Cooperation in the field of

[13] Interview #55.

renewable energy is certainly a way to overcome grievances and a lack of trust. Only recently, for instance, the UAE announced the construction of a solar plant in Iran. The normalization process between Israel and several Arab states might also diffuse to other countries in the Middle East and North Africa and bring new opportunities in terms of business activities and the transfer of technology and innovation. Lastly, it remains to be seen how the strong, although sometimes dialectic relationship between Saudi Arabia and the UAE will develop. There is a possibility that the leaderships in Riyadh and Abu Dhabi will continue their assertive policies of bidding for GCC hegemony that plays out in arenas such as the commercial and touristic sectors, but also in climate diplomacy. Still in the process of normalizing ties after a four-year spat between Qatar and Saudi Arabia, Bahrain and the UAE, this would lead the GCC straight into the next crisis. New regional reconfigurations, growing climate vulnerability and the geopolitics of environmental sustainability may result in new bloc formations across the whole region. Already now one can notice how countries such as Egypt, Morocco, Jordanian or Tunisia are dependent on the green technology and innovation from the wealthy and well-equipped countries such as Saudi Arabia, Qatar, the UAE or Israel. Other least developed and/or war-torn countries like Yemen might further fall behind this development of an unequal climate transition in the Middle East and North Africa. In short, climate transition will increase unequal power relations in the region.

Despite these challenges on various fronts, there is also hope that in the light of the upcoming COP27 and COP28 summits in Egypt and Abu Dhabi respectively, state leaders will make more efforts towards a more integrated and comprehensive environmental sustainability management, which encompasses strengthening participation in policymaking and greater willingness of regional cooperation. In the Anthropocene and a region that mostly lacking behind many of the SDGs, the Gulf states, with all their capacities, can play a constructive role and leading position in this development…if they are truly going green.

References

Ahmad, A., & Ramana, M. (2015). Prospects for nuclear power in the Gulf Cooperation Council (GCC). In G. Bahgat (Ed.), *The changing energy landscape in the Gulf: Strategic implications* (pp. 55–72). Gerlach Press.

Al Mubarak, R., & Alam, T. (2012). *The role of NGOs in tackling environmental issues*. Middle East Institute. Retrieved February 3, 2022 from https://www.mei.edu/publications/role-ngos-tackling-environmental-issues

Albrecht, H., & Schlumberger, O. (2004). "Waiting for Godot": Regime change without democratization in the Middle East. *International Political Science Review, 25*(4), 371–392.

Alharbi, F., & Csala, D. (2020). *GCC countries' renewable energy penetration and the progress of their energy sector projects*. IEEE Access 8. Retrieved January 31, 2022 from https://ieeexplore.ieee.org/document/9266039

Al-Sarihi, A. (2021). *Saudi Arabia and the Paris climate agreement*. KFCRIS Commentaries. Retrieved December 8, 2021, from https://kfcris.com/en/view/post/363

Al-Sarihi, A., & Mansouri, N. (2022). Renewable energy development in the Gulf cooperation council countries: Status, barriers, and policy options. *Energies, 15*(5), 1923. https://doi.org/10.3390/en15051923

Atalay, Y., Biermann, F., & Kalfagianni, A. (2016). Adoption of renewable energy technologies in oil-rich Countries: Explaining policy variation in the Gulf cooperation council states. *Renewable Energy, 85*, 206–214. https://doi.org/10.1016/j.renene.2015.06.045

BP. (2021). *Statistical review of world energy 2021*. Retrieved April 20, 2022 from https://www.bp.com/en/global/corporate/energy-economics/statistical-review-of-world-energy.html

Claude, I. (1988). *States and the global system: Politics, law and organization*. Palgrave.

Dourian, K. (2019). *Oman: A small oil player with big ambitions*. AGSIW Blog Post. Retrieved October 29, 2021 from https://agsiw.org/oman-a-small-oil-player-with-big-ambitions/

Ferguson, J. (1990). *The anti-politics machine. "Development," depoliticization, and bureaucratic power in Lesotho*. University of Minnesota Press.

Gardner, A. (2017). How the city grows: Urban growth and challenges to sustainable development in Doha, Qatar. In P. Sillitoe (Ed.), *Sustainable development: An appraisal of the Gulf region* (pp. 343–366). Berghahn Books.

Gaub, F., & Lienard, C. (2021). *Arab climate futures: Of risk and readiness*. European Union Institute for Security Studies (EUISS) Chaillot Paper 170. Retrieved March 19, 2022 from https://www.iss.europa.eu/content/arab-climate-futures

Gelil, I. (2016). Barriers to greening the energy sector in the Gulf Cooperation Council. In M. Raouf & M. Luomi (Eds.), *The green economy in the Gulf* (pp. 25–52). Routledge.

Griffiths, S. (2017). Renewable energy policy trends and recommendations for GCC countries. *Energy Transitions, 1*(1). https://doi.org/10.1007/s41825-017-0003-6

Griffiths, S., & Orkoubi, D. (2019). Energy and climate policies to stimulate renewables deployment in GCC countries. In H. Akhonbay (Ed.), *The economics of renewable energy in the Gulf* (pp. 139–166). Routledge.

Hanieh, A. (2011). *Capitalism and class in the Gulf Arab states*. Palgrave.

IRENA. (2019). *Renewable energy market analysis: GCC 2019*. Retrieved December 28, 2021 from https://www.irena.org/publications/2019/jan/renewable-energy-market-analysis-gcc-2019

Jones, C. (2020). Moving off the gold standard: Energy, security, "stateness", and the nuclearisation of the Gulf. *Journal of Arabian Studies, 10*(1), 190–204. https://doi.org/10.1080/21534764.2020.1794285

Karlsson, C., Hjerpe, M., Parker, C., & Linner, B. (2012). The legitimacy of leadership in international climate change negotiations. *Ambio, 41*, 46–55. https://doi.org/10.1007/s13280-011-0240-7

Koch, N. (forthcoming). Sustainability spectacle: Modernity and the contemporary imperative to be green. *Environmental Politics*, n/a.

Kostka, G. (2015). Command without control: The case of China's environmental target system. *Regulation & Governance, 10*(1), 58–74.

Krane, J. (2018). Political enablers of energy subsidy reform in Middle Eastern oil exporters. *Nat. Energy, 3*(7), 547–552.

Krane, J. (2019). *Energy kingdoms: Oil and political survival in the Persian Gulf*. Columbia University Press.

Krane, J. (2020). Climate strategy for producer countries: The case of Saudi Arabia. In G. Luciani & T. Moerenhout (Eds.), *When can oil economies be deemed sustainable?* (pp. 101–128). Palgrave.

Loewe, M., Zintl, T., & Houdret, A. (2021). The social contract as a tool of analysis: Introduction to the special issue on "Framing the evolution of new social contracts in Middle Eastern and North African countries". *World Development* 145, online first. https://doi.org/10.1016/j.worlddev.2020.104982

Luciani, G. (2021). Framing the economic sustainability of oil economies. In G. Luciani & T. Moerenhout (Eds.), *When can oil economies be deemed sustainable?* (pp. 9–30). Palgrave.

Luomi, M. (2012). The Gulf monarchies and climate change. *Abu Dhabi and Qatar in an era of natural unsustainability*. Hurst & Co.

Noach, K., & Guzansky, Y. (2021). *The Saudi drive to lead the green revolution in the Middle East* (INSS Insight No. 1486). Retrieved December 8, 2021 from https://www.inss.org.il/publication/green-saudi-arabia/

Ottaway, D. (2021). *Saudi crown prince gives up on kicking the kingdom's oil addiction*. Wilson Center. Retrieved January 31, 2022 from https://www.wilsoncenter.org/article/saudi-crown-prince-gives-kicking-kingdoms-oil-addiction

Ouis, P. (2002). 'Greening the emirates': The modern construction of nature in the United Arab Emirates. *Cult. Geogr., 9*(3), 334–347.

Pearman, G., & Parther, M. (2020, August 9). Don't rush into a hydrogen economy until we know all the risks to ourclimate. *The Conversation*. https://theconversation.com/dont-rush-into-a-hydrogen-economy-until-we-know-all-the-risks-to-our-climate-140433

Phelan, J. (2022, January 26). Desertification threatens food supply in Dubai. Can its fledgling green tech sector help to stem the encroaching sands? *BCC*. https://www.bbc.com/future/article/20220125-how-dubai-is-pushing-back-its-encroaching-deserts?s=09

Quaile, I. (2013, March 21). Green energy revolution in the Gulf? *Deutsche Welle*. https://www.dw.com/en/green-energy-revolution-in-the-gulf/a-16608352

Raouf, M., & Luomi, M. (2016). *The green economy in the Gulf*. Routledge.

Roefs, P., Moretti, M., Welkenhuysen, K., Piessens, K., & Compernollea, T. (2019). CO2-enhanced oil recovery and CO2 capture and storage: An environmental economic trade-off analysis. *J. Environ. Manage., 239*, 167–177. https://doi.org/10.1016/j.jenvman.2019.03.007

Saab, N. W. (2017). *Arab public opinion and the environment AFED 2017 Survey in 22 countries*. Arab Forum for Environment and Development (AFED). Retrieved October 29, 2021 from https://www.greengrowthknowledge.org/sites/default/files/downloads/resource/2017%20Report%20of%20the%20Arab%20Forum%20for%20Environment%20and%20Development_Arab%20Environment%20in%2010%20Years.pdf

Sever, S., Tok, M. E., & D'Alessandro, C. (2019). Global environmental governance and the GCC: Setting the agenda for climate change and energy security. In L. Pal & M. Tok (Eds.), *Global governance and Muslim organizations* (pp. 197–228). Springer.

Shehabi, M. (2020). Novel policy research on the resource exporters-energy policy nexus during the Coronavirus pandemic. *Environ. Resour. Econ., 76*, 447–517. https://doi.org/10.1007/s10640-020-00493-2

Sim, L. (2022). *Renewable power policies in the Arab Gulf states*. Middle East Institute. Retrieved February 10, 2022 from https://www.mei.edu/publications/renewable-power-policies-arab-gulf-states

Sowers, J. (2018). Environmental activism in the Middle East and North Africa. In H. Verhoeven (Ed.), *Environmental politics in the Middle East* (pp. 27–52). Oxford University Press.

Sullivan, P. (2021). *Under the volcano: Geothermal is key to Saudi Arabia's energy future*. AGSIW Blog Post. Retrieved January 30, 2022 from https://agsiw.org/under-the-volcano-geothermal-is-key-to-saudi-arabias-energy-future/

Tagliapietra, S. (2017). *The political economy of Middle East and North Africa oil exporters in times of global decarbonisation* (Bruegel Working Paper 05). Retrieved February 5, 2022 from https://www.econstor.eu/handle/10419/173150

Taher, N., & Hajjar, B. (2014). *Energy and environment in Saudi Arabia: Concerns and opportunities*. Springer.

Theeyattuparampil, V., Zarzour, O., Koukouzas, N., Vidican, G., al-Saleh, Y., & Katsimpardi, I. (2013). Carbon capture and storage: State of play, challenges and opportunities for the GCC countries. *International Journal of Energy Sector Management, 7*(2), 223–242.

Valeri, M. (2020). Economic diversification and energy security in Oman: Natural gas, the X factor? *Journal of Arabian Studies, 10*(1), 159–174. https://doi.org/10.1080/21534764.2020.1794284

Woertz, E. (2021). When "pariahs" go green: Energy transitions in the Middle East and the Biden administration. *Georgetown Journal of International Affairs*. Retrieved December 13, 2021 from https://gjia.georgetown.edu/2021/04/14/when-pariahs-go-green-energy-transitions-in-the-middle-east-and-the-biden-administration/

Wright, S. (2018). Qatar: The context of a hydrocarbon-funded social contract. In I. Overland (Ed.), *Public brainpower* (pp. 247–259). Springer.

Zaidan, E., & Abulibdeh, A. (2021). Master planning and the evolving urban model in the Gulf cities: Principles, policies, and practices for the transition to sustainable urbanism. *Planning Practice & Research, 36*(2), 193–215. https://doi.org/10.1080/02697459.2020.1829278

Zehner, O. (2012). *Green illusions: The dirty secrets of clean energy and the future of environmentalism*. University of Nebraska Press.

Zumbraegel, T. (2020). Beyond greenwashing: Sustaining power through sustainability in the Arab Gulf monarchies. *Orient, 61*(1), 28–35.

Zumbraegel, T. (2022): Between 'Suffering' and 'Surfing': Environmental sustainability management and its transnational dynamics on the Arabian Peninsula. *POMEPS studies 46: Environmental politics in the middle east and north Africa*. Retrieved August 22, 2022 from https://pomeps.org/pomeps-studies-46-environmental-politics-in-the-middle-east-and-north-africa

Appendix

List of Interviews

While all personally conducted interviews have been kept strictly confidential, some background information such as profession, affiliation and location can provide a rough idea about the discussed content and its relevance for the book's topic.

Interview 1. Professor political science of a Saudi university, Riyadh, Saudi Arabia, November 6, 2016.

Interview 2. Professor political science of a Saudi university and consultant to the GCC, Riyadh, Saudi Arabia, November 7, 2016.

Interview 3. Saudi businessman, Riyadh, Saudi Arabia, November 21, 2016.

Interview 4. Saudi-based energy expert at a Saudi research institution, Riyadh, Saudi Arabia, November 22, 2016.

Interview 5. Saudi political consultant, Riyadh, Saudi Arabia, November 24, 2016.

Interview 6. Saudi senior researcher at a Saudi research institution, Riyadh, Saudi Arabia, November 24, 2016.

Interview 7. Saudi political consultant, Riyadh, Saudi Arabia, November 30, 2016.

Interview 8. Saudi senior researcher at a Saudi research institution, Riyadh, Saudi Arabia, December 4, 2016.

T. Zumbraegel, *Political Power and Environmental Sustainability in Gulf Monarchies*, Contemporary Gulf Studies,
https://doi.org/10.1007/978-981-19-4431-4

Interview 9. Senior energy expert at a Qatari university, Doha, Qatar, February 9, 2017.

Interview 10. Doha-based researcher at a foreign think tank, Doha, Qatar, February 12, 2017.

Interview 11. Doha-based energy expert at a foreign think tank, Doha, Qatar, February 12, 2017.

Interview 12. Political scientist at a Qatari university, Doha, Qatar, February 13, 2017.

Interview 13. Professor of political science at a Qatari-based university, Doha Qatar, February 15, 2017.

Interview 14. Environmental expert at a Qatari research institution, Doha, Qatar, February 15, 2017.

Interview 15. Diplomat at a foreign mission, Doha, Qatar, February 15, 2017.

Interview 16. Political scientist at a Qatari university, Doha, Qatar, February 16, 2017.

Interview 17. Professor of history at a Qatari university, Doha, Qatar, February 20, 2017.

Interview 18. Environmental scientist at a Qatari university, Doha, Qatar, February 21, 2017.

Interview 19. Environmental expert and consultant, Doha, Qatar, February 21, 2017.

Interview 20. Senior environmental and climate expert at a Qatar-based think tank, Doha, Qatar, February 22, 2017.

Interview 21. Environmental scientist and advisor to the government, Doha, Qatar, February 22, 2017.

Interview 22. Political scientist at a Qatari university, Doha, Qatar, February 22, 2017.

Interview 23. Environmental scientist at a Qatari university, Doha, Qatar, February 26, 2017.

Interview 24. Political scientist at a Qatari university, Doha, Qatar, February 26, 2017.

Interview 25. Political advisor to the government, Riyadh, Saudi Arabia, March 1, 2017.

Interview 26. Senior research at a Saudi research institution, Riyadh, Saudi Arabia, March 2, 2017.

Interview 27. Senior official to the GCC Secretary, Riyadh, Saudi Arabia, March 4, 2017.

Interview 28. Senior environmental researcher at a Saudi research institution, Riyadh, Saudi Arabia, March 6, 2017.

Interview 29. Senior official in Saudi Arabia's ministry of energy, Riyadh, Saudi Arabia, March 7, 2017,

Interview 30. Economic expert at a foreign mission, Riyadh, Saudi Arabia, March 8, 2017.

Interview 31. Professor of political science and former advisor to the government, Kuwait City, Kuwait, October 16, 2017.

Interview 32. Senior official in Kuwait's environmental authority, Kuwait City, Kuwait, October 16, 2017.

Interview 33. Senior official in Kuwait's environmental authority, Kuwait City, Kuwait, October 17, 2017.

Interview 34. Senior researcher at a Kuwaiti research institution, Kuwait City, Kuwait, October 22, 2017.

Interview 35. Environmental scientist at a foreign university, Kuwait City, Kuwait, October 23, 2017.

Interview 36. Political scientist and historian at a foreign university, Kuwait City, Kuwait, October 23, 2017.

Interview 37. Assistant professor of political science at a foreign university, Kuwait City, Kuwait, October 23, 2017.

Interview 38. Kuwaiti businessman. Kuwait City, Kuwait, October 24, 2017.

Interview 39. Professor of political science at a Kuwaiti university, Kuwait City, Kuwait, October 25, 2017.

Interview 40. Former diplomat and political advisor to the GCC, Kuwait City, Kuwait, October 28, 2017.

Interview 41. Senior official in Bahrain's ministry of industry, Manama, Bahrain, October 30, 2017.

Interview 42. Senior researcher at a Bahraini research institution, Manama, Bahrain, November 3, 2017.

Interview 43. Economic expert and consultant, Manama, Bahrain, November 8, 2017.

Interview 44. Senior research at a London research institution, London, United Kingdom, June 29, 2018.

Interview 45. European diplomat and energy expert, virtually, February 18, 2019.

Interview 46. Former senior advisor to Saudi Arabia's ministry of energy, virtually, 24 April 2019.

Interview 47. Professor of political science at a university in UK, virtually, January 19, 2020.

Interview 48. Professor of political geography, virtually, April 19, 2020.

Interview 49. Senior environmental and climate expert in Saudi Arabia, virtually, June 9. 2020.

Interview 50. Senior environmental and climate expert in Oman, virtually, July 20, 2020.

Interview 51. Senior environmental and climate expert in Saudi Arabia, virtually, July 23, 2020.

Interview 52. Qatari political researcher, virtually, September 9, 2020.

Interview 53. Senior energy expert in Kuwait, virtually, September 11, 2020.

Interview 54. Senior official of Saudi Arabia's environmental ministry, virtually, October 10, 2020.

Interview 55. Senior researcher at a German think tank, virtually, October 20, 2020.

Interview 56. Assistant professor and energy expert at a Qatari university, virtually, October 23, 2020.

Interview 57. Senior economic expert at a German think tank, virtually, October 29, 2020.

Interview 58. Saudi-based entrepreneur, virtually, November 15, 2020.

Interview 59. Environmental and energy expert at a Saudi research institution, Riyadh, Saudi Arabia, September 21, 2021.

Interview 60. Senior expert and advisor at a Saudi-based energy agency, Riyadh, Saudi Arabia, September 21, 2021.

Interview 61. Consultant and former official in Saudi Arabia ministry of energy, Dammam, Saudi Arabia, September 22, 2021.

Interview 62. Director at an UAE-based energy agency, Abu Dhabi, UAE, September 26, 2021.

Interview 63. Senior official in UAE's ministry of climate change and environment, Abu Dhabi, UAE, September 26, 2021.

Interview 64. Senior researcher at a UAE-based research institution, Abu Dhabi, UAE, September 27, 2021.

Interview 65. European energy experts, Abu Dhabi, UAE, September 27, 2021.

Interview 66. Senior official in UAE's ministry of climate change and environment, Abu Dhabi, UAE, September 28, 2021.

Interview 67. Staff EXPO 2020, Dubai, UAE, September 28, 2021.

Interview 68. Energy and climate researcher at an Emirati university, Dubai, UAE, September 29, 2021.

Interview 69. Managing director of a UAE-based non-profit organization, Dubai, UAE, September 30, 2021.

Interview 70. Economic expert and consultant, virtually, July 16. 2021.

Interview 71. Environmental scientist at a Kuwaiti university, Berlin, Germany, September 7, 2021,

Interview 72. Kuwaiti-based energy expert and consultant, Berlin, Germany, September, 7, 2021,

Interview 73. Senior researcher at a Qatari university, Doha, Qatar, February 20, 2017.

Interview 74. Omani researcher and journalist, Berlin, Germany, September 6, 2021.

Interview 75. Economic expert and researcher, virtually, July 16, 2021.

Interview 76. Kuwaiti environmental scientist, Berlin, Germany, September 9, 2021.

Interview 77. Kuwaiti energy expert, Berlin, Germany September 9, 2021.

Index

T. Zumbraegel, *Political Power and Environmental Sustainability in Gulf Monarchies*, Contemporary Gulf Studies,
https://doi.org/10.1007/978-981-19-4431-4

FSC
www.fsc.org
MIX
Papier | Fördert
gute Waldnutzung
FSC® C083411

Kolibri 360 GmbH
Ferdinand-Jühlke-Straße 7
99095 Erfurt, Deutschland
produktsicherheit@kolibri360.de